The Age of
TOTAL WARFARE

The Age of
TOTAL WARFARE

H.W.KOCH

This edition produced exclusively for
W.H. Smith & Son Limited
Strand House
10 New Fetter Lane
London EC4A 1AD

First Published in 1983 by
Bison Books Corp.
17 Sherwood Place
Greenwich, CT 06830
U.S.A.

ISBN 0 86124 128 2

Printed in Hong Kong

CONTENTS

1. Clausewitz & Total War

Karl von Clausewitz, born 1 June 1780, has for many decades been one of the most misunderstood military writers. Professor John U Nef, writing shortly after the end of World War II, counted him among the creators of a new mysticism:

'which helped to fan the flames of the world wars. Unlike Napoleon, Clausewitz was not a remarkably effective officer on the field of battle. It is reasonable to regard his doctrines concerning the philosophical meaning of war as a product mainly of the mind at work in the study.

'Clausewitz and his followers in Germany and eventually in other countries gave warfare an intellectual justification in addition to the emotional justification it derived from the spirit of resistance, of defense, bred in the heat of the French Revolution. Clausewitz's philosophy of war made use of concepts and categories directly derived from the Christian and humanist philosophies of the past, but he put them to a new purpose. For him war became a great exercise, in which the intellectual as well as moral qualities of man had unique opportunity for fulfillment. The occasion for the use of the mind was slight, of course, in the case of the private, but even for him there was a respectable place in the new warfare. The choices offered him in great battles called for tremendous grit and for some intelligence. So battles conferred upon the common man a kind of dignity which ordinary economic existence was failing to provide. As one ascended the military hierarchy from the private to the general, the intellectual opportunities increased, until for the commander in chief they exceeded those accorded men in other callings.'

In short, Clausewitz's work is denounced as the gospel of militarism.

Yet nothing could be farther from the truth. As we shall see, he clearly recognized the danger of *total war* but the criticism leveled against him would be much more appropriate to a work published a century later, in 1935, by General Erich Ludendorff, *Der Totale Krieg*, in which this German general, as renowned as he was controversial, set out to replace the 'outdated' maxims of Clausewitz with a new theory of total war. Intellectually, there is no comparison between Clausewitz and Ludendorff. The latter's work is simply one of propaganda. Ludendorff maintained that the German government during World War I had failed to mobilize the physical and mental resources of the German people which would have made them invulnerable to allied propaganda. He therefore demanded that the next war, which was to erase the blemish of the 1918 defeat, be prepared for with propaganda and that in the war itself the propaganda weapon should have a rank equal to that of the other arms. In a future war which, measured by the experience of World War I, could only be a total war, psychological warfare would be one of the decisive weapons. Therefore the psychological mobilization would be as important as that of personnel and material. In such a war Clausewitz's idea of the *primacy of politics* would be abandoned; in its place should step the *primacy of the military*, in whose hands the political and military conduct of the war would be concentrated. In total war there was no longer any place for civilian politicians.

Nothing could contradict Clausewitz's maxims more than those of Ludendorff and a host of lesser writers of the post World War I period. Therefore it is important to discuss Clausewitz the man, his work and its fullest development up to World War II, retracing our steps in the last chapter so as to proceed to an analysis of the present military position.

Clausewitz's main work, *On War*, was published posthumously between 1832 and 1834 and was well received by his contemporaries, that is, by those who possessed the same wide intellectual horizon. In the field of politics, Marx and Engels were among the first to become captivated by the work and to immerse themselves in its study. Little wonder: Clausewitz

Previous page: Street fighting in the Franco-Prussian War. Right: French cavalry officer of the Napoleonic period. Above: Clausewitz. Next page: Napoleon wins at Ulm.

considered it his main aim to reconcile the theory and practice of war. What he intended was a structural analysis of the social phenomenon of war, which he took as simply one of the manifestations of social life, leaving its justification or condemnation to others. It is this motive which connects him with Karl Marx. Clausewitz did not consider reality as the testground of general maxims, but like Marx he elevated reality to a constitutive element of theory. What economics was to Marx, the history and theory of war were to Clausewitz. Both Clausewitz and Marx insisted upon the primacy of politics, a point with which even Bismarck agreed on the basis of his empirical experience, although late in life he admitted to and regretted not having read a line of Clausewitz.

The Wars of German Unification (1864, 1866, 1870–71) pushed Clausewitz's work to the fore, since it appeared that Prussia and Germany had conducted these wars fundamentally in accord with his maxims. Nowadays, since the early 1970s, there has been renewed interest world-wide in Clausewitz's work, in the United States, Europe and the Warsaw Bloc countries; indeed, in Russia, Clausewitz proved to be highly instructive to Lenin, and later to Mao Tse-tung in China and Che Guevara in Cuba as well.

Who was Karl von Clausewitz? He was born on 1 June 1780 in Burg, near Magdeburg, Prussia six years before the death of Frederick the Great. His ancestors were mainly parsons, but his father had served in the army of Frederick the Great and was retired after the Seven Years' War. Clausewitz's nobility is shrouded in mystery. There are strong indications that his father prefixed the 'von' to his name on his own initiative, without any real entitlement, and only in the later years of his son's career did King Friedrich Wilhelm III legalize this state of

he received his commission as a lieutenant, watching with great fascination the struggle between the new forces of the French Revolution and those of enlightened absolutism intent upon preserving the political and social *status quo*. Inevitably he witnessed the collapse of the 'rational art of war' and its replacement by the 'irrational warfare of the revolution.'

From 1795 until 1801 Clausewitz served as a subaltern in the garrison town of Neuruppin in Brandenburg and used his considerable leisure time there to study intensively the most recent military specialist literature. This proved a considerable asset when he was transferred in 1801 to the *Lehr-Anstalt für junge Infantrie- und Cavalerieoffiziere* – a teaching institute in the military sciences in Berlin, the forerunner of what ultimately became the Prussian War Academy.

This transfer represents the watershed in Clausewitz's career, because the head of the institute, Lieutenant Colonel Gerhard von Scharnhorst, quickly spotted the extraordinary talents of his pupil, 25 years his junior, and took him firmly under his wing, becoming not only his teacher but also his paternal friend. Scharnhorst was a military innovator born and bred. He was the first officer in Prussian service (he was originally from Hanover) to recognize that a new kind of warfare had been born in the American War of Independence, that the days were numbered in which military formations fought one another by linear tactics. His influence upon Clausewitz can be seen in Scharnhorst's paper on the military operations in Italy in May and June 1800, in which he drew particular attention to the relationship between war and politics. Scharnhorst made the point that the political and military leadership would have to agree about intentions and possibilities. If the Secret Cabinet (as it then still existed in Prussia) should act solely on military principles, it would come to grief in much the same way as if its political designs disregarded military necessities. Both elements, the political and the military, should act in concert. This was a line of reasoning which Clausewitz quickly absorbed and which was later to lead to his stipulation of the primacy of politics in warfare, the central theory in all his work.

Under Scharnhorst's guidance Clausewitz did not pursue the studies of a narrow military specialist but opened his mind to the currents of German literature and art, which were then at their strongest. Classics, literature, history, mathematics, philosophy, especially the writings of Kant and Herder, provided Clausewitz with ample stimulus.

In the campaign of 1806, when Napoleon broke Prussia's neutrality, Clausewitz fought at Auerstädt, commanding one of the modernized Prussian formations, a contingent of Prussian tirailleurs. But finally, on 28 October 1806, he became a prisoner of the French. He spent a year's captivity in fairly comfortable circumstances at Nancy. On his return to Prussia he immediately associated himself with the reform movement led by Freiherr vom und zum Stein and Scharnhorst, who had already begun the root-and-branch reform of the Prussian state and the Prussian Army. When Clausewitz was transferred to Königsberg where the Prussian government had taken temporary residence, in April 1808, he entered the inner circle of the reformers. Promoted to captain in 1809, he became adjutant to Friedrich Wilhelm III and the confidant of Scharnhorst. Also living in Königsberg was Marie Countess von Brühl who was to become his wife.

After the Prussian government had returned to Berlin – the popular risings in Spain against Napoleon had forced him to withdraw the bulk of his French forces from Prussia and evacuate Berlin – in August 1810, Clausewitz, then 30 years old and promoted to major, became instructor on the *Kriegsschule zu Berlin*, responsible for general staff courses and for Little Wars, that is, guerrilla warfare. In addition, he became the

affairs by issuing Karl von Clausewitz a patent of nobility.

Clausewitz was born into the world of enlightened absolutism and its imprint was made upon him in his early years. In Prussia, the period was marked by the centralization of all important powers including the leadership of the army in the hands of the king. It was precisely this unity which during the War of the Austrian Succession and the Seven Years' War provided Frederick the Great with a decisive advantage *vis-a-vis* his opponents in the field of political and military battle. After Frederick's death on 16 August 1786, that unity was soon lost in the hands of his weak successor Friedrich Wilhelm II, which became apparent to all when the War of the First Coalition, of Austria and Prussia against France, began in 1792.

How much the young Clausewitz observed the changes in the political and military order around him no one can say for sure. But it seems a fair assumption that he noted them in his early life and that in later years, when he was deeply engaged in the study of political and military changes, his deductions from his early experiences influenced his theoretical writings. This assumption becomes more probable when we note that at the age of nine he witnessed from afar the outbreak of the French Revolution, with its intellectual, political, social and military transformations. Seventeen years later, under the impact of the defeat at Jena, Prussia was also to be transformed.

Young Clausewitz was soon personally involved in what was to become the transformation of Europe. In 1792, at the age of 12, he entered the Prussian Infantry Regiment *Prinz Ferdinand* in whose ranks he participated between 1793 and 1794 in the First Coalition War. For Clausewitz, the high point of this war was the siege and capture of the fortress of Mainz and the expulsion of the French Revolutionary Army. At the age of 15

personal instructor of Crown Prince Friedrich Wilhelm, the future Friedrich Wilhelm IV.

Opposition to the reform movement was intense, especially from members of the traditional Prussian military aristocracy, including Yorck von Wartenburg. But nothing discouraged the reformers more than Prussia's failure to support Austria against France in 1809, and, what was worse, the alliance concluded between Prussia and France to invade Russia in 1812, in which Friedrich Wilhelm III supplied Napoleon with a Prussian contingent. Many members of the reform movement resigned from Prussian service, going to Spain, Austria and Russia. Gneisenau, a prominent reformer, wrote, 'Our fate will reach us the way we deserve it. With shame we shall go under, because we cannot deny to ourselves that the nation is as bad as its regime.' Clausewitz left the Prussian Army to serve as a Lieutenant Colonel in Russia's German Legion in the summer of 1812. King Friedrich Wilhelm III never really forgave him for this step.

In December 1812 Clausewitz played a key role as negotiator between General von Yorck commanding the Prussian forces fighting on Napoleon's side and General von Diebitsch (another German who had become a full general in the Russian Army) which culminated in the Convention of Tauroggen by which the Prussian forces declared themselves neutral. Clausewitz was the central figure in the negotiations, and it was really due to his immense efforts that the Convention was concluded in spite of much hesitation on the Prussian side. The Convention of Tauroggen was the precondition for the new alliance between Prussia and Russia and Prussia's declaration of war against France on 16 March 1813.

Nevertheless, Friedrich Wilhelm III was not ready to forgive Clausewitz's defection. Although prominent soldiers like Scharnhorst, Blücher and Gneisenau frequently intervened on Clausewitz's behalf for his reassignment to the Prussian Army,

Left: King Friedrich Wilhelm III of Prussia, whose alliance with Napoleon shocked Clausewitz and other Prussian officers. Below left: British infantry practising their rifle drill in 1807, when Britain was again threatened by a French invasion. Right: Napoleon's troops cross the Danube on their way to victory over the Austrians at Wagram in 1809. Unlike so many other campaign river crossings, this one shows no congestion; the rapid advance meant that the Austrians were too late to oppose the crossing. Below: General von Yorck, the Prussian commander who agreed to remove his troops from Napoleon's army.

the King remained unwilling for the time being and declined every such request. So for the campaign of 1813, Clausewitz, still nominally a Russian officer, became chief of staff of an army corps attached to the allied Northern Army.

However enthusiastically the Wars of Liberation were greeted throughout Germany, upper-level political and military arguments about the conduct of the campaign and its aims never ceased, a fact very instructive to Clausewitz. Thus after the Battle of Leipzig (16–19 October 1813) in which the French and their allies were decisively defeated, Blücher wanted to pursue the French Army into France and end the war by a battle of annihilation. To the Austrians, who feared a strong Russia and Prussia as much as a strong France, it was imperative that France not be completely eliminated as a military power. France's weight in a future balance of power was not to be destroyed. These differences of opinion were debated at length by the Congress of Vienna, convened in 1814 after Napoleon's first overthrow, and ended only with Napoleon's return from Elba and his journey through France to growing acclaim.

The Prusso-German forces which rallied to the aid of the hard-pressed Duke of Wellington at Waterloo in June 1815 included the III Army Corps under Lieutenant General von Thielmann, only a few months after Friedrich Wilhelm III had finally yielded to the numerous requests and taken Clausewitz back into Prussian service with the rank of colonel. Clausewitz became Thielmann's chief of staff. The relationship between the political and military conduct of war was most instructive in this case, with many of the hot-headed Prussian generals advocating a much more radical course than the politicians were willing to pursue. After the French defeat Clausewitz opposed the spreading of terror, the demand for large reparations and such extremes as blowing up the Jena bridge and the Arc de Triomphe in Paris. To his wife he wrote, 'You can imagine what kind of enemies we are making of the French and Louis XVIII, and this contrasts all the more with the English, who do not levy any contributions and do not plunder.' But then, of course, the English had not been plundered in the way that Prussia had been, nor had they ever paid the kind of tribute which the Prussians had paid to France. The main problem for Clausewitz was that the army was falling between two stools, spoiling its relationship with the French populace as well as with the French government. In the end, however, it was the politicians who won and not the generals.

After the war, Clausewitz became chief of staff to Gneisenau at the new army command at Koblenz. He also occupied this position under Gneisenau's successor, Lieutenant General von Hake. Both Gneisenau and Hake found only words of praise for Clausewitz and particularly admired his intimate knowledge of all aspects of military affairs and his wide intellectual horizon.

Early in May 1818 he was transferred and appointed Military Director of the Berlin War School. In spite of his promotion to major general in September 1818, he began to feel the onset of a policy reaction against the reform movement. His actual work

Top: A Russian artist's impression of the retreat from Moscow; Napoleon, escorted by his Imperial Guard, hurries out of Russia in his carriage, abandoning his army. Above left: Prussian infantry uniforms from (left to right) 1710 to 1845. The yellow-fronted jackets were worn in the Napoleonic wars. Above: Prussian generals' uniforms, with those of the Napoleonic wars in center. Left: Hungarian infantry officers and men about 1809. Top right: The coalition armies meet in Leipzig. The 1813 Battle of Leipzig was a crushing defeat for Napoleon at the hands of the Prussians, Russians, and Austrians. Right: · Prussian hussars.

was mainly administrative, and he had direct contact with the forces only in the role of an umpire at the annual maneuvers.

However, this enforced removal from the center of power provided him with sufficient leisure to reflect upon his experiences in peace and war and to begin to put them on paper. His initial studies concerned the relationship between attack and defense, the phenomenon of the popular war as practiced in Spain and the Tyrol, the Napoleonic strategy of annihilation and the problem of effective collaboration between the statesmen and the military leadership. This was, in fact, the genesis of his work *Von Krieg*, or *On War*.

This period of reflection was interrupted by a short tour of duty as a troop commander. In August 1830 he became Inspector of the II Artillery Inspection in Breslau. When popular unrest and risings occurred in the Russian-occupied part of Poland, a Prussian Army of Observation was stationed at the German-Russian/Polish frontier under the command of Gneisenau, with Clausewitz as chief of staff. However, Gneisenau died of cholera on 23 August 1831 and Clausewitz returned to Breslau. He died of heart failure on 16 November 1831 at the age of 51. He was buried at the garrison cemetery in Breslau. In 1971 his remains were disinterred by the East German authorities and put to rest in his birthplace, Burg.

What remained was an immense legacy of writings on military-political affairs, as diverse as it was voluminous. It ranged from treatises on military history to strategic memoranda, including official and private letters as well as biographical essays and detailed treatments of aspects of the Prussian Reform period. His most significant legacy was his treatise *On War*, which in time became the foundation of the modern theory of war, a status that it retains to this day. But at the time of his death, it existed only in draft form; Clausewitz himself had considered only a small part of it as complete. The closeness between Clausewitz and his wife, Marie von Brühl, is demonstrated by the fact that she was sufficiently intimate with the workings of his mind to edit his literary legacy into a coherent volume of 849 pages. The work was published between 1832 and 1834. So far, in German alone, there have been 22 editions, not counting unnumbered editions. The first translation of the work was into Russian, but otherwise it was ignored there for most of the nineteenth century. Then came the Bolshevik Revolution and Clausewitz was rediscovered. He now has a place with the essential texts for Soviet staff training, as well as staff training throughout the Warsaw Bloc countries.

On War is divided into three parts. Part One consists of Book 1: Concerning the Nature of War; Book 2: Concerning the Theory of War; Book 3: Concerning Strategy and Book 4: Concerning Combat. Part II contains Book 5: The Military Forces and Book 6: Defense. Part III comprises Book 7: The Attack and Book 8: The Warplan. In this work, Clausewitz endeavors to produce not a military manual but something timeless on the fundamental nature of war and the theory related to it. The empirical raw materials of his study are some 139 campaigns and his own personal experience in several wars, augmented by his reflections during his postwar career.

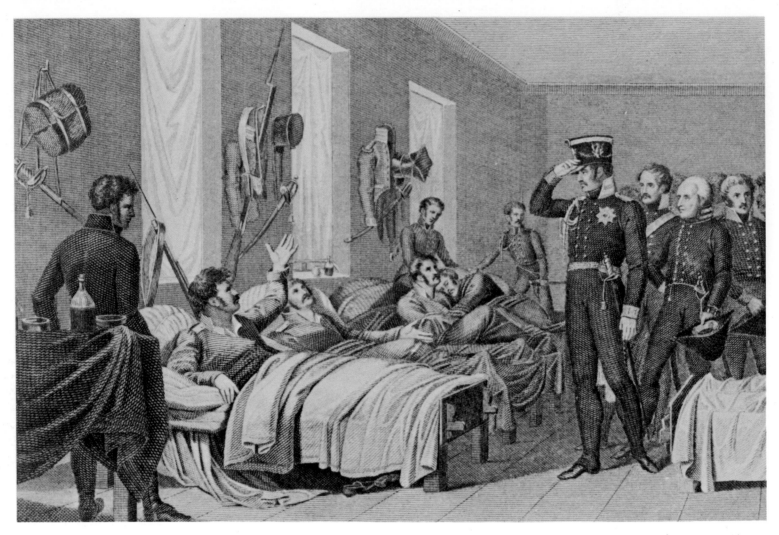

To understand Clausewitz one must understand the method with which he proceeded to examine his subject matter. He did not transform his thoughts into firm and unvarying rules. Instead he took the opportunity to treat the problems encountered dialectically, avoiding categorical statements and any tendency toward dogmatism. At every turn he viewed all sides of a given problem, examined its inner relationships critically and contrasted the advantages and disadvantages of any course of action. He rarely states his own opinions and convictions on a topic without first discussing it in detail. We find that every sentence has a counter-argument. Thus *On War* is characterized by three elements. First, it is a philosophical work, which has resulted from a dialectical method of thought and examination of the material. Second, it is a political work, since it never examines war as an isolated phenomenon, but always as an instrument of politics. Finally, it is a military-scientific work without equal, since it examines the fundamental questions of warfare. Clausewitz's thoughts on the relationship between war and politics are probably the most important and significant part of the work.

One term frequently encountered in his work is 'absolute' war. In Clausewitz's mind this represents an abstraction – a kind of war which had not yet been encountered, but to which Napoleonic warfare had come close. In other words, it means what we now call total war. If one looks for the foundations of Clausewitz's work, upon which his theory of the absolute war is grounded, one finds precise general ideas about the nature of war as such: what it can achieve and what it ought to achieve. In the first instance his ideas are deeply influenced by his outright rejection of the mechanistic theory of war prevalent in the age of absolutism and the enlightenment. Clausewitz reacted against an environment of mercenary soldiers, against armies

that fought one another while the bourgeoisie went about its business in a normal peace-time fashion. Military writers like the Swiss officer and later French and Russian general Jomini developed their art of war as a geometry and algebra of action, isolated from other forms of activity. Clausewitz repudiated these notions. In his view a theory of war was not necessarily an instruction for action. The task of theory was to make the empirical evidence subject to reasonable examination and reflection. Theory, in Clausewitz's context, provided a means of organizing the empirical evidence.

In the first instance his theory appeals to experience and directs all its consideration to those combinations which the history of war has already demonstrated. In contrast to Jomini, he aimed at no more than a limited theory here. In the second instance, however, Clausewitz includes in his examination all wars from the guerrilla war – the little war as he calls it – to the absolute war. His underlying purpose was to reconcile theory and practice. Soldier that he was, he left the justification or condemnation of war to the philosophers, preferably, one might guess, to St. Augustine and Grotius. His role in the history and theory of war was analogous to that played by Karl Marx in the field of political economy. Clausewitz's concept of the absolute war was based in part on 20 years' personal experience of Napoleonic warfare, which, as already stated, had not become really absolute but had been nearer to this point than previous wars. Since Clausewitz could not foresee the immense strides of science and technology in the century to follow, the absolute war was really an abstraction to him, because war usually appears in a limited form with all sorts of frictions and constraints, much as individual battles and campaigns are subject to unexpected hindrances. These frictions and constraints prevent war from escalating to the last and ultimate consequence.

Left: King Friedrich Wilhelm III visits his wounded Prussian officers after the Battle of Bautzen, one of several 1813 battles in which Napoleon attempted but failed to crush Blücher's forces.
Above: Marshal Blücher, who wore down Napoleon's army in 1813 and thereby brought about the French defeat of that year at Leipzig.

Although absolute war does not really happen, its mere possibility, however remote, makes it a subject for consideration and reflection. Transposed into the context of our own age, Clausewitz's absolute war is total war and its ultimate and probably final manifestation, *thermo-nuclear war*. The image of absolute war always hovers in the background for Clausewitz, a war that has reached the ultimate escalation. He vehemently opposed the notion that war follows its own inner logic, that it is 'like a mine which once exploded cannot be directed or conducted, except that one has provided it at the outset with a fuse.' Passionately he rejects this idea. 'War is only half a thing since it must be considered as part of a whole, and the whole is politics.'

What does Clausewitz mean by politics? He considers it as representative of all the interests of the community. In his view, the political process stood for all human interests, it was the harmonizing of all these interests and the conflicts among them, domestically as well as in the realm of foreign policy. For a man born into the *ancien régime*, this is almost a democratic definition and brings him into close affinity with his near-contemporary, the writer Alexis de Tocqueville. In a time when the forces of reaction had asserted themselves again in much of Europe, Clausewitz's conception of politics as the representation of interests is quite modern. From that conception came his famous dictum that 'War is nothing other than the continuation of state policy by other means,' a dictum that is by no means invalidated by its inversion in our own days that politics is nothing other than the continuation of war by other means. What has changed is the technological and scientific context.

According to Clausewitz, war has to be subordinated at all times to the primacy of politics. The art of war is a policy that delivers battles instead of diplomatic notes, exchanges the pen for the sword. But war has only a different writing and language, it does not have its own logic. All political purposes belong to the government alone; in no case can the art of war become its preceptor. All that a general can ask the politicians is that they do not over- or underestimate the military means available. In consequence, Clausewitz, very much affected by his own personal experience, rejected the influence of the military upon the formulation of political policy and did not want to leave the decision for peace or war in the hands of the military. One is reminded of the Schlieffen Plan for the German mobilization in 1914, or the conduct of World War I in general when politicians on all sides abandoned control of the war to their generals until Woodrow Wilson, with his Fourteen Points, restored the primacy of politics.

It was not simply Clausewitz's conviction, but the result of his reflections based on solid empirical evidence, which led him to the conclusion that war is an instrument of politics and must be measured in those terms. In short, Clausewitz postulates the primacy of politics at all times. He contrasts a *raison du politique* against an abstract, absolute war, perhaps with too much confidence in human reason, because the question remains open whether political constraints alone – without the transformation of the economy and society to a level which would ensure peace – are a sufficiently strong barrier against absolute war. Still, there are indications in his work that he recognized the danger of a radicalization of politics that could open the floodgates to absolute war. He discerned from far the consequences of the rise of totalitarian politics.

Wars conducted with the full deployment of a nation's resources of manpower and the economy expanded the whole spectrum of politics and warfare. The far-reaching effects of the Napoleonic Wars, according to Clausewitz, 'originated in the new social conditions which the French Revolution had brought about domestically.' In other words, because war necessarily carries the character of the politics which guide it, it can become more powerful and all-embracing, as in France in the 1790s, developing dimensions in which war comes close to its abstract form. In those insights, despite all essential differences, lies a point which is very close to the concept of total war. Clausewitz saw the specter of this development very clearly, and his efforts were aimed at avoiding it.

For a time Clausewitz's fears were held at bay, ironically by nothing other than the forces of reaction after 1815. The Congress System dominated European diplomacy after the fall of Napoleon I – effectively, a coalition of states organized for the defense of commonly accepted values and agreements. This meant no unilateral change of existing treaties or of the territorial *status quo* without the consent of the other signatory powers. The basis of this system was the defense of the principle of monarchic legitimacy and the existing social order by governments which, under the impact of the French Revolution, had combined to avoid any similar upheavals in future.

Although the Congress System was short-lived because of continuing and fresh conflicts of interest among the great European powers, this did not mean that the powers abandoned a platform comprised of mutual agreements. The Congress System was replaced by the so-called Concert of the European Powers, which could be upheld as long as monarchic legitimacy and the social *status quo* were to be defended, despite the relative

Left: Mid-nineteenth century uniforms. In the top picture four Prussians are at the left (infantryman, guard cavalryman, cuirassier, and officer) and five Austro-Hungarians to the right, with two British (sharpshooter and infantry guardsman) on the extreme right. The bottom picture shows French uniforms; from left to right they are a light infantryman from the African colonial forces, a chasseur (light infantryman), an infantryman, a zouave (member of an infantry unit recruited in north Africa), a cuirassier, a lancer, and a grenadier. The British examples are taken from about 1830, the Prussian from 1845, and the Austrian from about 1840. Below: Prussian dragoon uniforms from 1688 (left) to 1845. Third and fourth from right are of the Napoleonic period. Dragoons were heavily armed cavalry, capable of also fighting on foot. Right: The victorious allies enter Paris in 1814; the red and white banner is the Prussian state flag. The allies, including Russia, occupied Paris and France for some years afterward; the Russians in particular developed friendly relations with the French population. Below right: Wellington's campaign in Spain; the British defeat the French, commanded by Joseph Bonaparte, at Vittoria in 1813.

stagnation of economic growth and physical strength in the powers concerned.

On several occasions the Concert seemed close to disintegration, as when there was an attempt to extend it to the Ottoman Empire, over the Italian question in 1859 and over the German question in 1860, 1864 and 1870. But a closer look shows that these events had been preceded by a slower but remarkable change in the relative distribution of power, which had made the political premises of 1815 obsolete insofar as they concerned Italy and Germany. The real distribution of economic power was no longer in accord with that of 1815. The significance of this lies in the fact that these changes took place within the existing framework of power and of the power structure. Consequently, in spite of change, the principles of the Concert of the European Powers survived their occasional suspensions.

Between 1871 and 1890 the territorial *status quo* was still generally accepted, but from 1890 onward until 1914 it slowly decayed, and for the first time since the *ancien régime* the powers of Europe were compelled to rely upon a balance of power among themselves and the means generally associated with this – alliances and armaments.

The reasons for the decline of the European Concert are as manifold as they are debatable. Firstly, the Concert had developed within a European framework, but it was now increasingly subject to pressures originating from areas outside Europe, pressures which the Concert simply was not strong enough to withstand. The problem of the Straits (the Dardanelles) and that of the Egyptian question are but two illustrations.

Secondly, one notices the awareness of the growth of a power vacuum outside central and western Europe, which increasingly touched upon the older traditional interests of the European powers. International stability no longer depended simply on the distribution of power in Europe, but on the distribution of power in the global sense.

Thirdly, the growth of the democratic universal franchise, the entire process of democratization, brought the emotions of the masses into the spectrum of all those factors upon whose correct assessment a stable European policy was based. The growth of democracy brought forth the age of mass politics, with its emotionally rather than rationally formulated appeals to the masses, and thus unintentionally produced a new concept of the State which included a vast range of new functions. In 1815 the respective governments had been confronted by their respective societies. Although the conflicts between society and state had not been fully resolved, in 1914 and again in 1939, temporarily at least, behind every government in western and central Europe stood the solid, phalanx of a national community. The criteria of power had shifted from the degree of political stability, maturity and geographical advantages to factors that were industrial, economic and organizational in nature.

In such a changing environment, even the primacy of politics as understood by Clausewitz was bound to mutate and change. In Germany this was particularly noticeable among the generations of generals who followed Clausewitz. Increasingly, they studied him literally; they did not interpret the sense of what he was saying, but instead turned Clausewitz's work into the very opposite of what he had intended it to be, that is, into a book of firm rules and regulations – a dogma. It was gradually emptied of its theoretical-philosophical content and interpreted as an essentially technical theory of war.

This is true, for instance, of Helmuth von Moltke, probably the best military mind the Prussian Army ever produced. As Chief of the General Staff from 1857 until 1888 he was aware of the differences there had been between the politicians and the generals during the Wars of Liberation. In a letter to his brother in 1852 he claimed that the diplomats had regularly thrown Prussia into chaos from which only the generals could save it. The Austrians, by contrast, had lost many campaigns but obtained their major gains by their cabinet policy. Moltke was at the beginning of a process which can only be called a fundamental misunderstanding of Clausewitz.

It was Moltke's belief that the primacy of politics should exist only until the outbreak of war, when it should be suspended in favor of the primacy of the military for the duration of the conflict. This amounted to the sacrifice of the essence of Clausewitz's teachings. 'Political moments,' he wrote in 1870, 'deserve consideration only insofar as they do not demand something militarily inadmissible or impossible.' On another occasion he wrote 'The military and politicians work hand in hand as far as the ends are concerned, but in its action the military is completely independent.'

'For the duration of a war military considerations have pre-eminence and predominance, the exploitation of successes or failures is a matter for the politicians,' he wrote in 1882. Moltke demanded clearly defined areas of competency, thus rupturing the ties established by Clausewitz's theory.

This is borne out by Moltke's relationship with Bismarck. Bismarck always insisted that the determination and definition of the war aims, as well as the direct personal counselling of the monarch were the province of the manager of the political process and were therefore his own personal affair. It was he, the politician, who determined the political course of the war and not Moltke. In his view it was a difficult enough task to determine the best moment to make the transition from peace to war and from war to peace, which required thorough political knowledge. Bismarck demanded and succeeded in asserting the primacy of politics against great difficulties.

The relationship between Bismarck and Moltke often reached the crisis point, particularly during the Franco-Prussian War of 1870–71, when their cooperation often seemed to be on the verge of a breakdown. The first crisis occurred at a fairly early stage with the fall of Sedan and the capitulation of the French armies there under Napoleon III. It temporarily abated and then reached a simmering point again; by January 1871 the relationship between Bismarck and Moltke was on the verge of collapse. The issues included Bismarck's complaint that Moltke and his general staff kept him completely in the dark about the military campaign, that he was completely ignored in the planning of the second phase of the campaign after Sedan and finally, that Moltke refused, at least for a time, to bombard Paris by artillery, which Bismarck considered necessary for a speedy conclusion of the hostilities. But the main theme underlying the whole controversy was the army's failure throughout the war to keep Bismarck adequately informed.

Both political and military leaders were always present in the German headquarters, so in practice it should not have been at all difficult for the military to keep the politicians informed; there was ample opportunity for cooperation. Of course it was not absolutely necessary to inform the Prussian prime minister and German chancellor about the details of any tactical measures because these were purely military affairs in the hands of military specialists. However, the matter was different when it concerned the conduct of operations which exerted a profound influence on the course of the entire war, occasions when military strategic problems were closely interlocked with problems of political strategy. This was precisely the point at which Clausewitz had considered it essential that the politician and the general cooperate closely within a common war council. In Prussian constitutional terms, this would have meant that

Above: Wellington and Blücher meet after their joint victory at Waterloo. In this portrayal by a British artist the British commander, naturally, is dominant.

Bismarck and Moltke under the chairmanship of the King or the Emperor would discuss the situation and jointly decide upon a common course of action.

Moltke later wrote that neither in the war of 1866 nor in that of 1870–71 had such a war council existed. All he had done was to inform Wilhelm I regularly about the most recent developments and submit to him suggestions for any changes. On such occasions the Chief of the Military Cabinet, Lieutenant General von Tresckow and the Minister for War, General von Roon, had been present. Bismarck, who was also always present at Headquarters, was not mentioned by Moltke at all. Moltke defined a war council differently than did Bismarck. For him it was only an institution for the discussion of problems of military leadership and the conduct of a battle or a campaign. But this kind of discussion was by no means a substitute for a conference on the military and political strategies. Moltke and his subordinates were most anxious to do all they could to keep Bismarck at arm's length whenever they discussed military affairs with the monarch. In the course of these discussions they tried to gain the maximum share of military and political decision-making and simply to exclude the political leadership. The results were ever-increasing tensions between Bismarck and Moltke and the development of a dichotomy between the military and the political leadership.

As a case in point, after the capitulation of the French Army at Sedan it would have been advisable for Bismarck and Moltke to arrive at mutual decisions about the subsequent conduct of the war, especially since on 4 September the Republic was proclaimed in Paris and a government for national defense was formed. It would have been a matter for the politicians to decide whether the German Army should be satisfied with what had been gained thus far in the interest of a quick peace, or whether it should march on Paris to encircle it and go on to occupy further French territory. None of this happened. The second phase of the campaign was initiated by Moltke's order on 3 September 1870. Bismarck was left in the cold and did not participate in the discussions leading to that decision. Wilhelm I, himself more a soldier than a politician, failed to exercise his function as the supreme coordinator.

By 19 September Paris was surrounded and Bismarck favored an immediate artillery bombardment to make the French amenable to a rapid peace. Almost two months later Moltke argued that in the question of artillery bombardment only military opinion would be operative. What lay behind Moltke's argument was the simple fact that after Paris was encircled, heavy siege artillery was not available; it took considerable time to transport it from Germany and position it outside Paris. Even when the bombardment did start, the artillery and ammunition in place were not sufficient. Bismarck, meanwhile, forever afraid of the intervention of other European powers, was anxious to negotiate peace as speedily as possible. But only by the end of December 1870 was sufficient artillery and ammunition available to undertake the siege.

Below: The British infantry, drawn up in their squares, were basic units in the tactics of the Battle of Waterloo. Squares were highly resistant to cavalry attacks, although vulnerable to artillery; but since the enemy could not easily attack simultaneously with artillery and cavalry they were very strong formations, provided the infantry's discipline was tough.
Inset: Wellington, painted in the black cloak he wore at Waterloo.

Above: Gneisenau, with Scharnhorst the joint creator of the new Prussian army. Left: En route to his last exile; Napoleon paces the deck of HMS *Bellerophon*, closely observed by Royal Navy officers. Below: Wilhelm I, with Moltke and Bismarck in attendance, watches the siege of Paris.

Above: The climax of Prussian military success; King Wilhelm I stands on the parapet of a gun position as Paris surrenders. Right: Bismarck, who guided Prussian affairs from 1862 to his dismissal by the young Kaiser Wilhelm II in 1890. He is regarded as the virtual creator of the Prussian Empire and a skilful manipulator of diplomacy and military violence. But his success led to World War 1.

Bismarck was furious about the lack of information from the military. In a letter to Moltke, he demanded continuous reports about the military operation, or at least copies of the telegrams which the army headquarters sent to the press, since what he read in the papers was all new to him. He saw it five days after the event. Bismarck asked Wilhelm I to mandate his presence at the council of war, since the military operations inevitably influenced or touched upon political issues. Nothing came of that request, and he complained to Wilhelm again in early January 1871 that the political leadership had not been consulted in determining the conduct of the war and had been excluded from delivering opinions on its political ramifications. He repeated his request for consultation on the grounds that newspaper reports had been his only source of information except for rumors.

This time Wilhelm I responded favorably and ordered Moltke to cooperate with Bismarck by keeping him fully informed. The Prussian General Staff took a dim view of this, but a royal order could not be disobeyed. Indeed, Moltke's immediate reaction was to submit his resignation, but on second thought he held back. He insisted, however, that the Chief of the General Staff and the Chancellor represented institutions equal in rights but independent of one another. Technically this was correct, since the King and Emperor was the Supreme Commander of

the forces. But from this moment on Bismarck managed to establish the primacy of politics.

Bismarck's success is reflected in his letter of 26 January 1871 in which the statesman and politician informed Moltke, the soldier and warlord, that he had agreed with the French to the cessation of the bombardment of Paris beginning at midnight. This was followed by a meeting between Bismarck and Moltke which paved the way for the negotiations between German and French representatives culminating in the capitulation of all Paris fortresses and the conclusion of a three week armistice. On 17 February began the peace negotiations which ended in the preliminary peace of 26 February 1871. It seemed as though Bismarck and Moltke were reconciled. However, tensions built up between them again during the final peace negotiations. While Bismarck would have been content with the annexation of Alsace, border territory of which the German Empire had been deprived by Louis XIV 200 years before, Moltke insisted on obtaining a part of Lorraine as well, including the city of Metz, in the interest of a better line of defense in any future Franco-German conflict. Under great pressure, Bismarck finally gave in. The Treaty of Frankfurt of May 1871 put an end to the war between Germany and France.

Subsequently the relationship between Bismarck and Moltke ran smoothly; as long as Bismarck was at the helm of state, military-political relationships were very much in accord with Clausewitz's ideas.

Nevertheless, the trend within the Prusso-German army led away from the teachings of Clausewitz. Pure military thinking, divorced from a political context, was on the ascendant, checked only with great difficulty by Bismarck. The work of Chief of the General Staff General Alfred von Schlieffen was twofold: to eliminate frictions in war as much as possible in a period of rapid technological and scientific change in arms and industry, and to introduce an all-embracing military preparedness for any conceivable contingency in which political decisions were again subordinated to those of the military. Schlieffen's operational plans were the product of a perfected theory of war to which the political process was subordinated. Clausewitz's theory was thus reversed, and the dogma of the battle of annihilation established.

Another important factor was the social militarization of Germany after 1860. The immense prestige accumulated by the Prusso-German army in three successive wars put the military at the apex of the social pyramid. It was an army which, apart from its budget, was outside parliamentary control. Small wonder therefore that Bethmann Hollweg (who was chancellor from 1909–17) said with resignation that it was impossible for the layman to judge military possibilities, let alone military necessities. He confirmed that the politicians had abandoned Clausewitz's charge to them to lay down firm guidelines and establish a frame of reference for military function.

Schlieffen, who was the Chief of the General Staff from 1891 until 1905, left no fundamental exposition of his views on the relationship between civil authority and the armed forces. What he did leave were numerous memoranda about a campaign against France which involved the violation of the neutrality of Belgium, Luxembourg and the Netherlands. Military considerations preoccupied him to the exclusion of political considerations. The most important document he left for his successor was the Schlieffen Plan, which envisioned the distribution of the German forces on the western frontier with a right wing seven times stronger than the left wing. The weak left wing would hold the enemy at bay and the right wing would attack north of Diedenhofen and Metz. The army would then march through Belgium, which beyond Liege was ideal flat country for an army on foot, sweep around west of Paris and defeat the French forces decisively within a matter of weeks.

In his first few drafts Schlieffen contemplated violating the neutrality of the Netherlands as well, but he abandoned this idea in the plan's final form. Although the political leaders of the Reich had been informed, first Chancellor Bülow and then his successor Bethmann Hollweg, neither raised any objections. They left military affairs to those best qualified. And Kaiser Wilhelm II was not a man capable of coordinating the political and military leadership. He rather preferred making speeches. Indeed, he went so far as to state that in wartime the politicians had to keep their mouths shut until a successful strategy allowed them freedom of speech again. Thus the primacy of the military superseded that of politics throughout the Wilhelmine period.

The Schlieffen Plan has been much criticized, especially in the context of the July Crisis of 1914 when the military timetables were a major contributory factor to the outbreak of war because of the rapid mobilization and assembly of the military forces. But this development had been foreseen a number of years before, in 1892, when the Chief of the French General Staff, Boisdeffre, and the Chief of the Russian General Staff, Obruchev, upon concluding the Franco-Russian Military Convention, agreed that henceforth the mobilization of forces would have to be carried out at a speed which would make the outbreak of actual hostilities virtually inevitable.

Every general staff devises its plans with the objective of winning a war, or at least holding back the enemy until a cessation of hostilities can be reached. From this perspective the Schlieffen Plan was no novelty, nor was the envisioned violation of neutral territory. Great Britain showed no hesitation in breaking the neutrality of Greece in World War I when this was deemed essential to the outcome of the war. It is interesting to note that even the most incisive critics of the Schlieffen Plan, like the historian Gerhard Ritter, are really at a loss to suggest an alternative to it. One of the Plan's major determinants was Germany's geographic position. It has been suggested that she was favored by her internal lines of communication. To some extent this is true, but for Germany to fight a war on an interior

line of defense would have been tantamount to fighting a war of attrition, which can only be fought by countries rich in raw materials and foodstuffs. Except for coal and a very little low-grade iron ore, Germany had no raw materials of her own to speak of; most had to be imported. To a lesser extent this also applied to foodstuffs. In contrast, countries with exterior lines of defense and communication could not only draw upon their own resources but import all else that they needed.

Therefore, from a German point of view, the war had to be quick and decisive in the west before they could enter the fray in the east, where the going was expected to be rather more difficult. But the Schlieffen Plan failed as a result of the alterations made by Schlieffen's successor, General von Moltke, a nephew of Moltke the elder. Schlieffen's basic concept had been derived from the tactics employed by Frederick the Great at Leuthen in 1757. Moltke, however, was not satisfied with one outflanking pincer; the battle he wanted to emulate was Cannae, a double pincer movement of both right and left wings taking the offensive. But a strong left wing could be achieved only at the expense of the strength of the right wing. In addition, once war had broken out, the Russians invaded East Prussia much earlier than the Germans had expected. To meet the Russian danger, the German right wing had to be further depleted for defense in the east. The result was that German manpower in France was too weak to swing around west of Paris; instead it swung around east of Paris, exposing the entire German right flank to the city that was the center of the French communications network. As a result Joffre, the French commander in chief, was able to throw his forces against the German right wing. The Miracle of the Marne meant that the Schlieffen Plan had failed, and a war of movement degenerated into a war with firm solid fronts from the Channel to the Swiss frontier. It became a war of attrition in which slowly but surely the scales began to weigh against Germany.

Inside Germany it was hoped that this development could be countered by placing even greater emphasis on the primacy of the military, culminating in the virtual dictatorship of Hindenburg and Ludendorff. It was not within their power to change the ultimate outcome.

Left: In besieged Paris, 1870, even elephant meat becomes acceptable. Right: A French artist shows an allegorical France, confronted by real Prussians, signing peace preliminaries. Below: General von Schlieffen. Bottom: General von Kluck and staff.

Clausewitz was forgotten, and after the collapse of 1918 numerous writers in Germany and other countries began to patch together a new theoretical framework. Ludendorff's *Total War* in 1935, already mentioned, was one such attempt. Such lesser lights as General Friedrich von Bernhardi, a prolific writer on military affairs before 1914, postulated that statesmanship must limit itself to preparing for and exploiting military success, according to the directions given by the military leadership. 'This will ensure accord and harmony between military and political action.'

Modern war, so it was stipulated, has a planetary character. Therefore entire states and their populations are involved in it.

The differences between combatants and non-combatants had been blurred to the point of extinction. Consequently, intense propaganda must be employed to prepare the nation for the struggle and to sustain it throughout.

Not only military experts engaged in this kind of propaganda, but also writers of great distinction, such as the former shock troop commander Ernst Jünger, who in his *Total Mobilization* and *Der Arbeiter* pleaded for the primacy of the military. For Jünger, peace was only a preparation for war. The aristocracy of the trenches of World War I represented the true form of socialism. The shell crater and the trench were for him the harbingers of a new and healthier world.

Left: Joffre (left) and Foch. Joffre commanded the French army 1914–16 and has been described as 'a strategical vacuum within which buzzed his General Staff.' Foch later became supreme commander of the Allied armies on the Western Front. Bottom: A celebrated and perhaps crucial event of 1914; motor vehicles are commandeered to take French troops to the Marne.

Such eminent constitutional lawyers and experts as Carl Schmitt and Ernst Forsthoff added to this their demand for the total state, the pre-condition of total war. 'All instinctive, progressive and in substance revolutionary forces are engaged in the attack upon the legacy of our time. The age of the bourgeoisie will be liquidated. Any resistance will have to be exterminated ruthlessly.'

'In future,' to quote Forsthoff further, 'the total German state of Adolf Hitler will be governed by a highly qualified, racially homogenous and dominating leading class.'' The anatomy of the SS state was being sketched long before it existed.

Ludendorff in his own work denied that he wished to devise a new theory of war, but the essence of that work was to turn

Top: Recently-captured French prisoners of war under German guard in France late August 1914. In contrast to May 1940, the French army did not lose its cohesion in retreat, so there were no massive surrenders of French units. Above: Leading participants of the unsuccessful rising of 1923, the Munich 'beerhall' *putsch* of Hitler's National Socialists. The German Army's predilection for meddling in politics is well exemplified here; only two of the figures (Hitler and Frick) are in civilian clothes. General Ludendorff, whose ill-deserved military reputation was a major asset for the Nazis, stands in the center.

Clausewitz upside down. Clausewitz's maxim would have to be replaced by the postulate 'that all politics had to serve war.'

We might ask whether similar writings were to be found in other countries. Certainly in the United States, Homer Lea, before World War I or in Britain, H G Wells in his *Anticipations of Mechanical and Scientific Progress upon Human Life and Thought* forecast the garrison state in which all human endeavors were subordinated to the conduct of war. In France it was Rene Quinton in his *Maximes sur la guerre* and Albert Seche in *Les guerres d'enfer*, both of which ran to several editions. G Blancon and his work *Guerre nouvelle* and the right-wing radical Leon Daudet in *La guerre totale* preached the gospel of the new militarism. Perhaps it can be said of the French that their militaristic literature was a product of a time in which France was in extreme danger.

This can hardly be said of Ludendorff in 1935 when he demanded that all the lessons of Clausewitz must be thrown on the scrap heap on the grounds that war is the highest expression of the racial will to live. Politics has to serve the conduct of war at all times. His call was a plain and simple one for the establishment of a military absolutism, preferably with himself at the helm. What made these writings attractive to a wide readership? No doubt the memory of the days of August 1914, the immense physical and psychological effort made for over four years and the effort to distill some sense and purpose for sacrifices made apparently in vain. Also, the idea of a future multi-front war made Schlieffen's concept suitable to further radicalization in the sense of conducting maximum military preparations in peacetime. Total mobilization and racial cohesion appeared to promise a solution to the problems of German society. The community of the trenches seemed an alternative to the social relationships of a capitalist society.

What influence did these writings actually have? The question is easier to pose than to answer. In the German General Staff and the bulk of the officer corps, they appear to have had very little effect. Ludendorff was considered a crank. More importantly, after 1933 it was Adolf Hitler himself who firmly subordinated the military to the primacy of politics. The Chief of the General Staff, Ludwig Beck, and in 1938 his successor, General Halder, accepted Clausewitz's demand that the military commander subordinate himself to the statesman. But Hitler's concept of politics and of the political process was not only fundamentally different from that of his predecessors, it was in fact perverted. The results of this twisted understanding of politics changed the map of Europe and of the world itself.

In 1929 General von Seekt had said that if we accept Clausewitz's dictum that war is the continuation of politics by other means, then we may as well say 'War is the bankruptcy of politics.' A nation may be able to survive such bankruptcies as Germany did after 1807, 1918 or 1945, but in our own day and age, in the face of the apocalyptical weapons of war, defeats are unlikely to be assimilated or overcome. Hence it is perhaps a salutary sign that on both sides of the Iron Curtain a Clausewitz Renaissance has begun, since both sides realize how important it has become to maintain the primacy of politics *vis-a-vis* the alleged military and industrial necessities. In 1960 President Eisenhower warned in his Farewell Speech of the monster of the military-industrial complex which was about to subjugate the political process to its own ends. Thus Clausewitz and what he wrote are as topical and relevant today as they were 150 years ago. What he anticipated with some anxiety then, sometimes in blurred and shadowy outline, had become a program a century later, and in spite of that program's leading to utter disaster, the problem of the relationship between the military leadership and the civil power has remained with us.

2. Military Science & Society

The 19th century was an age of scientific and technological progress previously unknown in the whole of human history. It was dominated by the belief in progress, itself a product of the Age of Enlightenment. This belief influenced all the important philosophical and social structures of the time: German idealism, British utilitarianism, French positivism, American pragmatism, the socialism of a Proudhon as much as that of Karl Marx and Friedrich Engels. It influenced nationalistic and racial philosophies as well as sociological and anthropological theories and the philosophy of history. 'Progress' became an altar on which its most extreme exponents were ready to sacrifice old and proven values and institutions for the sake of perfection of the future. Progress became a slogan whose dynamism was considered irreversible. Little attention was paid to the anthropological background of the idea of progress; instead people surrendered to a vain optimism fed by utopian hopes for the future, and it was not long before attempts were made to put the idea of progress on firm scientific and empirical footing. The idea of progress owed its broad impact and popularity less to the speculative results of a political philosophy than to the impressive triumphs of the natural sciences, which apparently not only confirmed the belief in progress, but appeared to postulate 'the law of progress' as well. The question as to which direction change was moving in was raised only by a few lonely voices, by sceptics who in our own day would be labelled as cultural pessimists.

The essence of the idea of progress was the belief that mankind had always moved forward in one direction, in which it fulfilled its ethical norms, and it would continue to do so forever. This, of course, leaves open the question concerning the quality of the existing ethical norms and their potential mutability, as well as the possibility that these norms were determined by class or interest groups. As might be expected, this belief in progress was interpreted differently by its critical commentators, including its most fervent exponents. For the nineteenth century historian Alexis de Tocqueville, progress was a continuous movement of human society toward human equality, as inexorable as a divine law: 'It is universal, it moves on, in spite of all human interference.'

From a different point of departure, the English philosopher Herbert Spencer concluded that 'the development towards the ideal man is logically certain – as certain as any logical conclusion to which we can give our unlimited faith.' But he goes on to explain that although progress is a necessity, one cannot assume that it unfolds in a regular and uniform pattern. In spite of the differences between these two opinions, the emphasis of both lies more on the mechanism of progress and less upon its final result of the perfect man in a perfect society.

Naturally the progress of science left its impact in the military sphere. The Prussian reforms of 1807–1813 had already placed great emphasis upon thorough scientific training for new officers. Initially, of course, this took place on a rather limited basis, but when Wilhelm von Humboldt, another of the Prussian reformers, thoroughly reorganized primary, secondary and university education the army benefited accordingly. Humboldt's educational reforms were emulated first throughout Germany and later, wholly or in part, throughout the civilized world. No wonder that in 1866 the Austrians and in 1871 the French attributed the German victory to the German schoolmaster. It was realized that only an educated soldier could be entrusted with tasks which required independent action based on clear thought. The educational reforms had, of course, critics and opponents, even in Prussia, but the example provided by such intellectually versatile officers as Scharnhorst, Gneisenau and Clausewitz inevitably affected their subordinates. Moltke,

for example, reported that, at a lecture on Goethe held at the Berlin university in the winter of 1828–29, one-third of the audience were officers of the higher ranks. In the 1850s Friedrich Julius Stahl had many officers in attendance at his lectures on politics and political parties. The pressure for higher education in the course of the 19th century increased to the extent that by 1880 30 percent of the German officer candidates had university entrance qualifications. By 1912 this had increased to 65 percent; in fact, this became the precondition for a regular commission. The main emphasis of the university courses attended by officers was on international law, military history and politics. Since the General Staffs of all European armies had been given the task of preparing in peacetime all the measures necessary for war and defense, experts, linguists and specialists of all kinds were needed to serve at staff level.

The higher educational level of ordinary soldiers and officers allowed the introduction of large-scale open-ended maneuvers by large army contingents, while at the staff level the sand table exercise became a regular feature. Geography became a major subject of study for officers, no doubt influenced by the series of new discoveries made during the course of the 17th century. In Germany, Wilhelm von Humboldt's brother, Alexander, and Carl Ritter became the founders of scientific geography in the early 19th century, and among Ritter's students were the young Moltke and the young Roon. The latter acquired a reputation as an author of valuable works on geography.

Technological invention played a major role in these developments. In 1797 Aloys Senefelder, a native of Munich, invented lithography which allowed the rapid production of maps. Now maps were available not only to commanders and generals, but to all officers. The Prussian General Staff formed its own lithographic institute in 1817. From 1821 onward there were annual survey trips by members of the General Staff. This in turn led to the systematic survey of the whole of Germany and several foreign territories, including Turkey, which the young General Staff officers visited. Daguerre's invention of photography in the 1830s was a further help to cartographers. By 1866 most of the Prussian officers were equipped with accurate maps. This development was paralleled in Austria, which had its own Military Geographic Institute, and the syllabus of the *Thersianischen Militaarakademie* was thoroughly reorganized to make room for the natural sciences.

In France Napoleon I had founded the war academy of St Cyr in 1808 for the training of infantry and General Staff officers, while the cavalry had its training school at Saumur and the engineers theirs at Angers. Only those who had university entrance qualifications or the equivalent thereof were accepted. They had to sign up for nine years. The course lasted two years and on passing the examination successfully the candidates could choose their own branch of the service. St Cyr was something of a hybrid, with elements of both the Prussian cadet institutes and the Prussian War Academy.

In England, the Royal Military Academy, Sandhurst, is the product of two cadet institutes, the Royal Military Academy at Woolwich, founded in 1741, and the Royal Military College, Sandhurst, founded in 1799. In 1812 they were combined into one institution. At that time it comprised two sections, one to train future officers, the other to train commanders and General Staff officers. Among its many renowned instructors was Michael Faraday, whose inventions were profoundly important to the development of physics and modern technology.

Thus from the early 19th century onward there was nothing in the area of the natural sciences which armies could afford to neglect without seriously impairing their own efficiency. Henceforth no scientific discovery or technological develop-

Previous page: Something for the children, far from the battlefields; a 1944 Victory Garden in New York. Right: Krupp guns, already world-renowned, on show at the 1876 Philadelphia Centennial Exhibition. Below: Jean Henri Dunant (Henry Dunant in the USA), founder of the Red Cross movement. Bottom: Inflating a balloon in the US Civil War.

Left: The first Maxim machine gun under test in 1885. Two of the gentlemen are using stop-watches, presumably to check the all-important rate of fire. Below left: A Chinese diplomat attends a demonstration of the Maxim machine gun, and is duly impressed by a tree, cut down by the stream of bullets. Below: The Vickers machine gun, descendant of the first Maxim, in service with the British army in 1942. Bottom left: Gatling and his 1893 Bulldog machine gun. Bottom right: Gatling claimed his machine gun would cut down on casualties by reducing the necessity for so many men in armies; one of his guns in action in the Spanish-American War at the Battle of El Canay.

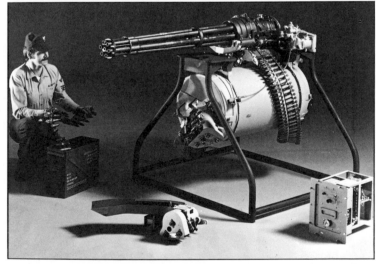

Top: German infantry in the Western Desert, using the standard general-purpose machine gun. Nominally a light machine gun, it could also be used in situations demanding an anti-aircraft weapon or a medium machine gun. Designed by the Mauser Works, it was the first light machine gun to use belt ammunition instead of a magazine; its telescopic sight attachment, to be seen here, is testimony to its utility over the longer ranges.
Left: A seven-barreled 20mm automatic gun mounted on a modern US warship. This weapon, the M61, was designed in the 1960s as an anti-aircraft gun with an exceptionally rapid rate of fire. It can despatch 50 rounds per second, presenting some problems of ammunition storage space. A ground version is part of a mobile air defense system used by the US Army.
Above: Manufacturer's picture of the M61 Gatling gun.

ment could be ignored by the armies, from the polarization of light in 1808 to the first model of the atom in 1911. Everything had now to be scrutinized and tested for its suitability in a military context: the determination of atomic weight in 1818, the synthesis of ammonia in 1913, the invention of the electric motor in 1834, the first motor-powered flight in 1903, the telegraphic writer in 1837, the picture telegraphy of 1902, the typesetting machine in 1890, the first cinematograph in 1895, the revolver in 1835, the tank in 1911, and building materials ranging from the iron concrete of 1867 to the cast concrete of 1907.

New discoveries in the fields of biology and medicine received equal attention. It became one of the most important tasks of the general staffs to observe the changing scientific and technological environment, to evaluate the results and to judge their applicability for military purposes. From that it was a short step for war departments or offices to contract work out to scientific institutes. The first example of this dates back to 1811 when British officers, watching the production of sulphur, noted that its by-product was a steam which poisoned the air and completely destroyed the vegetation on the ground. This experience was recalled during the siege of Sebastopol in the summer of 1855 and an attempt was made to smoke out the defenders from their fortress. It was the beginning of the deployment of chemical weapons in warfare.

In increasing numbers officers began to publish their own treatises in technical and scientific journals. Others had their main duties in the scientific sector and during the course of the 19th century they were absorbed into the general staffs.

As an example one can take the German General Staff as it existed on 1 April 1889. At the summit stood the Central Office, below which were three departments, each headed by an *Oberquartiermeister*. Department I concerned itself with military structural questions, mobilization plans and assembly of forces. It included a railway section responsible for the smooth organization of army transport as well as a section for airships. Department II was busy with intelligence concerning enemy fortresses and worked out plans on how best to attack these. It also included an engineers' section and a geographic and statistical section which had to supply the army in the field with maps. One section was responsible for the War Academy and also planned and supervised the fact-finding travels of the General Staff. Department III concerned itself with Russia, the Scandinavian countries, Austria-Hungary and the Balkans. Another section's area included France, Great Britain, the Netherlands, Switzerland and Italy. Later a special section for war history was established. Not part of the general staff, but subordinate to it, was a department with responsibility for land survey. This department united the former trigonometric, topographic and cartographic sections as well as one for non-German territories.

But as Moltke had emphasized in 1869, in the event of war the character of the officer weighed more heavily than his powers of reason. In action it was less a matter of what one did than of how it was done. Firmness of decision and the systematic implementation of what might be a simple plan were the ways to achieve a given objective. This argument, of course, was heartily endorsed by many, particularly those officers who felt themselves intellectually inferior to their peers. And the experience of warfare has shown that in most cases it is preferable to carry out a decision once taken rather than to reverse it several times. Or as Napoleon put it: 'Order – Counter Order – Disorder!'

Nevertheless by the middle of the 19th century the scientific education of officers had become indispensable, particularly for staff officers attached to the commanders of the various armies or army groups.

Another innovation with 19th century origins is what we now call troop entertainment. It was no profound psychological insight that gave a French captain and a lieutenant the idea of entertaining their troops and thus raising their morale during the siege of Sebastopol. They decided to found a Theater of Zouaves. While the captain directed the shows, the lieutenant wrote the spirited and humorous sketches which the Zouaves performed (in addition to their regular duties). When the French attacked the main Russian defense line on 28 June 1855, half of the theater members were killed. But the impact of the idea remained. The British Secretary for War, Lord Panmure, wrote to General Simpson, who commanded the British contingents after the death of Lord Raglan, that in order to reduce the habit of heavy drinking among the British forces he was going to send him artists and magicians for the entertainment of the troops. In both the World Wars, in Korea and Vietnam, troop entertainment became part and parcel of the highly organized business of conducting war. Thus the arts found a place in war, along with the sciences, for the creation of a kind of warfare which, imperceptibly at first, became more and more encompassing.

The discoveries in psychology and its auxiliary sciences gave birth to organized propaganda, which had already found its first expression in the mobilization of mass opinion in the War of American Independence, when pamphlets were as numerous as were bullets. A more sophisticated approach was seen just before the American Civil War whereby, for example, 'Uncle Tom' became the stereotype of the oppressed slave and Simon Legree the epitome of all the evils of slavery. In World War I both Great Britain and France took the propaganda offensive while the Central powers reacted at first hesitantly and, in the propaganda war, remained very much on the defensive.

The first testing ground of the new technology was the Crimean War, which began with an argument between Greek Orthodox and Roman Catholic monks about the holy places in Jerusalem. Czar Nicholas I took this as a pretext to intervene on behalf of the Greek Orthodox monks, which provoked Napoleon III who was striving to achieve pre-eminence in Europe. Supported by the British, the Turks rejected the Russian

Above: Some British east-coast towns were threatened by both Zeppelin bombs and naval gunfire in World War I; the picture shows damage at Yarmouth in 1915. Left: Savings drives were a feature of both world wars, the ostensible object being to encourage ordinary people to contribute to weapon purchase, and the real object being the control of wartime inflation; here a celebrity appeals on behalf of the US Liberty Loan in World War I. Right: Total war implies mass recruitment, which in turn means the replacement of men by women in civilian occupations. In this picture women are shown working in a US arms factory, using welding equipment. Similar scenes could be encountered in the other fighting countries, especially in Britain, but less so in Germany.

Top: Gas warfare on the Western Front in World War I. In the foreground German infantry equipped with gas masks are ready to go forward to take advantage of the demoralization and physical havoc that the gas is expected to inflict on the opposing troops. Gas was one of several technical innovations which might have decided the course of the war had they been used on a massive scale when they had also the advantage of surprise. Left: British officers are trained in anti-gas techniques in the 1930s; their gas masks are carried in chest packs. Above: US Marines in their gas masks. Right: Red Army men decontaminate their rocket launchers.

ultimatum, as a consequence of which Russian forces moved into the territories of the Ottoman Empire. Thereupon the Turks declared war on Russia in 1853. This caused France and Great Britain to attack Russia in the Baltic. Austria also mobilized but went no further. The only two ways of attacking Russia lay either through Germany or by landing at the Crimea. Prussia indicated that it would not permit the transport of French and British forces through Germany, which left only the Crimean solution.

Up to this point the British and French armies had had recent experience only in colonial warfare. The Napoleonic Wars had faded into history. Now for the first time the two western powers were engaged in an enterprise which could be carried out only with naval assistance. Effecting a landing on the open Crimean coast was not particularly difficult. Much more of a problem was the maintenance of supplies. Napoleon I, for example, had found it relatively easy to land 30,000 men in Egypt in 1798. But Nelson's victory at Aboukir cut his lines of supply and eventually Napoleon had to pull out. Similar problems had confronted the British in the War of American Independence. Therefore, for far-reaching global operations, dominance of the seas was essential. Great Britain and France had the naval supremacy and they had steamships which successfully braved wind and weather. In the Black Sea the Russian Navy had only small forces which dared not challenge the allies. But it was important for the allies to take a sizeable harbor.

The French Supreme Commander, Saint-Arnaud, intended to land at Feodosia and march upon Simferopol, the main Russian supply depot. Once this was taken, the Russian position was bound to collapse, since there were no railroads into the Crimea and in the autumn rains it would be impossible to keep the Russian forces supplied overland. However, the French plan could not be carried out because the British carried no supply trains. Therefore they were compelled to conduct their operations along the coast where their navy could keep them supplied. As a result, Sebastopol became the target, and the harbor of Eupatoria was chosen as the base of the navy, a navy which was to support the army simultaneously. To begin by capturing the small port of Balaklava, near Sebastopol, was out of the question because it could be effectively defended by the Russians from the surrounding heights as well as by the Sebastopol garrison. Eupatoria, in contrast, was surrounded by open land which could easily be taken under the fire of the naval guns if the Russians should defend it. The landing was made in September 1854 but it took seven days to disembark the combined British and French forces – an inordinately long time, but understandable in the face of strong seas and the total inexperience of the allies in amphibious operations.

The problem of getting regular supplies for the land troops was the greatest, especially after the Russians had succeeded in cutting off meat supplies from Turkophile Tartar tribes. At that time of the year it was impossible to guarantee regular supplies with sailing vessels and the available steamships were not sufficiently developed to transport large quantities of staple goods. The Royal Navy found a solution: steamships took the sailing vessels in tow from Constantinople. Thus for the first time in history a modern army of between 60,000 and 100,000 men was supplied for almost two years by a fleet of 84 warships and 300 cargo-carrying ships. Still, crises could not be avoided. The great storm of 14 November 1854 destroyed 55 ships, some of them inside the harbor at Balaklava which had fallen to the overland advance by then.

As already mentioned, the British commander, Lord Raglan, did not have his own supply trains for the coastal advance. Personnel and vehicles were denied to him in London. Although

he had hired Bulgarians and 6000 pack horses, in the end he decided to leave them where they were because he did not want to encumber himself with untrained personnel. But his progress remained slow, because the soldiers now had to carry everything themselves. The British forces were taxed beyond their resources before they came to the building of trenches and other hard work of emplacement which further depleted their physical stamina.

New technology was quickly brought in to help. At that time Great Britain had a railroad network of over 6400 miles. Throughout Germany, Austria and France, railroad networks had been built, and in the late 1840s Prussia had carried out its first maneuvers using rail transport. However, in the Crimea there was no railroad of any kind until the British, in December 1854, built the first field railway, about three miles long, which almost reached the heights of the Balaklava pass from the harbor. It supplied the forces with food and the tools and materials for building fortifications. The War Office in London had intended that it extend over ten miles and estimated the time for building it at three weeks. In point of fact even the much shorter line took over three months to build, since the terrain was extremely difficult and the technical and mechanical aids for constructing it were virtually non-existent. Nevertheless, from then on, field railways became an established means of supplying forces wherever the front had consolidated into firm lines.

Another major innovation which received its first test in warfare was the electrical telegraph, invented by the American, Samuel Morse, in 1837. It was to become of supreme importance to all armies. Up to that time orders and instructions had to be carried to their destination by messengers or by the cavalry. This was possible in an age when armies were still small, and the relative slowness of operational movements plus the frequent presence of the military leaders on the battlefield itself ensured that messages arrived in time.

Above left: The Spanish Civil War; armed women ready to fight for the Republicans on the streets of Barcelona.
Above: Hastily trained irregulars of the Spanish Civil War. The Republican forces included many women soldiers.

The problem was different once the armies of the French Revolution and the Napoleonic era had learned to fight over a vastly greater area. The invention of an optical telegraph or heliograph, by Claude Chappe, offered a major improvement but it had the disadvantage of necessitating a heliograph station every few miles within visible distance. Napoleon I used it to great effect, although building up a line of heliographs took considerable time and the instrument itself was dependent on the weather. The Prussian General Staff built a line of heliograph stations between 1832 and 1833 from Berlin via Magdeburg, Halberstadt, Höxter, Paderborn and Cologne, and then on to Koblenz and Trier. But heliographs were of limited usefulness to armies advancing on a broad front rather than in single columns. The telegraph was another matter. Major General von Etzel, a member of the Prussian General Staff, examined the new invention thoroughly, was impressed and submitted the first estimate of its cost to King Friedrich Wilhelm IV. The first line in Germany was built between Berlin and Potsdam in 1845, followed three years later by a second line between Berlin and Cologne, including Frankfurt on Main. Initially the telegraph was used not by the army but by politicians, the railways and the police, but in 1854 the Prussian Army established a mobile field telegraphy office for the use of the General Staff and the commanding generals of the most important army corps. Military field telegraphy was further expanded in 1859, particularly within the engineer corps. In the German-Danish war it took only 10 to 12 minutes to relay a message from Schleswig-Holstein to Berlin and the same amount of time to forward the message from Berlin to Vienna.

However, it was in the Crimea that for the first time in military history telegraphy became a significant influence in the conduct of operations. At the beginning of the war a telegram could be sent only as far as Varna in Bulgaria on the Black Sea and then had to be taken by ship across the Black Sea to Balaklava; it might take ten days to reach its destination. But when the British laid an underwater cable between Varna and the Monastery of St George near Balaklava they reduced the time of a telegram sent from London from 10 days to 24 hours.

One would think that everyone would have appreciated this invention. Certainly it was valued as far as questions of logistics and supply were concerned. But the distance between military leadership in the field and the War Office and Parliament in London had also been shortened and the wires were overloaded with all kinds of unrequested advice from politicians and everyone close to the court and the government who could, moreover, ask very deep and searching questions. The direct contact between London and the Crimea was considered by many officers and generals as an unwarranted interference in the conduct of operations and therefore as a great nuisance.

The Crimean War also demonstrated the immense superiority of seapower over exclusively land-based power. But it was not productive of great military talents or great generalship: the Charge of the Light Brigade is only one of many examples of this. In the main the war concentrated around the siege of Sebastopol, which was invested according to methods already in use during the 18th century. Also, at the tactical level, no innovations were forthcoming. The Russians still fought according to the methods introduced by General Suvorov and the British fought as they had at Waterloo. Linear tactics still dominated every battle. Only the French refined their tirailleur tactics, for which the bushland topography was ideally suited. But that development had its origins in French colonial warfare, especially in Algeria.

Ordinary soldiers still used muzzle-loading weapons but ammunition was now fired by percussion caps. This principle

Left: The beginnings of trench warfare in the US Civil War: wide excavations, with timber retaining walls. Bottom: British troops in France, in 1940, constructing a timber barrier on the Amiens–Rouen road in the hope of blocking German armored vehicles. Below: Trench warfare as it had developed by 1914; Austrian infantry on the Eastern Front. Trenches are now narrower, but easy access and movement is preserved by the provision of communication trenches in their rear.

Right: American troops of the 32nd Division in trenches overlooking Mulhouse, eastern France, in June 1918; the US forces arrived at the Western Front at a critical phase of the campaign. They are equipped with grenade projectors for their rifles. The hand grenade became a staple weapon in trench warfare, both in attack and defense. Bottom: The infantryman's foxhole, a quickly-dug excavation for one or two men, gave better protection against shrapnel; this belongs to a US Marine.

had been in use since 1807, mainly for hunting rifles but by 1840 this type of loading had come into general military use. Aiming was easier and more accurate, since the percussion cap did not result in as heavy a recoil as that of the 18th century muskets.

Most armies still relied on muzzle-loading weapons. When the Crimean War broke out the British and French were going over to rifled rather than smooth-bored weapons but the Russians still relied largely on muskets. Prussia was the exception on the question of muzzle loading, having used the breech-loading Dreyse gun since 1843. This type had first been constructed in 1827. Its rate of fire was double that of a muzzle-loading gun. The Dreyse weapon was also rifled and it had a moveable chamber with a gas-tight lock. It took the Austro-Prussian War of 1866 to demonstrate the advantages of the Dreyse rifle over the Austrian muzzle loader.

The artillery of the Crimean War was somewhat lighter than that used previously but little different in principle from that used during the Napoleonic age. However, at this time the first developments of breech-loading artillery pieces got under way though most weapons were still smooth-bore and muzzle-loading. The range of artillery had not increased significantly since the first two decades of the 19th century.

The Crimean War did not end because of a decision on the field of battle but as the result of an ultimatum delivered by Austria to Russia in December 1855. Peace was concluded in 1856, although none of the belligerent powers had exhausted its military strength. The Black Sea was neutralized and a European protectorate established over the Christians in the Ottoman Empire.

Left: Berlin in 1933. A uniformed Nazi keeps watch in front of a Jewish-owned shop during the boycott of such establishments. This was an early phase of the anti-Jew campaign which animated the Nazis and their supporters. The boycott notice is bilingual, presumably to deter Anglo-Saxon tourists. Below left: One of the German concentration camps in 1938. Such camps were established well before the war although this one, Dachau, reached its horrific peak only in the 1940s. Right: Berlin in December 1944. Impassive civilians enrolled in the *volkssturm* publicity parade, for which they have been provided with rifles but not uniforms. Below: In 1945 Germany there was increasing recruitment of the young, like these Hitler Youth soldiers.

In the meantime Prussia had become the laboratory of military experiments and innovation. Although the German Confederation had existed since 1815, its army was comprised of the armies of the different kingdoms, duchies and other principalities making up the confederation. There was no integrated command structure or general staff planning. The Confederation was led by Austria and the Army of the German Confederation nominally comprised some 292,000 men, allocated, on paper at least, into ten Federal Corps. Corps I, II and III were provided by Austria; IV, V and VI by Prussia; Corps VII by Bavaria. The VIII Corps represented Württembergers and Badensians as well as Hessians, the IX Corps was provided by the Saxons, while the X Corps came from Hanover, Brunswick, Holstein, Mecklenburg and the cities of the Hanseatic League. There was no supreme commander, since no one could agree on whether he should be an Austrian or a Prussian. In consequence, the German states only agreed to appoint a supreme commander in time of national emergency.

Every one of the German armies had a different training manual, a different method of conscription and a different uniform. Austrian uniforms were white, Bavarian light blue and Prussian dark blue. The Saxons were clad in green, the Hanoverians in red and the Brunswickers in black. Head-dress varied considerably – the Prussians had the Pickelhaube which after 1871 became the general headgear of the entire German Army until replaced by the steel helmet in World War I.

Rifles and artillery were supposed to be uniform throughout all armies of the German Confederation which, initially, was not very difficult. But because every army began to introduce new and different weapons in the 1840s, there was a potential problem should the Army of the German Confederation be called upon to act as a whole. Fortunately, when this did happen – as in the German-Danish war of 1864 – the campaigns were short and decisive. The army was not, in fact, a unified body but the army of a coalition.

In the Prussian Army the customary drill of the 18th century was not wholly eliminated; instead it was largely replaced by training under battlefield conditions. The battalion column was replaced by the company column in an effort to increase the tactical mobility of the army, which bore its full fruit once the Prussian Army was fully equipped with breech-loaders. In order to keep the infantry fire under control and thus prevent waste of ammunition, the infantry line was divided into so-called fire groups led by a platoon or section leader. He determined the target and the range setting for the rifle sights. Great emphasis was placed on firing from a prone position, while firing on the move was discouraged. Thus for the first time in military history the NCO's function was not simply to keep order among his troops; he had a new role in the framework of tactical leadership. The battle was henceforth determined as much by the quality of the NCO corps as it was by that of the officer corps.

Among the experts at the time the argument raged as to whether the increased rate of fire of the breech-loader was not simply a waste of ammunition. This argument was to recur during World War II when the Germans introduced the MG.42 machine gun with its 1200 rounds per minute. But the bloody practice demonstrated that it was less important for the rifleman

Top left: Samuel Morse, the American pioneer of the telegraph and inventor of the telegraphic code that bears his name. Although its requirement of semi-permanent lines made it unsuitable for tactical use, the telegraph proved an invaluable means of speeding communication between a general headquarters and outlying units, or between an admiralty and its ports. It has only in modern times been superseded by telephone and the more flexible radio. Left: French troops in the Franco-Prussian War cutting down telegraph lines. This became standard procedure in retreat, on a par with the destruction of railroad tracks, intended to prevent the advancing enemy making immediate use of local communication facilities. Below left: German *jaegers* (riflemen) using field telephones in 1914. It was in World War I that the telephone proved clearly superior to the telegraph and was found suitable for battlefield use. Below: The standard German field telephone of World War I. This particular example is being studied by a US Signals Corps officer, having been abandoned by the retreating Germans. Right: Laying telegraph lines in the US Civil War. Center right below: U-boat control center; the operator's hand is resting on an 'Enigma' cipher machine. Bottom far right: US field radio of 1943.

to shoot accurately each time than to have massive and rapid fire power to keep the enemy down. Once this was generally accepted, it was only a short step to semi-automatic and ultimately fully automatic infantry weapons.

In Prussia, artillery was divided into siege and field classifications. The field artillery was divided into regiments, each containing three horse-drawn batteries, three detachments on foot with each battery. Up to 1843 the uniform of the artillery included a tailcoat, but thereafter they were garbed like the infantry except for a black collar and piping where the infantry wore red.

From 1860 onward engineers were divided into engineer battalions, each composed of four companies and including the field telegraphy troops or simply the communication detachments. Also among the engineers were the rail-road troops, not only to supervise the loading of men and equipment onto trains, but to keep the rail communications intact as well. They underwent their first test, and successful at that, during the Prussian mobilization in 1859 occasioned by the war in Italy. In 1864, during the war against Denmark, the Prussian railroad communications network was used most effectively by the railroad detachments of the engineers. Without them the speedy assembly of the Prussian forces in 1866 against Austria and of the German forces against France in 1870 would have been virtually impossible. Separate supply units, field bakeries, field hospitals and medical troops were also organized.

After the Prussian Army reform and reorganization, the Prussian field army was structured into units of two to three army corps each. Each corps consisted of two infantry divisions, each comprised of two infantry brigades and a cavalry brigade of two regiments, an artillery brigade, a light infantry battalion, an engineer battalion and two supply companies. The division as an operational and tactical unit was the product of a later time. Up to and including the Franco-Prussian War, brigade headquarters were the focus of tactical leadership.

The Prussian General Staff kept a close eye on military and technological developments all over Europe. When the French and Italian forces decisively defeated the Austrians at Solferino in 1859, the role played by the railways in the quick assembly of the French forces was not lost on the Prussians, who embarked on a new boom in strategic railway building. Neither was the inadequate logistical support of the French overlooked, with appropriate conclusions drawn therefrom. On the evening of 25 June 1859, 22,000 dead and wounded littered the battlefield of Solferino. The Swiss writer and philanthropist Henri Dunant witnessed the scene with horror, which led him to found the Red Cross, and in 1864 the International Committee of the Red Cross met in Geneva, where the Geneva Convention was to be drawn up in 1906, with the stated aim of making an 'improvement of the fate of the wounded and sick of the armies in the field.'

If Scharnhorst, Gneisenau, Clausewitz and a host of others had by their reforms pulled the Prussian Army from the Frederician Age firmly into the 19th century, the elder Moltke not only continued this tradition but advanced it into the 20th century. Helmuth Carl Count von Moltke was born on 26 October 1800, like Scharnhorst and Gneisenau a Prussian by choice. He was a subject of the Danish Crown and entered the Danish Army first. As a result of his extraordinary ability, he was called to attend the War Academy in Berlin and in 1828 he was given an appointment to the Prussian General Staff. From that moment on he never again served as an officer in the field. This gave him a reputation as a pure theoretician who was not well informed of the problems of the troops on the front line. Moltke must have found some justification in this charge, because once he became Chief of the General Staff he insisted on a regular rotation of General Staff officers to service in the line. His exceptionally wide intellectual horizons and his profound historical and political knowledge were rounded off during a five-year period spent as an advisor and instructor with the Turkish Army. After his return to Germany in 1840 he served in the Prussian General Staff until 1857 when, with the rank of major general, he became its chief.

Institutionally, the General Staff was still subordinate to the Prussian Ministry of War. Moltke's initial function was solely that of an advisor. Therefore he did not participate directly in the reforms of the Prussian Army between 1859 and 1862, which were carried out by Roon, the Minister for War. He was not party to the plans and intentions of the Prussian government. This, of course, made Moltke's own work rather more difficult. Even the operational orders issued by the General Staff required the previous sanction of the Minister of War.

However, this state of affairs was a blessing in disguise for Moltke, since it allowed him to deploy his entire energy to the reorganization of the General Staff and to the instruction of General Staff officers. It was they who worked out all the details for troop transport in the mobilization of 1859. Although Prussia did not enter the war between Austria and Italy supported by France, it was a major test successfully carried out. Moltke recognized the great significance of the cooperation between the administration of the railroads and armies of the allied German states, as well as the inseparable connections between strategy, operational planning and politics. He further realized that only he and his General Staff could carry out the operational preparation of the war, and believed that only he and his subordinates should advise the Supreme Commander (the king) – much the same point over which he fell out with Bismarck.

An army commander or commanding general not party to the detailed planning of an operation would be unable to lead his forces properly, since he was by definition unable to act according to General Staff plans. Therefore each army commander had as chief of staff a General Staff officer entrusted and familiar with the broad aspects and objectives of his leadership. Moltke subjected the campaign of 1859 in Italy to detailed scrutiny and concluded that the lack of coordination at the apex of the Austrian command, and lack of communication from the command to the forces in the field, were the primary reasons for the Austrian defeat. He addressed several memoranda to King Wilhelm I in which he elaborated his principles of leadership, principles without which, to this day, the command and training of units and large contingents would not be possible.

This was not enough for Moltke. He dispatched General Staff officers to the returning Austrian, Italian and French armies and to the battlefields to gain even more detailed and firmer impressions. The offshoot of this was the establishment of military attachés at every German embassy abroad. The first such attaché was sent to Paris.

In the realm of operational leadership, Moltke placed a premium on rapid mobility, the speedy assembly of the army for battle by rail and road. Operations, he believed, should be so designed that the battle virtually grew out of the assembly. Supply was another problem to which he addressed himself, since too much time was wasted by troops cooking for themselves. But the problem was not solved until shortly before World War I when the German Army introduced mobile field kitchens. Moltke insisted that supply officers participate in maneuvers so that they would come face to face with the relationship between adequate supplies and the morale of an army in the field. 'Adequate supplies are the mother of discipline' he used to say.

БЕЙ НЕМЕЦКИХ ЗВЕРЕЙ!
УНИЧТОЖИТЬ ГИТЛЕРОВСКУЮ АРМИЮ—МОЖНО И ДОЛЖНО.

Above: A Soviet poster of 1943.
The message is 'Kill the German
beasts!' and the bottom line reads
'Destroying the Hitlerite Army; it
can be done and must be done.'
Soviet posters were savage, which
is not surprising in view of the
nature of the war; their aims
included the instilling of national
confidence, and of hatred for the
enemy. Even in 1943 the
wholehearted loyalty of the Soviet
people was not certain. Above
right: A Russian poster of World
War 1. This is actually
recommending a war savings bond
known as the 'Freedom Loan', but
the inscription on the flag reads
'War until Victory.' The poster
dates from 1917, when there was a
growing anti-war feeling in Russia.
Right: German poster advertising
an anti-Semitic film, Der Ewige
Jude ('The Wandering Jew').
Several such films were made in
Nazi Germany, and their posters
had the same aim of inspiring
revulsion. Far right: A German
World War II poster bidding
citizens to watch out for spies and
avoid careless talk. All the
belligerent countries issued such
posters.

The most important of his innovations concerned the training of General Staff officers. Here he came to three conclusions. First, that the railroad network and its capacity determined the operational possibilities of future warfare. From 1863 onward, his war plans were exclusively based on it. Secondly, the General Staff should issue directives and not orders, since army formations assembled often widely apart until the area of concentration was reached. Commanding generals must be given a free hand in the choice of how to implement the directives. Ultimately they had to act in the interest of the whole. This was the origin of the German *Auftragstaktik*, according to which a directive, not an order, is issued even at a lower level and it is left to the officer on the spot to decide the ways and means to his objective. This contrasted strongly with the practice in other European armies and in America, where an order had to be followed to the letter, thus curbing the initiative of soldiers and officers on the scene. Only after World War II did the US Army introduce this innovation in the form of the 'mission-type-order.'

Moltke's third conclusion was that the best strategic method consisted in concentrating only for battle while moving in dispersed formation between engagements. This, in Clausewitz's terms, was bound to produce friction, so Moltke described strategy as a system of improvisations that were really not teachable. He was the enemy of any firm and inflexible 'system,' and no doubt would have rejected the Schlieffen Plan on these grounds. The best operational effort would be a short march from different directions against the front and the flank of the enemy, as indeed Moltke practiced at the Battle of Sedan. Such a course would depend on calculations of time and space, the weather, small military engagements en route and intelligence about the enemy. The march should be followed by the concentration before the battle. Concentration on the battlefield was the exception for Moltke. In his sense, concentration meant directing the columns onto a single point but, having reached it, not dividing immediately into a prearranged order of battle. The final decision on where to attack was to be taken only once concentration was complete.

Moltke did not believe in the single decisive battle. To devise such a campaign plan would be a mistake, because nobody could know what would happen after the battle. Even though an army might be victorious the enemy could still have an opportunity to assemble other forces elsewhere. What mattered most was how a battle was carried out; one could not plan it mathematically.

Considering Prussia's geographic position, a major problem for Moltke was the battle on interior lines. This no doubt favored Prussia because of its advanced communications network, but Moltke failed to see the disadvantage of interior lines once a war became a war of attrition. The decisive advantage was in the possibility of having the element of surprise in an offensive. The way Moltke used terms like strategy and tactics shows that they do not correspond entirely to what they mean in our day. Implicit in Moltke's use of these terms is Clausewitz's definition of tactics as the lesson of the use of forces in combat and strategy as the lesson of the use of combat for the purposes of the war.

When the war against Denmark broke out in 1864, Moltke's influence upon operations was very limited at first. Connected by telegraph with the supreme commander of the Austro-Prussian forces, General von Wrangel, he was rather dissatisfied with the conduct of operations. He considered the capture of Fredericia and the conquest of Alsen unimportant. Instead he demanded the occupation of Funen. This island held a flanking position from which the allies could dominate the Danish

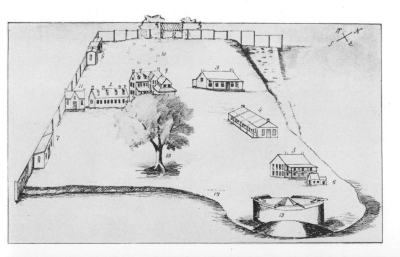

Left: As war became professionalized and technically advanced, the proper training of officers became indispensable. During the nineteenth century, therefore, in many countries, existing officer-training institutions were modernized, losing some of their more barbaric customs and acquiring better-educated specialists to teach a wider range of courses. This is a general view, made in 1845, of the Naval School which five years later was to be renamed the United States Naval Academy at Annapolis. Its members were selected on the basis of recommendations from politicians, but also included meritorious veterans. Below: A recent view of West Point, the US Military Academy, founded in 1802. Bottom left: Turn-of-the-century West Point cadets at summer camp. Bottom right: Old traditions on display at West Point.

mainland and the Danish islands. Moltke did not then consider the annihilation of the Danish forces as the paramount operational objective, but politics imposed its limits upon that war much as they did two years later at the Battle of Königgrätz during the war against Austria. Moltke always resented the interference of politics in the sphere of warfare, which put him in opposition to Clausewitz's teachings. He was the most important, though not the only advocate, of the primacy of the military over that of politics as long as a war lasted.

The German aim in the war with Denmark was to achieve quick victories in order to occupy the whole of Schleswig but to stay away, as much as possible, from Danish soil in order to prevent the intervention of the neutral powers, particularly Britain. Finally, on 30 April 1864, Moltke took over the operations and decided to cross over to Alsen. It was his first major success. Moltke had been hampered in the operations by a total lack of information about Bismarck's plans. It was a deficiency so obvious to most that in 1865 Moltke was invited to participate in sessions of the Crown Council. But this did not result in an upgrading of his position; he was still dependent on the War Ministry and he still did not have any direct access to the monarch. In later years this did become common practice and it was institutionalized in 1879.

Immediately after the war, Moltke set about evaluating his experiences. His main conclusions were concerned with the tactical level. He recognized that the modern breech-loading rifle, or even the muzzle-loading musket, proscribed the traditional advance of infantry across open territory. Instead, the topography of the battlefield had to be fully exploited. Nor was it advisable to have the infantry attack without preliminary artillery bombardment and general artillery support, even if the attacking side was far superior in numbers. Considering the increased rate of fire of infantry weapons, it seemed advisable to provoke the enemy into the attack from a well-chosen defensive position and then to destroy him by a counterattack in the flank or from the rear. Therefore Moltke tried to achieve two things: first, on the offensive to attack the enemy's flank, encircle him and attack from the rear; second, on the defensive, to construct a defense in depth.

At the operational level he recognized that in the future it would be impossible to circumvent or surround the enemy in close proximity to him. The depth of the marching column had increased many times, along with the range of modern artillery. The preparations for battle had to be made over a wide and deep geographic area, which led him to the maxim that armies should march separately and strike united. For the commander, the problem was that he could no longer oversee every phase of the development of the operations and was therefore dependent on the sometimes unreliable system of telegraphic communications. This had by no means been perfected in 1866 or 1870–71; indeed, it still showed serious weaknesses during the early phase of World War I. The German withdrawal from the Marne in September 1914 was very much the result of a failure of communication between the General Staff and generals in the field. A commander also had to be absolutely sure of the ability of his field commanders for the *Auftragstaktik* to succeed.

Moltke first put this thought into practice at Königgrätz (also known as Sadowa) in 1866. His aim in that war was to obtain a victory over the main Austrian force in Bohemia. He believed he could ignore Austria's allies, such as Bavaria, at least for a time; he strengthened his army and invaded Bohemia. For his operational advance he had five railroad lines over a front of approximately 350 miles. Austria had only two railroad lines available. Moltke and the Prussians thus had much greater mobility. In addition, Austria was conducting a war on two

fronts, one against the Prussians, the other against the Italians. The inherent advantages of fighting on interior lines were nullified because Austria did not have the kind of communications which would have allowed rapid deployment of superior forces against the Prussians.

At Königgrätz the Austrian and Prussian forces were about equal in number. Moltke had divided the Prussian forces into three armies which invaded Bohemia over a width of about 300 miles. Each army had its own road for the advance from the rail heads. His operational plan was not devoid of risks but as he said, 'in war everything is dangerous.' However, during the Battle of Königgrätz he was more than once overcome by the fear that this could become Prussia's Solferino. By the end he was completely exhausted. But the Prussians won the day and thus the war, since Bismarck wanted and achieved a speedy end to the hostilities. He had attained his political objectives in Germany and he had expelled Austria from the German Confederation. What more could he ask?

In the hands of the Prussians the Dreyse breech loader had

Left: An SS recruiting poster for Norwegian ski troops. Right: A United States Marines recruiting poster. The inscription 'We're looking for a few good men' exploits the Marines' reputation as an elite force. Below right: A US Marines recruiting poster of World War 1. Again, the emphasis is on the Marines' reputation as a somewhat exclusive high-grade body of men. The German soldiers' description of the Marines as 'devil-dogs' adds to this image.

Left: Map of the Battle of Königgratz, in which Prussia's defeat of Austria was crushing and final.

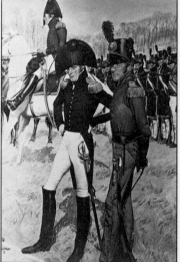

Top: US uniforms of the American-Mexican War. Above: US officers uniforms of 1814. Right: By the end of the nineteenth century bright uniforms had given way to subdued browns, greens and grays. American troops wore khaki in the Spanish-American War.

proved its value; the Prussian rate of fire compared with the Austrian was three to one. But this was not the only reason for the victory. It was the combination of better armaments, the company columns and excellent exploitation of the geography of the battlefield. The Prussian cavalry had been kept mainly in reserve. It would serve only for reconnaissance purposes, Moltke concluded after the war.

On the artillery side, this was the first war in which the belligerents had confronted one another with rifled artillery pieces. Austria had introduced rifled artillery weapons in 1863, but they were muzzle loaders. The Prussian artillery was caught off guard to some degree, because when the war broke out it was just in the process of re-equipment. The new guns had rifled barrels and were breech loaders, but the re-equipment was incomplete and the new crews inadequately trained, let alone the artillery reservists who had been called to the colors. The Austrians and Prussians each had about 400 artillery pieces. But the Battle of Königgrätz definitely showed that the smooth-bore muzzle loader had outlived its usefulness on land and that the breech loaders were superior in both range and accuracy. Moltke himself voiced his criticism about the state of the Prussian artillery after the war, which resulted in increased artillery training and the maintenance of the cadres of artillery regiments.

The artillery had to be ready at any moment. It opened the battle and continued it until all the other arms could join in. Therefore part of the artillery had to be at the head of the marching columns, the bulk of it was to be with the main force, but it was never in the rear. At the early stage of combat a commander had to be in a position to bring the full effectiveness of his artillery to bear upon the enemy. Moltke used the years between 1866 and 1870 primarily to improve the standards of Prussia's artillery.

During the same period the degree of cooperation increased between the forces of the North German Confederation, successor to the German Confederation, and its south German allies. Moltke became convinced that it was not the brigade but the division that was the most suitable large tactical unit. Army corps he considered superfluous, since they duplicated what already existed in the command structure at army and divisional levels. The ideal size of an army was 100,000 men, but under no circumstances was it to be larger than 150,000 to 200,000 men because this would impede its mobility, create problems of supply and make it difficult to command. But until 1871 much of this remained on paper.

For his achievement in 1870–71 Moltke was promoted field marshal. The French war plan of 1870 was that the French

Army, based on the railroad lines to Metz and Strasbourg, would cross the Rhine north of Karlsruhe and then turn toward Berlin. The French mobilization system was so faulty that of the 400,000 men envisioned, by early in August 1870 only about 240,000 had reached their garrisons. Under the supreme command of Emperor Napoleon III they formed a left wing army under Marshal Bazaine and a right wing army under Marshal MacMahon. Both marshals had made their reputations in the colonies, in the Crimea and in Italy.

The French forces were opposed by German armies which were 460,000 strong within a few weeks of the outbreak of the war. Reserves were also held back in Germany in case of a landing on the German coasts. Altogether, Germany mobilized 1,180,000 men in the course of the conflict. The armies were divided into corps consisting of two infantry divisions, each division of two brigades with two regiments each. Each division had a light cavalry component of four squadrons, four artillery batteries with six guns per battery, two engineer companies and a medical corps detachment. The corps artillery consisted of a foot regiment and a mounted detachment of two batteries. The train carried infantry and artillery ammunition as well as supplies, pontoon bridges, field bakeries, horses, additional medical detachments and twelve field hospitals. The six available cavalry divisions were detached to corps and armies according to need. During the war their main task was one of reconnaissance. Furthermore, there were five battalions of railroad engineers and four field telegraphy detachments. One of them remained with the headquarters and the General Staff, the others were attached one to each of the three armies.

As a rule in combat German infantry battalions divided up into company columns, thus providing a smaller target for the enemy and, supported by strong artillery fire, moved toward the enemy. While advancing, the topography was to be exploited to the maximum. When in defense, infantry fire was not to be opened until the enemy had approached as near as 300 paces. Throughout the war the German forces displayed a remarkable fire discipline.

In contrast to France, the German states had possessed a detailed mobilization and assembly plan since 1867. All officers down to platoon commanders were issued excellent maps. The French officers had maps of Germany but none of their own country, a cause of much difficulty when the war, against their hopes, began to be fought on French territory. Although the French had established supply depots in various fortresses such as Metz, the troops had to requisition food from their own countrymen when on the march, which did not make the army very popular with the French peasantry. The supply organization was controlled by civilian contractors.

On 4 August 1870 the German armies crossed the French frontiers and two days later the Battle of Wörth was fought and the first defeat inflicted on the French. This battle showed that the French Chassepot rifle was superior to the German Dreyse gun, that the south German troops were not as well trained as the Prussians and that cavalry attacks were no longer a means for deciding a battle. On the same day the heights of Spicheren were taken, much against Moltke's intentions, but this had the favorable result that Bazaine's supply magazines in the Saar were lost and he had to withdraw toward Metz. Meanwhile, at Chalons-sur-Marne, MacMahon formed his forces into the Army of Chalons while Bazaine concentrated his around Metz. Troubled by illness, Napoleon III delegated supreme command to Bazaine.

Moltke had received further reinforcements from Germany, which enabled him after various engagements to bottle up Bazaine and his army in Metz. MacMahon wanted to retreat in

Above: Censorship of newspapers by the Allies in World War I. The scene is the press bureau set up in the Paris *bourse*, with French, British, US, Belgian and Serbian censors at work. In previous wars censorship had been rare, and intelligence services made good use of their enemies' press reports. Above right: Air raid practice in a Japanese school; the pupils dash from classroom to shelter, holding handkerchieves to their faces as a partial defense against smoke and poison gas. Right: In many respects the USA was in a state of war months before Pearl Harbor. The need to conserve home resources led to some shortages. Here, in August 1941, a gasoline station supplies night-time motorists for the last time.

the direction of Paris, but the French government ordered him to move toward the Belgian frontier, where the German III and IV Corps had arrived near Montmédy. Attacked by the Germans, MacMahon's forces withdrew to the small fortress of Sedan. Bazaine, locked up in Metz, could not launch any support operation and on 1 September 1870 the Battle of Sedan was fought, putting an end to MacMahon's army. The French capitulated, among them Napoleon III who had arrived to join MacMahon.

At the beginning of the war both German and French Armies showed a high degree of bravery and discipline. But the French had drawn the wrong conclusions from 1866. Though the French rifle was superior to the German, with a range of 1000 to 1200 yards versus about 800 yards for the Dreyse rifle, superior German infantry and artillery tactics were decisive. Also, the French appeared to think only defensively, with the result that many a French tactical victory became an operational defeat. Conversely, the Germans drew the wrong conclusions from 1870–71 and put the emphasis on the offensive, which in World War I, especially during its early months, led to atrocious losses among the German forces. Of course it was superior generalship that won the war for the Germans, based as it was on detailed general staff work, which in the field exploited to the full the railroads and field telegraphy.

French resources were still formidable enough to prolong the war into the first month of 1871. Leon Gambetta, the new French leader, however, failed to produce the *levée en masse* which the French Revolution had brought forth; basically the country was tired of this war, and of wars in general, into which Napoleon III had drawn them all too frequently. Still the French managed to enlist another million men, but they were mainly untrained and no match for German professionalism. Another French novelty were the *franc tireurs*, irregulars from private rifle clubs. They conducted the war in the rear of the German forces, but since they were few in number they could never contribute decisively. Furthermore, not recognized as regular combatants, they were usually shot on the spot when caught.

By the end of January 1871 the French admitted defeat. This was followed by a temporary armistice and ultimately by the Peace Treaty of Frankfurt in May 1871. In the less than seven decades since 1815, the nature of war, the technological environment and the society which suffered and sustained war had changed beyond recognition.

3. Army & Society: France

In contrast to most other European armies, the French Army during most of the 19th century was a garrison army which lived its own life, separate from the society of which it was a part. It was as much an instrument of domestic politics as it was one of foreign policy. In domestic politics it represented the means by which the various French governments suppressed revolutions.

Within French society there was for a long period a horror of the type of conscription introduced by the Revolutionary *levée en masse*. Clausewitz, during his captivity in France in 1807 when Napoleon stood at his zenith, reported many instances in which two or three policemen took thirty or forty conscripts roped together to the prefect's office. There were manhunts for deserters and missing conscripts, and their number rose by 1811 to 60,000, of whom only half could be caught. Communities, families and even entire administrative districts were held responsible for the escape of a conscript.

After the defeat of Napoleon I, his army as such was dissolved and the French officer corps was subjected to a royalist purge which introduced 14 categories of guilt. No wonder that the country was soon swamped with ex-officers who were suspected to be sources of political disquiet. A new army of volunteers was formed around the royal guard and the Swiss mercenaries, in effect no more than a police force. It was hardly an instrument to inspire popular confidence and enthusiasm. For the officer corps it was more important to display loyalty to the monarchy than to possess any valid qualifications.

Still it was an army which met the needs of France as long as the allied occupation forces were still in the country, and indeed the abolition of conscription was probably the most popular measure enacted by the restored Bourbon king. However, military service had become so unpopular that after 1815 the normal requirement of volunteers could not be met. Many of those who were recruited came from the dregs of society, attracted only by the high initial payment received upon signing up. Very often, they deserted after receiving this payment.

After the allies had left France the question arose as to what kind of an army France should have. To return to the mercenary armies of the 18th century was impossible, since most of France's neighbors had adopted the French principle of the people's army. One answer was the Army Law of 1818 drawn up by Marshal Gouvion St Cyr, which remained in force for over two generations, although the July Monarchy of 1832 and Napoleon III in 1855 made a few changes. It reflected very much the needs and fears of French society and it was bound to be, therefore, the product of compromise. It maintained the Revolutionary principle of each citizen's duty to serve in the army. However, this principle was applied to only a small portion of the male youth, not simply because of the general disinclination to do military service, but out of fear that genuine general conscription could arouse the nation as a whole to the extent that the people would become a danger to the government. The army was to comprise 244,000 men. What numbers could not be filled by volunteers were to be drafted into the army. To alleviate the draft, the choice was made by lottery, which produced 40,000 recruits in a country of 30 million. Prussia raised the same number of recruits annually from a population of only 11 million. In practice, the greatest number of recruits actually inducted in any one year in France was 34,000; in some years there were no more than 10,000 and in the 1860s the annual average was 23,000.

Those Frenchmen who pulled the right lottery ticket were exempt from military service in peace or war. Of those who had the bad luck to be conscripted, a certain proportion had automatic exemptions on the basis of physical unfitness or

family hardship, or simply because they were able to pull the right strings. Students in theological seminaries and certain universities, and those who had won prizes in the sciences and literature, were automatically deferred. In addition there was also the old system of providing a substitute. Those families who could afford to hire a substitute for an attractive monetary payment saved their sons from military service.

The period of service was first six, then eight, and from 1832 on seven years, a term during which the conscripts had to live in barracks and remain unmarried. The middle classes did not mind, since in most cases they were able to buy a substitute. But others argued that the army was bound to become alienated from the nation by this system and arch-reactionaries looked back on what they considered the good old days of the *ancien régime*. The fact that the army had failed the monarchy badly in the French Revolution was conveniently forgotten. One explanation was that this had been due to insufficient discipline, and that the long period of conscription would inevitably prevent such problems. For the bourgeoisie the army was an instrument for the protection of private property from the forces of revolution, but as the events of both 1830 and 1848 showed, despite their original loyalties the soldiers were quick to put their services at the disposal of a new regime. Nevertheless, even after 1871 Adolphe Thiers, the representative of the liberal bourgeoisie, argued on behalf of maintaining the eight-year conscription period.

What was overlooked was the fact that the increasing standards of education had made a long-serving conscript army unnecessary, as long as there was a firm nucleus of professional officers and NCOs. Also, modern warfare as it developed during the 19th century did rely less on long-serving conscripts and more on the availability of well-trained and well-led reserves, since modern war demands from the outset the mass army, which can hardly be sustained without strong reserves. The availability of seemingly inexhaustible reserves, who had trained for three years or less and could immediately be integrated into the regular army, was the source of Prusso-German superiority.

France did not lack for men who recognized the Prussian and German advantages very clearly, as well as the shortcomings of their own system, but they did not find the ears of those in power. What France lacked in 1870 were trained reserves. Despite the great achievement of Gambetta and his supporters in raising numerous armies very quickly after Sedan, not only was it too late, but the personnel were largely untrained. To emulate the Prussian system was suggested on various occasions in the French Chamber of Deputies, but those who did so found no support. For most deputies, such an army posed too great a threat to the crown and its institutions, indicating a distrust of the revolutionary undercurrents of the French population. Instead the liberals denounced the Prussian system as barbaric. As for transforming the entire country into a barrack square, it might be suitable for the territories east of the Elbe River with their subject peasants, but it was totally unsuited for such a highly cultured and civilized nation as France.

The net result for the French Army for most of the 19th century was a very low social position. Although the officer corps still represented a closed corporation of the nobility for most of the century, after the overthrow of the monarchy in 1830 and again in 1848, the space within which such a caste system could be exercised became rather limited. The French nobility did not, in fact, represent a homogenous body; it included old pre-Revolutionary officers and the new Napoleonic nobility as well as that created after the Bourbon restoration. It was a body very much rent asunder by internal quarrels exemplified by frequent duelling and lawsuits.

Suspicions of the alleged monarchist spirit of the officer corps and its support of the Roman Catholic Church were always present among the parties left of center, culminating in the great explosion represented by the Dreyfus case at the end of the century. (Captain Dreyfus, an army officer, was falsely accused of spying for Germany, and later evidence of his innocence was suppressed in a cover-up which reached to the highest levels of the army. Dreyfus was Jewish and anti-Semitic prejudice within the largely Catholic hierarchy was undoubtedly a factor in the case. He was eventually pardoned after a long and violent public debate.)

For a long time an army commission was not very attractive to the new middle classes because of the extremely low pay. The shortage of officers became so great that rapid promotions had to be made from the NCOs to fill the vacancies, another factor disturbing to the homogeneity of the French officer corps. But the officers were still in a rather more favorable position than the NCOs and the rank and file. Sons of respectable peasants, artisans and workers had to spend six to eight years with the dregs of society. The substitutes amounted to one quarter of the army and were mainly men of low reputation. But which peasant, artisan or laborer could afford 2000 francs to buy off his son? Those who were really interested in the profession of arms became regular soldiers, but they were in the minority. Soldiering on the whole was an affair of the poor and

Previous page: High noon of the *Entente Cordiale*; officers of France and her allies in a Parisian cafe. Left: Marshal Soult, one of Napoleon's best officers. Below: French troops charge a Russian Baltic fort in 1854.

Above left: The Battle of the Alma, first engagement of the Crimean War. French colonial troops attack Russian positions after scaling the Heights. Trained never to advance without artillery support, the French advance soon petered out after its brave beginning. Left: Marshal de St Arnaud, the French commander at the Alma. St Arnaud failed to pursue the defeated Russians despite British urging; he said his men could not proceed without their knapsacks, which they had left in the rear, and their artillery, which had run out of ammunition. This prevented the early capture of Sebastopol.
Above: French infantry board a British warship for the 1854 Baltic expedition. Right: French zouaves at the time of the Crimean War, equipped with percussion muskets.

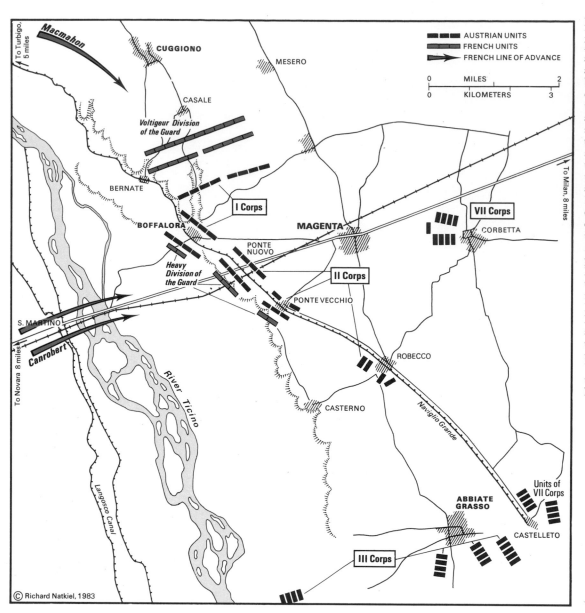

To Turbigo, 5 miles
Macmahon
CUGGIONO
MESERO
CASALE
Voltigeur Division of the Guard
BERNATE
I Corps
BOFFALORA
MAGENTA
PONTE NUOVO
Heavy Division of the Guard
II Corps
PONTE VECCHIO
VII Corps
CORBETTA
To Milan, 8 miles
S. MARTINO
Canrobert
To Novara 8 miles
River Ticino
Langosco Canal
ROBECCO
CASTERNO
Naviglio Grande
Units of VII Corps
ABBIATE GRASSO
CASTELLETO
III Corps

	AUSTRIAN UNITS
	FRENCH UNITS
	FRENCH LINE OF ADVANCE

0 — MILES — 2
0 — KILOMETERS — 3

© Richard Natkiel, 1983

Left: Map of the Battle of Magenta. Both the French and the Austrians lost heavily in this engagement, but as the latter retreated it was adjudged a French victory. It may be regarded as the first of a series of costly battles which culminated in the loss of Austria's predominance at the Battle of Königgratz in 1866, seven years later, at the hands of the Prussians. The French war against Austria of 1859 may therefore be regarded as opening the way for Prussia's emergence as a great military power in the 1860s. Right: On the battlefield in the evening at Magenta. The French emperor, Louis Napoleon, confers the rank of marshal on General MacMahon. Louis Napoleon, perhaps because he was a Bonaparte, campaigned with his troops although he had little military experience or competence. Below: French crowds outside the Eastern Railroad terminus in Paris, applauding reservists about to travel to the front in 1870. Although the railroad was well organized, the War Ministry was not, and many troop trains left for the war zone half-empty.

of social outcasts, squeezed together in barracks two to a bed, with eight men eating from one bowl. Consequently, it was impossible to produce a real military spirit within the army; the large number of deserters and cases of self-inflicted wounds spoke for themselves. The army, as the institution it was, helped to sharpen the social tensions and the hatred of the poor for the rich. In order to avoid the militarization of the whole nation, France had produced an army of her lowest social strata, left to vegetate in barracks apart from the national life.

During the first third of the 19th century the majority of French politicians did not see in this the source of a danger potentially lethal to France. In view of the general economic upsurge, the rise of industrialization, the belief in progress and the ultimate perfectibility of man, it was thought that armies had become old-fashioned and would sooner or later outlive their usefulness. But anti-militarism and pacifism could exert their influence only for so long as France did not develop any new ambitions in the realm of foreign policy. These currents did not necessarily deny the need for an armed force, but as socialists throughout Europe were to advocate, the standing army should be replaced by a national militia, supplemented at most by a small body of professional soldiers to guard the frontiers. Various attempts were made in this direction but the National Guard was never a real national militia. It saw its task solely as the protection of the property of the bourgeoisie. The last time the National Guard played a significant part was in the civil war situation in June 1848. Thereafter the rise of Napoleon III,

beginning with a military *coup d'état*, put an end to pacifist dreams and pointed French foreign policy into new and dangerous directions.

However, Napoleon III was neither a trained soldier nor a military reformer, although even a layman could not fail to see the weaknesses of the French military establishment. One of his measures was to secure the loyalty of the army by improving its material position and its public prestige through the generous allocation of honorary posts, the granting of pensions and a general increase of pay throughout the army. The substitute system was changed so as to increase the financial intake, which was used as a fund to tempt well-trained and proven soldiers to re-enlist. This strengthened the character of the French Army as a professional army, establishing a body of *troupiers* able to fight on European soil as well as colonial battlefields. The French Army certainly improved its general image in Europe, especially in the Crimean War.

However, there was still a question as to whether it was equal to any of the other European armies. Napoleon defeated the Austrians at Solferino, but he was immediately hampered by lack of supplies. He also lacked the reserves necessary to cover his Rhine frontier against Prussian intervention, which forced him to a negotiated peace in which not all that the French desired was achieved, let alone the aims of the Italians. Indeed, for the Italians, French support had become rather costly. They had had to hand over Savoy and the Côte d'Azur, including Nice, to France.

Aware of these shortcomings as shown in the war of 1859, Napoleon tried to make up for them by calling only some of the conscripts to long-term service from 1861 onward, the others being trained for only a few months to create a viable reserve. It was a half-measure which did not achieve its objective. This was demonstrated again in 1866 when Napoleon III was not in a position to intervene effectively on Austria's behalf; Austria collapsed too quickly and a preliminary peace was speedily signed which deprived Napoleon of any new opportunity.

The lesson was not lost on him. Napoleon entrusted Marshal Niel with the task of preparing a thorough military reform which came very close to emulating the Prussian example. However, the reform was mutilated beyond recognition in the Chamber of Deputies. Hence the Defense Law of 1868 was not only a bad compromise; in retrospect it was a disaster. The army was slightly enlarged through greater annual recruitment, and the period of service was reduced to five years. What was eliminated from the original bill was Niel's provision for the creation of an effective reserve. The parliamentarians were satisfied with the creation of a *Guard Mobile* in which all should serve who did not serve in the army and in which no substitutes were allowed. This newly created force received little military training. An organizational structure existed on paper but not in practice; the most it could be used for was guard duty.

What remained was the old traditional army, traditional, that is, since 1815, with all its weaknesses and deficiencies, especially in its administrative apparatus, its mechanism for mobilization and the completely out-dated structure of the supreme command.

After the defeat of 1870–71 it was said that military leadership was incapable, that the army had lacked order and discipline, that corruption was rife and that the officer corps showed a remarkable lack of education, while the General Staff was alleged to have been totally out of touch with the soldiers in service and the regiments of the line. There is much truth in these accusations, but they ignored the fact that the French public, and particularly the French politicians, had effectively prevented any thorough-going reform. Although the French enjoyed *la gloire*, they were unwilling to pay the price for it in military terms. There was a dichotomy between the foreign

Left: Prussian troops in occupied territory requisitioning food at pistol-point. Above: Bazaine, commander of the French Army in 1870, an unsuitable appointment imposed by ill-informed public opinion. Below: The German advance during the Franco-Prussian War.

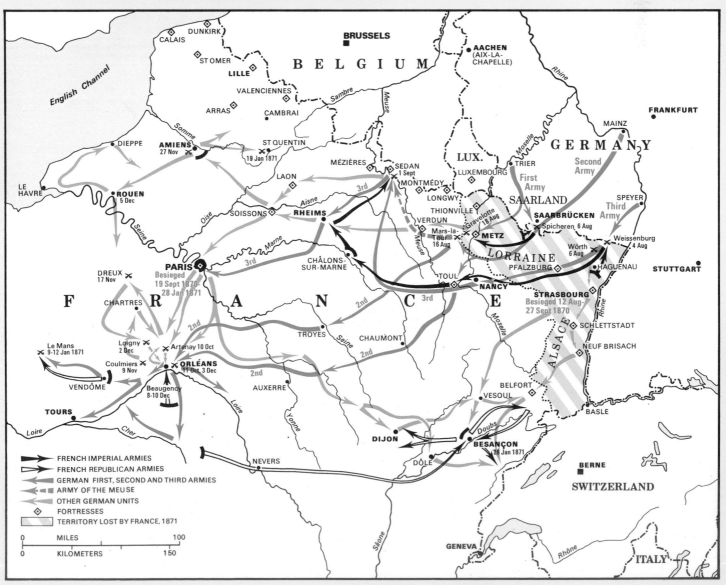

Above: French infantry in a
skirmish over a railroad track in
the Franco-Prussian War. The
artist, portraying a touch of glory,
has seen fit to renounce the use of
the excellent cover provided by the
railroad. Above right: French
troops await the Prussians in 1870.

Below: Another combat over a
railroad track; the French infantry
have the Chassepot rifle. Railroads
played an important role in this
war, as supply and reinforcing
channels and as targets for
both regular troops and French
guerillas.

policy aims of Napoleon III, widely supported by the French public, and the same public's unwillingness to provide the efficient instruments that would have formed the backbone for that policy. The moment of truth came in 1870. Within a period of one month all the prevailing illusions were ruthlessly destroyed. Gambetta's attempt to resurrect the *levée en masse* was only the sad and abortive epilogue to decades of mismanagement.

For France the war of 1870–71 was a watershed in its military history. The French National Assembly, which discussed a new Defense Law in 1872, was dominated by the categorical statement of the Republican General Trochu (governor of Paris in 1870–71) that the German Army was the only modern instrument of war in Europe. Like him, many others now wished to emulate the German example. The Defense Law of 1872 did away with the substitutes. The length of military service was reduced to five years, but service in the reserves ranged from 9 to 20 years. Now every Frenchman was genuinely liable to be called to arms – not only those who could not afford to pay a substitute. As in the German Army, short service commissions were introduced. But the optimism about the new military instrument was tempered by the fears engendered by the Paris Commune – that a nation in arms could become dangerous to the prosperous middle classes.

However, the new Defense Law was partly neutralized by financial considerations; some of those who should have been called to the colors were again excused in order to keep expenditures down. Of every annual age group eligible for military service (approximately 300,000 men) 110,000 were enrolled for a period of five years, a second group whose fate was decided by lottery served for six months and officer candidates who were to become reserve officers served only one year. So basically there was a division among those serving five years, one year and six months. These inequities were cause for the further development of the French military system. After 1876, when the conservative regime made way for more radical political sentiments, the idea of the nation in arms was raised again. It found support among the socialists, many of whom thought they could bring back their idea of a militia. Had this point of view prevailed, France would have, in effect, left the ranks of the Great Powers.

Although France was isolated in Europe for some years after 1871, the conclusion of the Franco-Russian military convention in 1892 and the Franco-Russian Alliance in 1894 broke that isolation. Allied with Russia, supplemented in 1904 by the Anglo-French *entente* and in 1907 by the Anglo-Russian *entente*, France attained a new feeling of security, which in the last years before 1914 led it to transform the Franco-Russian Alliance, which had had purely defensive intentions, into an offensive one.

The acts of the politicians should not be equated with the mood of the population. It is doubtful whether the new spirit ever existed that was so frequently invoked when speaking of the generation that went to war in 1914. The memories of 1870–71 had faded. French literature provided ample evidence that the people were fed up with arms and armies, and criticism of the army and the officer corps was widespread and frequent. Primary school teachers are alleged to have preached pacifism. The syndicalists called upon the soldiers to mutiny. But nothing divided French society more than the Dreyfus case. In the context of our analysis, the actual case of Captain Dreyfus is less important than its byproducts. When the case came to public attention in 1898, the French Army could inform the government, for the first time since 1871, that it was in a sufficient state of readiness to defend France's eastern frontier successfully.

True, the French Army, especially the officer corps, was not fully integrated into the republic. It was a state within a state. Rather like the *Reichswehr* of the Weimar Republic, the French Army accepted the Third Republic as the least of several evils. But it considered itself the actual receptacle of all national virtues and traditions. The army represented the historical continuity of *La France*. It kept out of politics, with the exception of the Boulangist affair, but the fact that General Boulanger had no backing was amply shown by his end. Nonetheless the army acquired allies within parliament which it could well have done without, particularly the monarchists of various brands who made themselves the self-appointed spokesmen of the army's interest – this in turn provoked opposition on the center and on the left. Whether or not it was willing, the army could not be kept out of politics. The officer corps was especially vulnerable to attack because of the alleged over-representation of the nobility there but that was the Republic's own fault: it blocked the careers of scions of the nobility except in the army and the foreign service. The case of Captain Dreyfus made public all the accumulated resentment. The call went forth that the army had to be reformed and the officer corps purged.

This crisis at the public level began and continued during a period in which France had entered dangerous waters in its foreign policy. The Fashoda Crisis of 1898 occurred at a time when the nation was divided over the Dreyfus case. French policy would have been much firmer *vis-à-vis* the British had it not been for the deep divisions at home. Under these circumstances the French had no other option but to step onto the golden bridges built for them by Lord Salisbury and withdraw from their venture. When the Rouvier government came into office the purge of the French officer corps was begun by General André. The criteria for dismissal or denial of promotion were whether an officer was a practicing Roman Catholic, whether his wife or close relatives were of the same persuasion and whether his children were educated in a convent school. Public confidence in the army was shattered and the officer corps was deeply divided. Precisely at that moment Foreign Minister Delcassé decided to pursue a forward policy in Morocco. Germany opposed it on solid legal grounds, but diplomatically the French were better prepared. Even so, at this point in 1906, when the annual class of officer cadets at St Cyr had declined from 2000 to 870, France took great risks by provoking Germany; France's only firm ally, Russia, had been neutralized by her recent defeat at the hands of Japan. If the Germans had been bent on carrying out a preventive war against France, it could have been a repetition of 1870–71. As it happened, the French were fortunate, but it was the task of subsequent governments to make good the damage inflicted on the French Army between 1898 and 1906. And an important factor in this was the realization after 1906 that France was again threatened by Germany. This caused a serious decline in the hitherto prevalent pacifist currents and the French introduced an armaments program to rival that of the Germans.

Reforms had to be carried out not only to restore public confidence in the army, but to heal the breach within the officer corps. In 1889 the five-year period of military service was reduced to three and the short service period was abolished with certain qualifications which were later nullified when a general conscription on a two-year basis was introduced in 1905. This corresponded with the German example of calling up a greater proportion of those eligible to create large reserves. Divisional or corps commands were firmly institutionalized and distributed throughout France, which facilitated the quick integration of the reserves into the existing cadres. The system of mobilization was vastly improved and the General Staff

Right: A crowded meat market during the siege of Paris. This scene, published in a British magazine, and evidently intended to shock the reader with its absence of anything apart from horsemeat and sausages of doubtful content, for some reason omits a vital indicator in the form of prices. Below: Thiers, French president from 1871. Bottom: Barracks in central Paris, 1870.

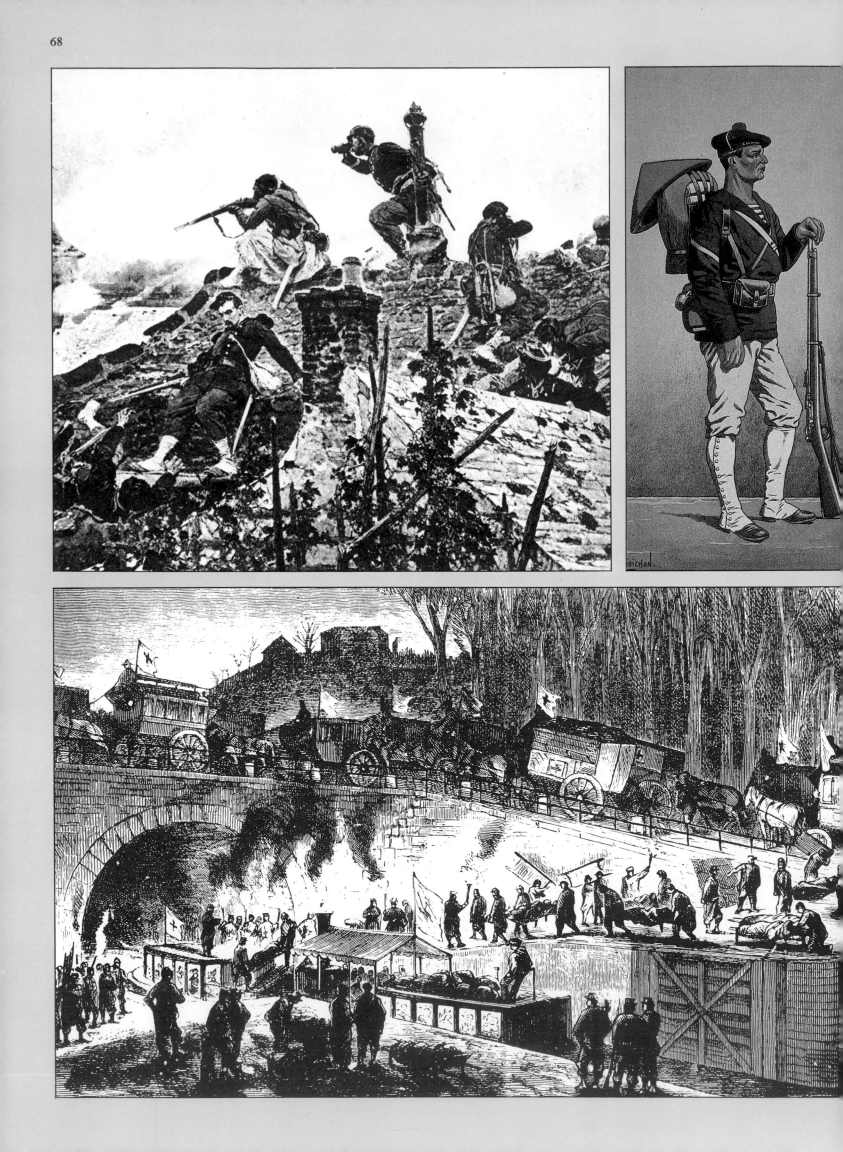

Far left: A French depiction of the Franco-Prussian War, showing French infantry in urban fighting. House-to-house fighting has been a feature of wars for centuries, becoming more destructive with the advance of weapons technology. Left: French marine infantry of the 1880s.
Below left: Horsedrawn ambulances transfer wounded to steamships on the Marne Canal during the Franco-Prussian War. Below: French colonial troops of the 1880s, armed with the Lebel tubular magazine rifle.

completely reorganized. From 1905 onward the French Army became more and more like the German in its structure and organization. There was one important difference: France could do this only at the expense of a maximum effort, since its birth rate compared unfavorably with that of Germany. Eighty percent of those eligible had to be called into active service and even that was not sufficient to produce the required number of soldiers. Against that background the French panic in 1913 is explicable; when the Germans changed their call-up arrangements, the French responded by increasing the length of military service from two to three years.

What is important to note at this point is that in France the primacy of politics was maintained at all times, however disastrous this may have been on certain occasions. Apart from Boulanger, the generals never questioned their subordination to the politicians. The legacy of Napoleon I cast its shadow over the entire 19th and early 20th century. The whole organization of the army was designed to prevent generals from playing an independent role. Before 1873 no permanent centers of command existed; in peacetime the largest formations were corps or even divisions. Every regimental commander was the direct subordinate of the Minister of War. The supreme power of decision for army and navy campaigns lay with the Superior Council for National Defense, which was chaired by the Prime Minister and comprised the Ministers of the Exterior, the Interior, Finance, War, the Navy and the Colonies. The Chief of the General Staff and of the Navy had advisory roles only. However, between 1871 and 1914 this council convened on only 17 occasions and so the opportunity to coordinate all aspects of national defense planning, including the planning of armaments was not fully exploited.

One question which posed a problem concerned the supreme command of the army. It was desirable that it should be held by one man responsible to parliament but still capable of acting militarily. Formally the President of the Republic was the Supreme Commander of the Army. He could take the initiative to convene the Superior Council for National Defense but he had only one connection with the army and that went via the Prime Minister and the Minister of War who had only political responsibility. Constitutionally, the Minister of War had the full power of command but the trouble was that in most cases he was a military administrator totally lacking in military expertise. One of the most important institutions operating under the Ministry of War was the permanent Supreme War Council which convened monthly, comprising 10 prominent generals under the chairmanship of the Minister for War. The senior general would become the commander in chief in time of war and was vice-chairman of the Council while the ordinary members were designated to become army commanders. None of these appointments carried executive authority in peacetime and in any case they were changed annually. The Chief of the General Staff was also in a weak position and was usually a comparatively junior general. A further indication of the fears that officers could develop a personal following was the rule that no general should lead an army corps for a period longer than three years.

Thus the generals were strictly subordinate to the civil power, their role at the political summit being that of technical advisors only. They were not, in a political sense, a state within a state. The drawback, of course, was the annual rotation of the Chief of the General Staff, which made for considerable discontinuity in military planning, especially in a General Staff beset with mutual animosities arising from the Dreyfus case, a division that went through the entire French officer corps. Formally, even in time of war, the Chief of the General Staff held a purely ad-

Far left: A French rail-mounted heavy gun under camouflage on the Marne. The sheer volume of artillery activity was one of the several unexpected features of World War I, and the accompanying voracious demand for shells was hard to satisfy; in the Allied countries ministers of munitions occupied a key but vulnerable office. Left: Aviation became a third arm in World War I; the French premier, Clemenceau, visits a frontline air base. The most important role of aircraft was reconnaissance, but air battles and bombing attracted most public attention.

Below: A remarkable photograph showing the last seconds of a French assault on the German line, taken on the Western Front in 1917, and showing in human terms the advantage of defense over offense.

visory position *vis-à-vis* the political leadership. He was subordinate to the Minister of War who acted as the executive organ of the Supreme Council for National Defense and to the Prime Minister who carried the political responsibility. He was also subordinate to the President of the Republic who was the Supreme Commander. Therefore, in contrast to the monarchical system as in Germany, there was never a full integration of the military leadership.

There was, of course, always the possibility that in case of war a successful military commander could gain the full support of public opinion and thus tilt the scale in favor of the military. This was a potential development continually feared by successive French governments, which tried to prevent it by frequent changes in command. They would also play one general off against the other and subject the generals to continuous and intensive control by parliament. This was bound to produce the frequent intrusion of dilettantes into military affairs.

During World War I one of the main guarantees of political predominance was the simple fact that none of the generals was ever able to achieve decisive and final results. Joffre, acclaimed as the victor of the Battle of the Marne, for a time possessed strong authority which he tried to exploit to expand his headquarters into a kind of central command operating independent of the government. He kept the ministers poorly informed, but he could only maintain this position until the end of 1914. Under Clemenceau, the French politicians took the offensive and reestablished their primacy. The Battle of the Marne, after all, had not brought the Germans to their knees. They were still deep in France. The following year showed that it was virtually unforeseeable if and when the tables could be turned against Germany. Joffre was subjected to severe and widespread criticism. Parliamentarians appeared at military headquarters and among the front-line troops to carry out their own inquiries and press their own half-baked solutions. More and more the army became involved in party politics. Politicians exercised great influence on promotions. Clemenceau in particular took personal satisfaction in taking generals down a peg or two and deflating their self-esteem.

From November 1917 Clemenceau was the strongest man in the French state, partly as a result of the many failures of the French armies to expel the Germans. He was a great manipulator of parliamentary commissions and exercised considerable influence upon public and printed opinion. Viviani's previous cabinet had failed and was toppled as a result of the abortive Dardanelles venture which Viviani had pressed upon his generals despite their opposition. Briand, who had followed him, tried his hand at the Saloniki landings. They were commanded by General Sarrail whom Joffre had earlier relieved of a command. So one commander was played off against the other. Briand also called General Galliéni to the post of Minister for War. Parliament was on the verge of entrusting him with the Supreme Command – something which Joffre just managed to prevent. But continuous military failures had begun to undermine Joffre's own position, especially the failure of the Somme offensive. Parliament clamored for his replacement, and Nivelle was appointed as his successor. But Sarrail was not subordinate to him and was responsible directly to the Prime Minister. Briand also reclaimed the right to appoint army commanders himself. When Briand fell, Ribot became his successor. He maneuvered very carefully and tried to secure all his flanks before giving General Nivelle permission to launch a series of offensives. Nivelle had first to submit his plan for a large-scale Anglo-French offensive to the prime minister. When he met with criticism he offered his resignation, but President Poincaré insisted that he stay in office. When the offensives failed, sus-

Above: French heavy artillery on the move in World War I. The heavy gun, with a range sufficient to place it in a safe position well behind the front line, and firing high-explosive shells capable of blasting great holes in earthworks, became a key weapon in trench warfare.

taining heavy losses, Nivelle was sacked and even put up before a court martial. In the meantime, large contingents of the French forces had begun to mutiny. It was up to General Pétain to restore order, which he did successfully though not without bloodshed. Pétain's position, in turn, was controlled by the appointment of General Foch as Chief of the General Staff and direct advisor to the French government. Painlevé, Minister of War during the summer of 1917, bears the credit for thus putting the two ablest French generals at the head of the French Army and also for the creation of an Interallied War Council which at

long last established effective coordination between the French and British Armies. After he had been toppled, the hour came for Clemenceau.

Clemenceau's very dynamism made him a highly popular leader who was able to get his way even in the Chamber of Deputies. He also assumed command of the Ministry of War and began to conduct the war his way. He was a frequent visitor to the front line, and branded any opposition simply as defeatism; he succeeded in revitalizing the energies of the French nation and army. Clemenceau also prevailed in his insistence that Foch be appointed Supreme Commander of the Allied Forces. And to him is due much of the credit for overcoming the crisis produced by the German offensives of March to June 1918. It was largely his will that prevented the outbreak of widespread panic when the German armies succeeded in approaching Paris again for a short time.

In August 1918, under the leadership of Foch, the allies finally managed to gain the initiative in the west. This carried with it the danger that under Foch the military power might become supreme. Foch gained decisive influence in the armistice negotiations. His struggle with Clemenceau was intense, but Clemenceau brought him to heel. When it came to the making of peace, he maintained the upper hand and the military remained firmly in the control of the politicians. The inter-war years did nothing to change that relationship, nor for that matter did the outbreak of World War II. Even in the dark days of Vichy the politicians remained in control. The primacy of politics has been maintained since 1945, despite the political troubles of the Fourth Republic and its wars in Indo-China and Algeria. Even for the Fifth Republic, led for its first 10 years by a soldier, General de Gaulle, the principle of political control has remained unchallenged.

4. Army & Society: Britain

Cromwell's standing army had left a lasting legacy which had weighed particularly heavily upon British public opinion. For a long time the British were deeply averse to maintaining a large standing army on British soil. Successive British governments preferred to fight their wars by paying the armies of other countries to do their fighting for them. Their own army included a large number of mercenaries. Even Wellington's army at Waterloo was made up for the most part of foreigners, Germans and Dutch-Belgian forces. Conscription for the army was out of the question. No British Parliament in the 19th century would have sanctioned it. Therefore, in the imperial context, India was particularly important to Great Britain. Not only did India pay for itself, unlike many other British colonies which were heavily subsidized by the British taxpayer, it also supplied much of the manpower for the Indian Army which could be used not only in India but also in Africa and the Middle East.

The transformation of the British Army into a modern fighting force was a very slow one, not least because the army came only a poor second to the Navy. For many, an army was the curse of the nation. They believed there was no need for Great Britain to maintain large land forces in the British Isles. The Royal Navy was sufficient to guard her interests in the world and maintain the *Pax Britannica*. Furthermore, the British governments of the early Victorian period showed little interest in army reforms, since they would be expensive. Their foreign policy was generally conciliatory and there was even a feeling that it would be wise to reduce the existing colonial commitments. In the public mind, dominated by ideas of free trade, there was little room for interest in anything military, apart from glorious memories of the past.

Nevertheless, slow and piecemeal reforms were carried out during the 19th century in two spheres, namely the increased control of Parliament over the military establishment and military reform to overcome the shortcomings that the Crimean War had made so blatantly obvious. The technological backwardness of the army had to be cured as well as the problem of replacements and supplies. But it took the Boer War to alarm the nation sufficiently to back a thorough-going overhaul.

For continental powers, and especially for Prussia, it was a source of utter amazement that since 1688 the continued existence of the British Army has depended on an annual vote by the House of Commons to grant the necessary funds. The Mutiny Acts which provided the legal framework of military discipline had also to be renewed annually. From 1721 Parliament had also voted the peacetime strength of the British Army. Thus the Army was forever unsure about its continued existence. Once the Congress of Vienna had begun, but long before it had come to any firm decisions about the future of Europe, the House of Commons drastically reduced the strength of the British Army. As a result, when Napoleon returned from Elba and Wellington prepared to encounter him, the forces available were only a shadow of the army Wellington had led prior to 1815.

Public distrust and dislike of the army turned the army itself into something of a provisional instrument. No large garrisons were built; instead barracks, old prisons and other disused public buildings were employed to house the army. The welfare of the rank and file concerned no one, and the extremely low level of the soldiers' education gave no cause for alarm. Nothing was done to improve the education of the officer corps or to create a modern general staff. Indeed, soldiers of the British Army were social outcasts even more than in France, where the situation was bad enough. The army consisted entirely of volunteers who had 'taken the King's shilling,' some of them not strictly voluntarily. Since it was a period of great economic and industrial growth,

Previous page: The well-led charge of the Heavy Brigade at Balaklava, a bold and hard-fought move against a surprise approach by Russian cavalry, was a brilliant British success which received considerably less public notice than the fiasco of the charge of the Light Brigade which followed it. Above: William Pitt, the British statesman who organized the coalition against Napoleon. Above right: Sir John Moore, who carefully trained his infantry and with them conducted a brilliant retreat to Corunna during the Spanish Peninsula campaign. His hero's death at Corunna in 1809 was celebrated for years afterwards. Right: A last stand by the British during the Second Afghan War.

the bulk of the soldiers were men virtually unemployable in any other position. A deep gulf divided the civilians from the soldiers. The former considered the latter roughnecks and drunkards, not without some justification. Soldiers were excluded from such public amenities as theaters and even public parks. As late as 1902, when the future Sir Henry Wilson wanted to take a marching exercise with his troops through Clacton-on-Sea, the mayor implored him to circumvent Clacton and spare the tourists the sight of soldiers. After the end of the Napoleonic Wars, Londoners complained about the number of soldiers being seen in the streets, and even in 1817 the Prime Minister raised serious objections to the building of an officers' club. The country seemed devoid of compassion for its soldiers, who were badly housed, poorly paid and underfed.

Even in times of peace the mortality rate among the soldiers exceeded that of the civilian population. They were especially prone to tuberculosis. Physical punishment was still in use, up to 300 strokes; it was abolished only in 1867. Nor did it favor the public image of the army that it was used as an instrument to enforce public order. No regular police force existed in the early 19th century and the army was often used to protect private property against 'the revolutionary actions of the

workers.' The Peterloo Massacre in which cavalry charged a demonstration, killing a number of people, is but one example. The public image of the soldier was still that of a mercenary, popular in wartime as long as he was victorious, but an outcast at home. Nothing was further from the British mind than the notion of a national army.

This was also reflected in the public's attitude to the officer corps. To be an officer in the British Army was not a treasured honor as elsewhere in Europe, but a means of providing for the younger sons of the gentry. Social origin apart, entry qualifications were very low, a private income essential and the required duties easily discharged in a few hours a day. The rank and file who served for 21 years, or virtually for a lifetime, needed no extensive training, especially when the army was fulfilling only a police function. Maneuvers were out of the question; they cost too much money. Apart from this, large troop formations did not normally exist in peacetime. The officer corps had no close contact with its men, and the ratio of officers to men was the highest in Europe.

During the 18th century, when the British aristocracy was at the apex of its power and influence, political patronage was essential to obtaining high commands in the army and a career in the army was very often combined with a seat in the House of Commons or the House of Lords. Venality was the rule; commissions were normally purchased. Good connections in Parliament and with the Secretary for War could prevent well-deserved disciplinary punishments.

In 1793 the office of Commander in Chief was created, an office of a purely military character. Its incumbent was not to be

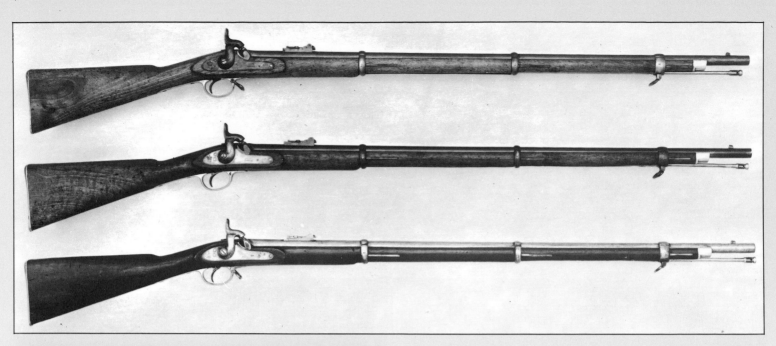

Above: The Enfield rifle (second model) of 1853. The rifling of firearm barrels, imparting spin to their projectiles, was the fundamental advance which brought accurate fire, making long-range shooting practicable and thereby necessitating great changes in battlefield tactics. Left: The percussion lock of the 1853 Enfield rifle; this too, was an advance, but the firing mechanism of rifles and pistols was still far from perfect, subject to ignition failures. Below: Kinburn, a late Crimean War engagement which is hardly remembered by the Russians or by their opponents. Above right: A general view of the Battle of the Alma, fought by the Franco-British-Turkish forces soon after they had landed in the Crimea. The Russians held a strong, elevated, position, but withdrew after some hard fighting. Below right: British horsedrawn artillery of the 1850s.

Below: The British infantry, after wading the River Alma under fire, advance in good order in the final stage of the Battle of the Alma. Explosive shells saw extensive use in this campaign, although the solid cannonball still had a role. Far left: Another view of the Battle of the Alma, the artist having contrived, it seems, to show as many different units and personalities as possible. In the center, wearing a red jacket, is the Duke of Cambridge, Queen Victoria's cousin, promoted to command a division at the age of 35. Prince Napoleon is encouraging his French infantry at the extreme right. Center left: British and Russian infantry get to grips at the Battle of Inkerman, in ruggedly mountainous terrain. Left: French chasseurs advance at Inkerman.

a member of parliament, since he was to represent the military prerogative of the Crown. The first Commander in Chief, the Duke of York, introduced stricter discipline into the army and the officer corps, and opposed with great fervor and success backstairs intrigue and influence emanating from Parliament. He also created his own personnel office staffed by proven officers and founded a training institution for officers. In 1866 royal ordinances prohibited members of the armed forces participating in party political affairs. Thus much abuse was abolished, but it was not by any means a root-and-branch reform of the armed forces. The aristocracy still occupied the best positions, since they still exercised considerable influence at court and in parliament. Although a more regular promotion system gradually took over, the purchase of commissions continued well into the 19th century, a great hindrance to many deserving officers. A final stop was put to this only in 1871; examinations for officer candidates were introduced and pensions awarded to retired officers as a right rather than an occasional reward. Formerly every regiment of the regular army had been the virtual property of an aristocratic colonel. The unit had carried his name and he hired the forces from the lump sum supplied to him by the government. Whatever he could save went into his own pocket. A more uniform system of administration was being introduced by the late 18th century, particularly after financial reforms introduced in 1782, but these were carried out only slowly, by fits and starts. Up to and including the Crimean War, the supply of uniforms was managed by the colonel. Higher tactical bodies than the battalion were permanently formed in peacetime only in the course of Haldane's army reform of 1905.

The supreme command of the armed forces was the product of a series of *ad hoc* measures, not of a clearly conceived overall plan. It was divided among numerous offices distributed over several locations in London and in the country whose cooperation left very much to be desired. On the other hand, from the parliamentary point of view, this provided security against any growing independence of the army from the political institutions of the nation.

Formally, the supreme command rested with the King who had his deputy in the Commander in Chief. The Crown defended its prerogatives in the military sphere tenaciously until the end of the 19th century. Queen Victoria especially put great store by this and even made attempts to expand it. Undoubtedly influenced by her husband, Prince Albert, she was concerned that without royal influence the genuine military experts in the army would be pushed back by the place-seekers and that dilettantes in politics, especially in parliament, would exert undue and harmful influence. There was a plan to appoint Prince Albert Commander in Chief, but it was cut short by his death.

In 1856 a cousin of the Queen, the Duke of Cambridge, was appointed to this post, which he held until 1895. However, his conservatism, allied to a very narrow intellectual horizon, was such that he proved an obstacle to the introduction of technical innovations and a new command structure, even though his authority was limited. He could award commissions and promotions, hand out medals and maintain the discipline of the forces, but he had none of the powers of a chief of the general staff, a post which did not yet exist in the British Army, nor was there a general staff as such. Even the royal command power was vague and undefined.

Parliament retained its major influence particularly in the matter of the annual army appropriations. At the beginning of the 19th century, no less than 13 other institutions competed with the Commander in Chief for authority. For all questions of armaments, from rifles to artillery, from engineers' equipment to cavalry lances, the Master-General of the Ordnance was responsible. Induction of auxiliary forces such as the militia, the yeomanry and volunteers, the deployment of the forces for police purposes and the transfer of forces from one part of the country to another was the responsibility of the Home Office. Matters of discipline and military courts were supervised by the Judge-Advocate General. All colonial forces belonged to the sphere of the Secretary for the Colonies. The feeding of the forces was in the hands of the Commissary, itself a department of the Treasury. Furthermore, there were additional offices responsible for the control of payments to the army, two Paymasters-General, a board of General Officers, an Army Medical and Hospital Office and separate commissions for the housing of troops and for recruitment.

The Commander in Chief was largely dependant on the Secretary at War in financial and administrative matters without being directly subordinate to him, but it was the Secretary for War who was directly responsible to Parliament for all operational affairs; thus in terms of influence he occupied a rather more important position than the Commander in Chief. It was Pitt the Younger who had added this office of Secretary for War, an institution that was in the future expanded into the Ministry for War and the Colonies. He was to conduct the entire military policy in peace and war, and had Cabinet rank and represented the War Office there. Until 1914 only civilians occupied this office. It soon became obvious that the Secretary for War was overburdened, mainly with colonial affairs, another factor which obstructed successful cooperation among the military authorities. The rivalry between the civilian political institutions and the military institutions remained unresolved until the end of the century.

The civilians' powers dominated, much more so than in France where military experts at least had an advisory capacity and where, with few exceptions, generals headed the War Ministry. Politically, the civilian dominance had great advantages. The British Army never slipped out of control to pursue policies separate from those of the government, but in purely military terms the civilian influence proved an obstacle to its transformation into a modern force. The Commander in Chief was really nothing more than an administrator with very limited competence. Wellington once said that he could not order a corporal and his men to march from London to Windsor and back without the approval of the civil authorities. Military plans were drawn up and marching routes for the army determined in Pall Mall and not Horse Guards Parade. In the Crimean War the Secretary for War and the Commander in Chief together exercised supreme command.

The Crimean War was the first eye-opener to the mismanagement within the British Army. In Great Britain the war enjoyed great popularity. The small opposition raised, notably by Cobden, Bright and the Peace Society, was dismissed; Cobden and Bright were even burned in effigy. Great Britain's contingent amounted to 27,000 men and *The Times* sent out its own correspondent, William Howard Russell, in itself a novelty since heretofore British newspaper had relied on reports copied from the continental press or sent to the newspapers by junior officers. Russell pitched his own tent alongside those of the British forces and sent his dispatches to London.

What he had to report was far from inspiring. Within a few days of his arrival at Gallipoli he dispatched a message to his paper to the effect that 'the management is infamous, and the contrast offered by our proceedings to the conduct of the French most painful. Could you believe it – the sick have not a bed to lie upon?' Throughout the war Russell sent messages in a

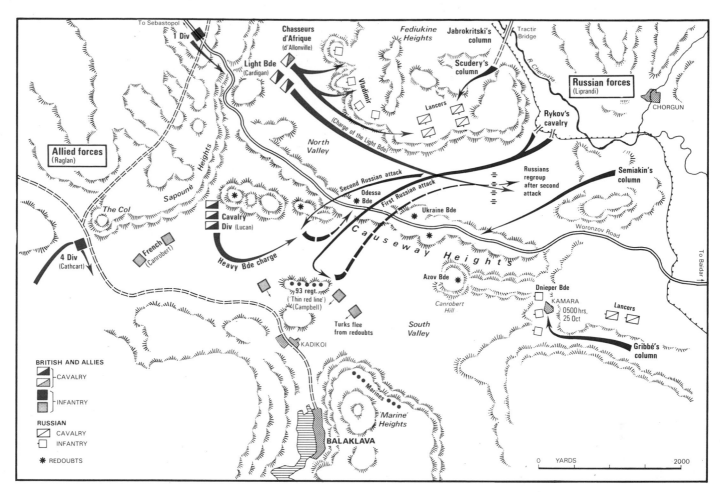

Above: Map of the Battle of Balaklava. This, the best-known battle of the Crimean campaign, resulted when the Allies decided to capture, and then defend, Balaklava, instead of pressing on to Sevastopol without delay.

similar vein. Early in November 1854 he wrote, 'I am convinced that Lord Raglan [the British Commander in Chief in the Crimea] is utterly incompetent to lead an army through any arduous task,' and later in the month he followed up with the dispatch:

'It is now pouring rain – the skies are black as ink – the wind is howling over the staggering tents – the trenches are turned into dykes – in the tents the water is sometimes a foot deep – our men have not either warm or waterproof clothing – they are out for twelve hours at a time in the trenches – they are plunged into the inevitable miseries of a winter campaign – and not a soul seems to care for their comfort or even for their lives.'

In December *The Times* published a vehement leading article:

'Incompetency, lethargy, aristocratic *hauteur*, official indifference, favour, routine, perverseness, and stupidity reign, revel and riot in the camp before Sebastopol, in the harbour of Balaklava, in the hospitals of Scutari, and how much nearer home we do not venture to say. We say it with the extremest reluctance – no-one sees or hears anything of the Commander-in-Chief.'

The Crimean War cost the British nation more in terms of human lives and money than had the Napoleonic Wars. Army reform seemed essential by way of a Parliamentary Committee of Inquiry.

However, during the Crimean War most of the various army administration offices had been merged and reorganized under the control of the Secretary for War. He was relieved of his colonial responsibilities, so the previous diversifications had been largely eliminated or reduced. The office of the Secretary

at War was merged with the War Office, but the Secretary for War remained a civilian and a member of the Cabinet. Queen Victoria, however, was most anxious that the role and functions of the Commander in Chief should not be diminished. Indeed, his functions were expanded to the extent that he assumed actual military command and that artillery, engineers and the colonial troops came under his control. The open question was still the degree of independence with which he could carry out his command under the direct control of the crown. The Queen wanted to hold back parliamentary influence in the matter of appointment and promotion of officers, and in this she appears to have enjoyed the support of public opinion. But all bodies concerned with the reform of the British Army insisted that the Secretary for War was ultimately responsible for all military questions and that therefore he would have to exercise full control over the Commander in Chief.

To all intents and purposes it appeared that through this reorganization the relationship of the politicians and the military had found its final solution, but experience was soon to show that this was not so, that in the end it was always a problem to find a compromise solution between military needs and political requirements. Unlike France, Great Britain always pursued a peaceful policy in Europe. Only in the latter part of the century, with the onset of the New Imperialism, did a profound change affect the course of British policy and its consequences.

As it was, friction between Horse Guards and the War Office never completely ceased and after 1863, even increased. The military complained about the financial meanness of the civilians, while the civilians accused the generals of extravagance.

The most influential and effective Secretary for War in the years after the Crimean War was Edward Cardwell, who in 1870 transferred the office of the Commander in Chief from Horse Guards Parade to Pall Mall, which demonstrated clearly his subordination to the Secretary for War. He now occupied and administered a department of the War Office, although he

Below: British hussars (light cavalry) in a close engagement with Russian infantry as they overrun a Russian gun at Balaklava. Far left: The charge of the Light Brigade at Balaklava. The artist has depicted the attacking British cavalry units too close together; they would have been more widely spaced from front to rear while not filling the whole valley from flank to flank. Nevertheless the picture, unlike other artistic and poetic efforts, does suggest that the achievement of the Light Brigade in overrunning the Russian guns was not so much a result of bravery, but of the iron discipline which enabled it to maintain under intense fire its regular alignment, so important in maximizing the impact of a cavalry charge. Right: A German painting of the Light Brigade's celebrated charge.

Above left: The survivors of the charge of the Light Brigade line up for inspection after their costly exploit. Left: One more of the many pictures celebrating this event; this one gives a fine impression of the mass and momentum of a well-disciplined cavalry charge.
Above: Lord Cardigan, commander of the Light Brigade. Although a fellow-officer exclaimed 'Cardigan has as much brains as my boot,' the suicidal charge of the Light Brigade was not his fault, despite subsequent allegations.

still had a direct connection to the crown. The War Office itself was reformed and its many sections structured into three main departments: one for questions of command and discipline headed by the Commander in Chief, a second responsible for finance and a third responsible for the arsenals and fortifications. Subsequently there were still other alterations in the structure of the War Office. The departmental chiefs of the last two departments were Members of Parliament, while the Commander in Chief, as a peer of the realm, had a seat in the House of Lords.

The difficulties between the departments on the one side and between the War Office and Parliament could not be eliminated. In order to deal with this problem, a new division was attempted in 1888: one side was to be a purely civilian sphere, the other a military one to whom all purely military departments and offices were responsible. This put the head of the military section into a position akin to an advisor of the Secretary for War which caused a wave of protest, especially since the man in that position was the Duke of Cambridge, renowned for his arch-conservatism and resistance to all military innovations. This put him particularly at odds with his more progressive and reform-minded subordinates. As far as the Secretary for War was concerned, the Duke of Cambridge made a nuisance of himself by continually using his direct access to the crown. The royal prerogative became, in a very direct way, an obstacle to further reform. The only way out was to integrate the army within the parliamentary democracy and its institutions. In 1870 a reform commission had tried to do away with the office of Commander in Chief, or at least reduce its functions and remove it altogether from the War Office. It was advocated that in its place a Chief of the General Staff should be appointed, similar to the German and French example. He, together with the civilian and military department chiefs, would form a kind of council. This plan was bitterly opposed by Queen Victoria and her supporters. The Duke of Cambridge retired in 1895, but his office continued to exist. The chiefs of the military departments could now advise the Secretary for War without interference from the Commander in Chief who was neither a responsible minister nor the sole advisor of the Secretary for War, let alone a Chief of the General Staff or even commander of the troops. All that was left to him was routine day-to-day administration. But it was still not clear who actually held the responsibility for military planning and for the condition of the army. It could not be the Secretary for War, because as a civilian he was not a military expert and he was wholly occupied with parliamentary affairs. It could not be the General Staff, because there was no such institution. Nor could it be the departmental heads who administered only specific aspects of the military.

Little wonder, therefore, that the War Office acquired the reputation of being a 'circumlocution office' whose various departments tended to work against one another rather than to cooperate. The army administration was excessively centralized, which led to a great deal of administrative work being given to officers who would have been better deployed in service with the troops. But large troop formations still did not normally exist in Great Britain. Unlike France and Germany, Great Britain was not divided into military districts, each with its own command and administrative apparatus. This underlay more serious shortcomings: the lack of training during peacetime, the absence of any organization for mobilization and the inadequate training of staff-caliber officers. In case of emergency officers and generals suitable for command and staff duties had to be collected from all parts of the country. On the whole, the British war machine was intended to do no more than protect the coasts (which, in fact, the Royal Navy did much better) or to participate in small colonial wars.

One wonders what might have happened if Great Britain had entered World War I with this kind of army and organization. Fortunately, the British Army and Parliament received a timely warning in the form of the Boer War. There could hardly have been another campaign in modern history which was as badly prepared and improvised as the British intervention in South Africa. Again, as in the Crimean War, the public supported it wholeheartedly. Kipling's poem of October 1899 reflected the sentiments of the majority of the nation as well as their somewhat ambivalent attitude to the ordinary soldier:

When you've shouted 'Rule Britannia,' when you've sung
'God save the Queen,'
When you've finished killing Kruger with your mouth
Will you kindly drop a shilling in my little tambourine
For a gentleman in khaki ordered South?

The poem was written as part of a fund-raising campaign to save soldiers' families from material hardship. It raised well over one quarter of a million pounds, appearing on tobacco tins and general bric-a-brac and was set to music by composer Sir Arthur Sullivan for rendition in music halls, drawing rooms and on bandstands.

Field Marshal Viscount Wolseley expressed his utter confidence in the supremacy of British arms. He had no doubts whatsoever about the commander of the expeditionary force, Sir Redvers Buller. Initial news from South Africa sounded favorable. A host of newspaper correspondents were sent out, but most of their reports were inaccurate because their messages were heavily censored by the army, on whose lines of communication they had to depend. The seriousness of the reverses suffered by the British Army was discovered by independent visitors to the scene of war and rarely by the correspondents. The terrible state of the military hospitals, in which a great proportion of the 16,168 deaths from wounds or disease occurred, was revealed by William Burdett-Coutts, a British Member of Parliament who toured the hospitals personally. The conditions in the concentration camps established by the British later in the war were revealed by a Quaker, Emily Hobhouse. As the quick victory did not materialize, and the war wore on, the early enthusiasm for it waned.

Gradually the consequences of the disastrous campaign could no longer be concealed; in many quarters of the world, and especially in Europe, the real strength of the British Empire was seriously questioned. In Britain immense efforts were made not only to turn the reverses in South Africa into an ultimate victory, but also to reform the entire structure of the British armed forces. Almost immediately upon the conclusion of the hostilities in South Africa, Britain, whose Navy still reigned supreme, began to try to produce an equally efficient army. The entire military structure was reformed and modernized. New equipment was introduced, major attention given to the training of officers, and provisions made for an effective reserve at all times.

Prime Minister Balfour formed a committee headed, between 1903–04, by Lord Esher, which initially referred to recommendations for reform made as far back as 1890. The reforms recommended by the Esher Commission were carried out by Orders in Council, which meant that the government's wishes were implemented by royal command without any parliamentary discussion.

The reforms put an end to the previous squabbling between the army and parliament and healed the conflict between civilian and military authority. The office of the Commander in Chief was abolished. The Secretary for War was still to be the executive organ for the royal prerogative. To a large extent the army's administration was modeled on that of the Admiralty. Under the chairmanship of the Secretary for War (a Cabinet-rank politician), a seven-man committee would decide all important questions. A Chief of the General Staff was appointed, as was a Quarter Master General, a General responsible for Ordnance and an Adjutant General. Their civilian colleagues on the committee were the parliamentary undersecretaries (junior politicians), the senior departmental civil servants and a representative of the Treasury. Military men and civilians were no longer to work separately but to cooperate in a committee with common responsibility. This was one of the features borrowed from the Admiralty. Seven military districts were formed, each having its own administration. The top-heavy centralization had been abolished.

The most important step was the creation of a General Staff. This had been recommended in 1890 but it was ignored at that

Below: A French painting of the Battle of Balaklava, showing the
outnumbered Scots Greys, of the Heavy Brigade, engaged with Russian
cavalry. Before the courageous fiasco of the Light Brigade's charge, the
Heavy Brigade routed the Russian cavalry and, had the Light Brigade
been ordered to attack then rather than later, a great and possibly decisive
Allied victory would have been ensured. But the Allies, and especially the
British, were encumbered by commanders who had been appointed not
for their competence but because of their wealth, family, or connections.
However, the aggressiveness shown by the British cavalry at Balaklava
unnerved the Russians, giving the British an advantage of morale which
lasted throughout the remainder of the Crimean War.

Top: The 'thin red line'; the 93rd Highlanders at the Battle of
Balaklava. This unit, strengthened by invalids, stood firm against a strong
Russian cavalry attack at an early, critical, stage of the battle. Above:
Florence Nightingale, who improved the deplorable British military
medical service. Right: The Allies bombard Odessa.

Above: In the Crimean War Russia was also attacked halfheartedly in the Baltic. Here the Royal Navy is using small paddlewheel ships to bombard the fortress of Bomarsund. Right: HMS *Driver*, a small and shallow-draught vessel, off the Baltic fort of Kronstadt.

time, since British politicians tended to view generals and general staffs as warmongers. Another innovation was the Committee for Imperial Defense which was chaired by the Prime Minister and included Cabinet members of his choice (usually the Secretary for War and the First Lord of the Admiralty and others) as well as a staff of officers drawn from all parts of the army and from the dominions. These, however, did not have a vote; their role was an advisory one. It was a fairly cumbersome organization but it did give a more coherent direction to military policy-making. The Prime Minister also continued to seek the advice of a cabinet committee in which military experts were included as advisors. The Boer War represents a watershed in the history of the British Army. Having started late, the British could avoid most of the problems that still affected the organization and workings of the French and German armies.

The actual reorganization of the army was begun during the Boer War, with the placement of younger and more efficient officers in important posts. A nationwide campaign to rouse the public's interest in the army and to popularize it was launched with considerable success. Not only was Great Britain called upon to carry its share, but the dominions and colonies as well. The dominions (Australia, New Zealand and Canada) re-

sponded accordingly and during World War I sent larger forces than Westminster and Whitehall had ever expected.

The general living standard of the army rank and file was vastly improved and veterans received more care than they ever had before. The Cardwell reforms had reduced the enlistment period from 21 years to 12 years, of which seven were spent in the army and five in the reserve. This provided the basis for reserve formations. Most regiments now had two active battalions, of which one was based in the British Isles training recruits while the other served in the colonies. The 'overseas' battalion could draw on the 'home' unit for replacements. National service based on short-term recruitment was not considered adequate to British requirements at that time, because a period of one or two years' service overseas was judged to be uneconomic.

What proved to be a viable source of recruitment was the Militia, an institution which had existed since the days of the Tudors. In the 18th century service in the Militia, of which each county had its own, was intended to be compulsory but the system of substitutes existed here as well. Since the middle of the 19th century the Militia had been called upon only when the

country was virtually denuded of regular troops, as during the Crimean War, for example. The Militia underwent a very elementary and superficial training. Recruits had six months' basic training under regular soldiers and thereafter had to participate in an annual exercise lasting three or four weeks. Service in the Militia was limited to six years.

Militarily, they had been of only limited value, but in course of the reforms inspired by the Boer War they attained a new status as reserves for the regular army, one of the achievements of Secretary for War R B Haldane. He foresaw that sooner or later Great Britain might well have to participate in a continental war against Germany. 'Splendid isolation' was, in Haldane's view, no longer a practical policy. Together with the Foreign Secretary, Sir Edward Grey, he backed military conversations with the French of which only the Prime Minister and some of his colleagues (but not the entire Cabinet) were informed. Haldane's objective was the creation of an effective expeditionary force which could be mobilized within a few days and shipped across the Channel. The expeditionary force was to consist of six infantry divisions and one cavalry division, all equipped and structured according to their continental

Above left: A French painting of the stand of the Highlanders against Russian cavalry at Balaklava. Above right: The harbor at Balaklava, used by the Allies as a supply port for the operations against Sebastopol, Barrack huts of the Guards are in the foreground. The British laid the first military railway here, to carry supplies from the port. Above: General Simpson, who became commander in chief after Lord Raglan died of cholera. Right: The storming of the Redan at Sebastopol; British guns and mortars at work.

counterparts. Haldane studied the German tactics for mobilization very thoroughly and then applied them to the British Army.

Having an expeditionary force was one thing, but having adequate reserves for it another. A reserve force was created in 1907, not by the introduction of universal military service, but by way of the reorganized Militia which became the Territorial Army. A typical regiment with two regular battalions would have two territorial battalions attached to it to allow wartime expansion. In some parts of the United Kingdom the Militia system had virtually disappeared, and where this had happened

Above left: The siege of Sebastopol; a captured Russian battery. The rope mantlets were to protect the gunners. Above: Artillery emplacements for the bombardment of Sebastopol. The nearest piece is a siege mortar, used for lobbing heavy projectiles. The protective earthworks are also being used to provide covered shelters. Left: An Allied gun battery at Sebastopol.

it was now re-established. The nascent Labour Party was not slow in raising the cry of 'Militarization' and 'Germanization.' Irrespective of that, by 1909 the Territorial Army comprised 270,000 men. Propaganda for the army and for volunteers for the Territorial Army in particular was promoted at all levels of British society. Schools and universities had their own cadet forces and the Boy Scouts became one of the most important organizations for youth para-military training. Field Marshal Lord Roberts headed the National Service League which advocated the introduction of conscription. Within the British General Staff this idea was seriously considered in 1912 and 1913, but dropped because it was likely to increase the existing international tensions still further and would, in any case, be strongly opposed in Parliament.

How successful these measures were in the long term is a matter of debate. The commanders of the British Expeditionary Force complained bitterly after the war that they had been sent to France with under-strength forces and insufficient equipment in arms, artillery and ammunition. They argued that Great Britain had been in no way prepared for the kind and scale of war they encountered. Then, with a very few exceptions, the generals of all belligerent armies had believed in the short war.

A slaughter of the dimensions that was to take place between 1914 and 1918 was beyond the imagination of most. Nevertheless, Haldane's reform laid a firm basis for what was ultimately to become a large national army. At conferences with the dominions between 1907 and 1911 it was laid down that the successful cooperation of the British Empire could be guaranteed only if uniforms and equipment were standardized throughout the Empire. All the officers of the dominions and colonies received British-style training. Joint plans of operation were worked out. Hence the British chief of staff had the official title Chief of the Imperial General Staff. The objective was twofold: firstly to put the dominions in a position to defend themselves without aid from the mother country, and secondly for the dominions to transfer large forces to the European theater of war. Behind these measures stood the growing 'German threat' as interpreted by Grey.

Once the war had broken out Great Britain, as compared to its allies, had one decisive advantage; Parliament tended to refrain from interfering in military affairs. Then, of course, Great Britain was not as directly threatened as France. The more the war became a *total* war, the more the whole of the nation was involved in it, the more strongly public opinion supported its own army. To this end official and semi-official propaganda was organized on a scale hitherto unknown in Europe to sustain the moral fiber of the nation and extend it to the neutral countries. Even such an eminent scholar as Lord Bryce considered it his duty to organize British propaganda in the United States and to spread the blatantly untruthful stories of the German atrocities in Belgium and France. The stories of the amputated hands and gouged-out eyes of the Belgian children disgusted the

Below: Inside an Allied battery at Sebastopol. Sailors maneuver a 32-pounder into the sandbagged emplacement. Both sides used sailors for land operations in this war, often to operate guns landed from ships. The picture also shows how guns could be dismantled, so that the heavy barrel could be moved on a separate vehicle. Left: Another view of a battery in action at Sebastopol. Shellbursts in the air are another reminder of the great use made of explosive shells in this campaign. Their time fuzes were neither precise nor reliable. Right: Night action at Sebastopol.

Left: The Russians blow up their Fort Nicholas at Sebastopol. With their highly-competent and resourceful military engineers, the Russians mined many of their defensive works. If captured by their opponents, the works could be blown up, to the discomfiture of the captors. Fifty years later the Russians had brought this technique to a high level of refinement, which they used effectively in the Russo-Japanese War. Below: A French painting showing the death of General Campbell during an initial, and disastrous, assault on the Redan at Sebastopol. Campbell was killed as he urged his reluctant men forward in this mismanaged attack.

public at home and abroad and were believed until they were finally refuted after the war's end.

The political leadership in Westminster was never formally questioned by the military and this remained the case because, as in France, no British general could achieve the kind of victories which had given Wellington not only military but also political eminence. The British role in the war was initially limited to holding the positions in Flanders and supporting the French, very much the senior partners in the alliance. Only in the colonies and in the Middle East, in East Africa and Mesopotamia, were the generals relatively free from government control.

Even the immense energies produced by Kitchener, the first military Secretary for War, and the efforts of first Field Marshal French and then Haig, his successor in command of the British forces, could do nothing to break through the German lines and put an end to the enormous blood-letting that used up almost all the available reserves of manpower. Only in May 1916 could Parliament be persuaded to introduce general conscription. It produced new manpower but no decisive change in the front line. In the face of the lists of fatal casualties, the early enthusiasm for war began to evaporate; like France, Great Britain became war-weary. Lord Lansdowne – Sir Edward Grey's predecessor as Foreign Secretary – published a 'peace letter' arguing in favor of a negotiated peace. *The Times* of London refused to print it but it reached the public via the press of the Labour Party. Although parliament's political primacy was never questioned, it was parliament and the government itself which had abandoned its responsibilities to the generals.

First French and then Haig said that the next great offensive would bring the decisive breakthrough. Such a breakthrough was not achieved, at least until the summer of 1918, and the casualty list grew. Although Prime Minister Lloyd George was rather contemptuous of his generals, he could do nothing but leave the conduct of the war in their hands. The only other alternative would have been to begin negotiations for the cessation of hostilities, but that was not politically acceptable.

In any case, a British Cabinet, 30 ministers strong, would have found it difficult to intervene in military operations. They simply lacked the expertise to do so, with one exception: Win-

ston Churchill. As First Lord of the Admiralty (navy minister) he developed the concept of pushing into the soft underbelly of Europe by means of the Gallipoli operation. It was ingeniously conceived, but when carried out it lacked the wholehearted cooperation of the Army, Navy and French allies. It turned out to be a disaster. Churchill was made the scapegoat and had to resign.

At the beginning of the war, when Asquith was still Prime Minister, Lord Kitchener, a soldier, was appointed Secretary for War. But when the cabinet discussed the war plans, for instance, on 5 August 1914, the Chief of the Imperial General Staff was not invited to give his opinion. Instead a number of other officers were invited who did not possess all the information in the hands of the General Staff. Kitchener mobilized the nation, but he could do little to transform the cabinet into a more decisive instrument for the conduct of war. His achievement was to build up the new army and his actual aim was to produce the largest land army in Europe and thus to put Great Britain in a position to determine allied policy during and after the war.

The cabinet proved such an unwieldy instrument that by the end of 1914 Asquith had created a cabinet committee of six members, later increased to 12, which became the War Council.

In 1915 it was renamed the War Committee of the Cabinet, but the General Staff remained excluded. It was not until December 1915 that the then newly-appointed Chief of the Imperial General Staff, Sir William Robertson, gained access to it in an advisory capacity and it was up to him to issue all operational orders – one sign that the politicians preferred to leave military operations in the hands of those qualified. But he remained subordinate to the Secretary for War. Robertson attempted at first to restrict the competencies of the Secretary for War to purely administrative matters, but Kitchener opposed this and proved more than a match for Robertson.

One of the byproducts of the abortive Dardanelles offensive, besides Churchill's resignation, was the fall of the Asquith Cabinet and the formation of a coalition government under Lloyd George. Lloyd George had earned his laurels as Minister for Munitions and as Secretary for War after Kitchener's death in 1916. He was a man who kept his head in times of crisis like the German offensives of the spring of 1918 but he lacked the ability to think through strategic problems and was very erratic in many respects; his own high self-esteem frequently got the better of him. Like Churchill, though with less justification, he prided himself on his strategic talents, and he devised many plans, none of which, fortunately, was ever carried out, partly

Below: Sebastopol on 8 September 1855. The Allies make their final assault on the fortifications. In this picture the French under MacMahon and Bosquet have captured the Malakoff, the key strongpoint of the defenses (marked 1 in this French painting). Meanwhile the Russians, already keen practitioners of scorched-earth tactics, have set fire to the town and have commenced an orderly evacuation across a bridge of boats. The siege lasted almost a year, and was bravely and very competently managed by the Russians, thanks largely to their skill in military engineering and to the assistance of their sailors and naval officers, whose ships had been immobilized. The last act of the retreating Russians was to place water at the side of the Allied wounded. This picture overlooks the scene from the north; the Allied assault was from the south, and the badly-led British suffered enormous casualties.

British colonial wars. Above far left: The British infantry make a bayonet charge against the Ashantis of West Africa in 1874. Above left: Lances, carbines and pistols against spears and knobkerries; the 17th Lancers pursue the Zulus at Ulundi, 1879. Far left: Carnage as the British cavalry achieve the final repulse of the Zulus at Ginghilovo in the 1879 Zulu War. Above: A celebrated battle of the Zulu War, the defense of Rorke's Drift. Queen Victoria later described the Zulu warriors as 'singularly honest' and 'merry.' Left: The British magazine *Illustrated London News* gives the Zulu War first-page coverage. This sketch of a Zulu attack on a British regiment at the Intombi River was drawn by an officer who had taken part. Those who opposed the British prime minister, Disraeli, regarded the Zulu War which he instigated as not only immoral but also shortsighted; subsequent events proved them right.

because at the last moment he feared the risk if they should miscarry. His cooperation with the sober, hard-working and systematic Robertson was uneasy, and he finally had him replaced by the politically more agile Sir Henry Wilson.

In the realm of politics Lloyd George usually managed to get his way; he was resourceful and the most powerful orator of his time. It is often asked why Great Britain never succumbed in times of dire economic trouble to another orator of equal caliber: the British fascist leader of the 1930s, Sir Oswald Mosley. The usual answer – although it ignores many other important aspects – may have a core of truth. Having once trusted a powerful orator in the person of Lloyd George, none of whose promises came true after the war, once was enough for the British: they now distrusted a splendid orator. Lloyd George had an intuitive feeling for the masses, a phenomenon of the age of mass democracy.

In the House of Commons, however, Lloyd George frequently had a deputy speak on his behalf while for his own use he created a war cabinet comprising five to seven civilian ministers temporarily freed from their other departmental duties. The generals and admirals had to submit their plans to this war

Below: An attempt to find a bright side to the humiliating British defeat by the Zulus at Isandhlwana in 1879; two dashing horsemen save the colors. It was in this engagement that the son of the exiled French emperor Louis Napoleon was killed while serving in the British army. This defeat disillusioned many Britons who hitherto had rejoiced in Disraeli's colonial excursions. Right: An incident in the Battle of Omdurman; a long line of British riflemen prepares to receive the assault of the insurgent Sudanese. A field hospital, sign of improved medical care, can also be seen.

Left: The First Boer War of 1881. With the Zulu threat removed by the British Zulu War, the Boers of the Transvaal felt strong enough to assert themselves against Britain. Their defeat of British forces at Majuba Hill weakened the conciliatory voices in the British cabinet, but Gladstone managed to negotiate an agreement with the Boers which retained a British claim to the Transvaal. This picture shows British cavalry and infantry advancing in one of the engagements of this small-scale war, the Battle of Laing's Neck. Below left: Another British last stand, this time during the punitive 1879–80 Afghanistan campaign. Below: Tribesmen of the Indian North West Frontier, long-term tormentors of the British. Then, as now, their rifles were often home-made copies. The picture dates from about 1890.

Right: Eleven men and their dog make a last stand in the Third Afghan War of 1879–80. The British press had an unjustified obsession with heroic last stands during this war; this was perhaps an echo of the disastrous Afghan War of 1842, the first of the three Afghan Wars which Britain undertook to check undue Russian influence in Afghanistan, which was thought to represent a threat to India. The British commander in the 1879–80 campaign was the future Lord Roberts, whose 10,000 men marched 320 miles in 23 days from Kabul to Kandahar. Below: A British infantryman of the 1890s, with magazine rifle and equipped for colonial service.

cabinet for approval; they served in an advisory and executive capacity. He also organized a huge staff and auxiliary offices to guide two essential sectors, the war economy and propaganda. On the domestic scene, Lloyd George's role came very close to that of a dictator. But the generals, aware of the civilian authorities' ignorance in military matters, were anything but servile to him and largely got their way as far as the conduct of operations was concerned. After General Foch had been appointed Supreme Commander of all the Allied Forces in France, the weight finally shifted to the generals until the war had been won.

The primacy of politics had finally been preserved but in what turned out to be a very perverse primacy of mass politics. The nation had been exhorted to mobilize all its physical resources; it was asked to bear a hitherto unknown loss of life. Mass democracy now asked for its price – and the price was the Versailles Treaty. The German Navy, scuttled in Scapa Flow, was no more. Her colonies had passed into the hands of the victors and for the time being German commercial competition had vanished. The formidable instrument which the German Army had once been was reduced to 100,000 men. What more could Great Britain want?

The end of the war brought the abolition of conscription. Great Britain returned to a policy in which imperial considerations were paramount, and thus the military establishment was pruned to the requirements of colonial warfare. Great Britain was determined never again to intervene with a land expeditionary force in Europe. If intervention was needed, it could be made by means of the Royal Air Force on the principle that the bomber would always get through. The appointment of Adolf Hitler did little to change this attitude at first, but finally his expansionist policies could no longer be ignored. Great Britain was committed once again on the European continent. When Churchill succeeded Chamberlain on 11 May 1940, a man of uncommon energy and military knowledge led the country through very adverse times until finally, largely through his own initiatives, the tide turned and with the aid of the Grand Alliance the German foe was smashed again. Churchill's political and military abilities were evenly balanced, and the question of the primacy of politics versus the military never seriously arose during World War II – at least as far as Great Britain was concerned.

5. Army & Society: Germany

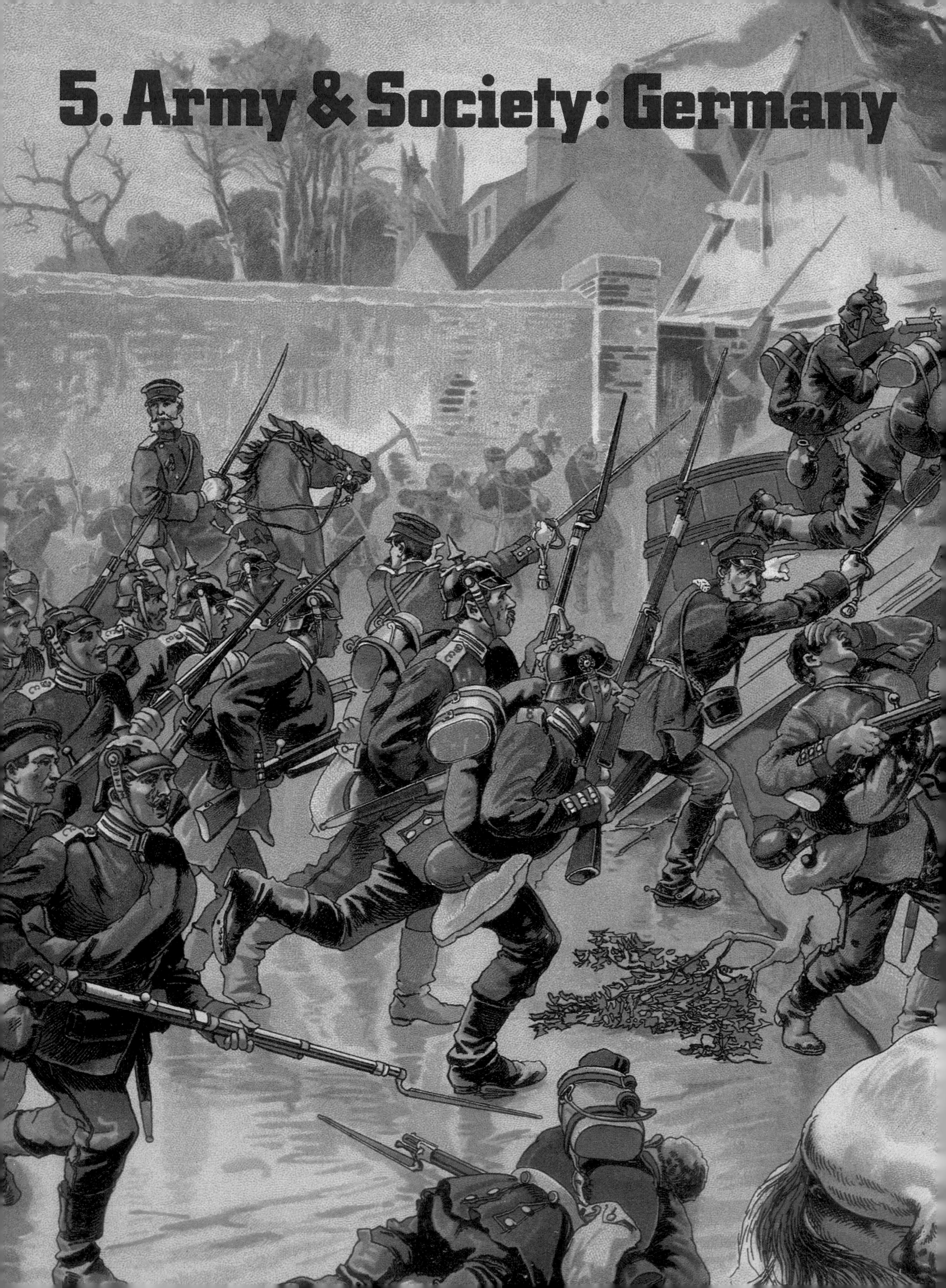

As we have had occasion to note before, the reforms carried out in Prussia between 1807 and 1813, particularly the military reforms, had excited the passion and opposition of many. An army which had previously been manned by the two pillars of the Prussian state, the aristocracy and the peasantry, had been opened to the middle class, precisely that part of the nation suspected by reform opponents to be most vulnerable to the ideas of the French Revolution. It had indeed become a national army. During the War of Liberation criticism abated somewhat, to be taken up with renewed vigor after 1815.

One of the institutions created was a Ministry of War, headed by the reformer General von Boyen. This body became the focal point of struggles for and against the army reforms enacted between 1807 and 1813. Conscription had been introduced for the duration of the war only. By a cabinet order of 27 May 1814 it was lifted again, causing anxiety among the reformers that a return to the *cantonal règlement* would take its place. Boyen's efforts prevented this, but he too had to pay his price, namely to sacrifice the *Landsturm*, the reserve formation for the *Landwehr*, the militia which had been created by the reformers and in which every able-bodied Prussian male had to serve. Thus before State Chancellor Prince Hardenberg's and King Friedrich Wilhelm III's departure for the Congress of Vienna, the king signed the law making conscription a permanent feature on 3 September 1814, to be supplemented a year later by new regulations governing the *Landwehr*. From then on Prussia had a relatively small regular army of approximately 136,000 men (whose members had to do three years' active service plus two years in the reserve) and a *Landwehr* of 163,000 (whose members did seven years' service) which, after receiving basic training from officers and NCOs of the regular army, met for a few weeks every year except in time of war when it was integrated into the active army. There was also a second line of *Landwehr* for purposes of territorial defense, but this did not participate in peacetime exercises.

Conscription and the *Landwehr* were institutions viewed with immense hostility by Prussian conservative reactionaries like Prince Charles of Mecklenburg and Prince Wittgenstein. The latter declared that 'Arming the nation means the organization of revolution.' Attempts were made to abolish both conscription and the *Landwehr*. The Minister of Finance, von Bülow, argued that they resulted in a financial burden which the Prussian state was unable to carry. Boyen, in reply, demonstrated that the financial burden per head of Prussia's population, considering its actual earnings and rising prices, was lower than it had been in the days of the old army, which had shown itself to be ineffective at Jena and Auerstädt. In this he found the support of the King. The issue of the *Landwehr* was more explosive. Through faults of its own, it had allowed such standards as it had possessed between 1813 and 1815 to deteriorate and now gave cause for serious complaint.

Up to the rank of captain it was commanded by its own officers, virtually elected by the men. Within each governmental district it had its own inspectors and, being a part-time army, *Landwehr* soldiers and officers were naturally deeply involved in the lives of their own communities. Only the general of the province was their direct superior officer. Boyen was emphatic in maintaining the militia traditions of the *Landwehr* because he considered it vital that it preserve its character as a people's army. Hence he insisted upon strict segregation between the regiments of the line and the *Landwehr*, which he feared would be jeopardized if the line regiments exerted a greater influence. The King, however, counseled by his generals who were especially critical of what they considered lax discipline in the *Landwehr*, wanted

greater influence for the regular army and the removal of the *Landwehr* inspectors, as well as the combination of line and *Landwehr* regiments into divisional formations. These wishes prevailed.

In 1819 the *Landwehr* was reduced in size and put under the direct command of the regiments of the line. Boyen resigned his post, as did the Chief of Staff General von Grolmann. With their departure the spirit of the officer corps of the regiments of the line began to determine the development of the Prussian Army. It was the beginning of that ministerial crisis which resulted from the reactionary policy of Friedrich Wilhelm III and culminated in the struggles of the conservative State Chancellor, Prince Hardenberg, who had originally been a reformer, and his former associates. For all practical purposes, the reform movement had come to an end. It remained a promise only half-fulfilled with a legacy of betrayal and bitter frustration that was exacerbated by the King's failure to keep his promise of 1815 to grant Prussia a constitution and a representative assembly. Though Prussia was in dire financial straits, there was no need to consult the populace about raising taxes, since a very large loan contracted from the House of Rothschild in London made Prussia independent of public sanction for increased taxation.

The King remained supreme commander of his army without any parliamentary interference. But by 1847 political and economic pressure had mounted to the point that King Friedrich Wilhelm IV found it necessary to give way by publishing a decree which called a Prussian Diet into being on 3 February 1847. It was to meet as often as called for by the requirements of the state, as when there was a need for new loans, new taxes, or an increase in existing taxation. The United Diet, as it was called, was to represent the three estates; the higher nobility such as princes were to deliberate separately as a kind of upper house, the *Herrenhaus*. However, the concessions made were too few and too late. Ultimately, in the wake of the Revolution of 1848, Friedrich Wilhelm IV had to grant a formal constitution to Prussia, but not one produced by a Prussian representative

Previous page: Prussian troops, nearing Paris, storm a street barricade to enter Le Bourget, in 1870. Above left: The Prussian army in action against Berlin revolutionaries in 1848.

Above: Infantrymen of the Prussian *landwehr*, founded 1813. Below, left and right: The 1848 revolutionaries defend their barricades.

Far left: A Prussian artillery park in 1864, at the time of the war against Denmark. The method of moving the increasingly heavy guns over longer distances involved detaching the barrels and carrying them on 4-wheel transporters formed by joining two pairs of artillery wheels by a stout beam. A derrick for lifting the barrels can be discerned in this picture.
Below: Two heavy cannon serving the Prussian campaign against Denmark in 1864. The Prussians, helped by the Austrians, were quickly successful in this campaign; Denmark's provinces of Schleswig and Holstein were ceded, respectively, to Prussia and Austria. Prussia made war against Austria shortly afterwards and gained Holstein, the whole affair being regarded as a triumph for Bismarck. Left: Prince Frederick-Charles of Prussia (fourth from right) in the 1864 war.

assembly. Instead it was drafted by the King and his advisors, although it did include many features which liberals had been demanding for decades.

General and representative elections were planned (but under the pressure of the liberals the franchise was whittled down and a three-class voting system introduced that favored the propertied class) and two chambers were to convene to discuss the final version of the constitution. The full executive powers of the Crown were retained, including its prerogative in military and foreign affairs, although these were limited by the framework of the constitution. A vital feature omitted was that the armed forces should swear loyalty to the constitution; a clause was included which stipulated that the army and civil servants swear loyalty and obedience to the King.

What had not been finally decided was whether the army was to be an instrument of the state and thus under the Minister for War and subject to parliamentary control, or whether it was the exclusive instrument of the monarchy. Discussions on this soon preoccupied the Prussian Diet, but Friedrich Wilhelm IV insisted that the constitution had given him supreme command of the army and that it was therefore removed from the diet's influence. In other words, the Minister of War was an administrator, responsible both to parliament and to the King. The immediate military advisors of the Crown did not answer to parliament at all.

The question of the status of the *Landwehr* was raised again, without, however, changing the ideas of the King and his generals. Even a man like Friedrich Engels spoke up against change: 'As long as one has a French Army on the one side, a Russian Army on the other, and has to consider the possibility of combined attack by both, one needs forces which do not have to acquire the first principles of soldiering in the face of the enemy.' As a matter of fact, the issue of the *Landwehr* was no longer very important in itself; it served only as a point of departure for those parliamentarians who endeavored to expand parliamentary control over the entire Prussian Army. As far as the regular army was concerned, the more the *Landwehr* was allowed to deteriorate, the stronger would become the influence of the regular army, or 'the spirit of the line.'

In 1858 compulsory military service for three years was reintroduced, but it was the experience of the war in Italy in 1859 that impressed upon the military party in Prussia the need for a thorough overhaul of the entire army. This view extended to the Minister for War, Roon, and the Prince of Prussia, later the King and Kaiser Wilhelm I. The reform was nothing unique, because both the Crimean War and that of 1859 had impressed upon the staffs of the armies of Europe the need to carry out drastic reforms. Prussia's peacetime army had remained the same size between 1820 and 1859, although her population had increased during that period from 11 to 18 million. During those years, the Prussian Army inducted 40,000 recruits annually. Those who had not been drafted served in the *Landwehr*, which, in case of mobilization, was no longer an instrument with which one could seriously reckon.

One of the lessons of the Prussian mobilization of 1859 was the need to increase the cadre of the regular forces. This was done by recruiting 63,000 men annually instead of the previous 40,000. The regular army comprised all men between the ages of 20 and 26. The *Landwehr* itself was reduced to the status once occupied by the *Landsturm*, a force to guard bridges and other militarily important objectives. In this way the Prussian Army became younger and more mobile; there was no longer any need to rely on middle-aged men.

Since all this was carried out without seeking the advice,

Bottom left: Hanoverian dragoons attack a Prussian infantry square. Hanover wished to stay neutral in the Austro-Prussian War, but soon found itself fighting on the losing side, which gave Bismarck the opportunity to absorb the state into Prussia. Below: Helmuth von Moltke, commander of the Prussian army in its victories over the Danes, Austrians, and French, and subsequently the first Chief of the Great German General Staff. Below right: The Battle of Uttingen in Baden. Baden was another unwilling participant in the Austro-Prussian War, having been dragged in by Austria. Bottom: Cavalry moves by rail in 1866, and arrives faster and fresher. Moltke had noticed the military uses of railroads in the American Civil War.

counsel or approval of the Prussian Diet, differences hardened on the domestic scene. The new reformers, Generals von Manteuffel and Roon, along with Wilhelm I, acted completely independently. The army was the King's, or as Roon put it, 'The army is now our fatherland, because here the impure and fermenting elements have not yet entered.' They looked at the Prussian Army from a viewpoint that identified it with the state: the army was the state and the state the army. However, the army reforms were violently opposed by Parliament, not because Parliament saw them as unnecessary, but because it considered them and the additional revenue they required as a lever with which to subordinate the army to parliamentary control. The opposition became so vehement that Wilhelm I

Bismarck's advice which prevailed against that of the military. The same applies to the Franco-Prussian War of 1870–71, in which he ultimately asserted the primacy of politics.

Three successful wars gave the Prusso-German Army a reputation it had never before possessed. From these successes it came about quite naturally that the Prussian Army system should be emulated throughout the states of the German Empire. This had already begun in 1867 with the creation of the North German Confederation and the alliances with the south German states. Bavaria, Württemberg and Baden took over Prussian methods of training, weapons and manuals. True, the allied states reserved rights to the extent that their Kings and princes retained supreme command over the army in peacetime, but in case of war all their armies were subordinated to the Kaiser.

Bismarck, as Prime Minister of Prussia, as Chancellor of the North German Confederation and as Chancellor of the German Empire reasserted and maintained the primacy of politics, but his concept of politics was very much his own and kept large areas of governmental activity from the Diet and the Reichstag. He was not responsible to them, but only to his King and Emperor, and his position remained unchallenged throughout the reign of Wilhelm I. Even so, he needed the cooperation of the Reichstag, which, from its establishment in 1871, had the power of the purse. This explains Bismarck's continuous endeavor to find workable parliamentary conditions that would secure him the vote on vital issues.

One factor which he had initially ignored was Germany's rapid industrialization and the rise of the Social Democratic Party which, up to the mid-1890s, adopted an explicitly revolutionary attitude never reconciled to the empire. As long as German Social Democracy was led by Ferdinand Lasalle there were few problems, but with his death in 1864 and the transfer of leadership into the hands of Wilhelm Liebknecht and August Bebel, the Marxist internationalist ideology gained dominance. (In the years before his death in 1913, Bebel even gave German naval secrets to the British.) This revolutionary attitude was bound to confront the army with serious problems.

With the induction of new recruits into the army, the monarchic legitimist conception and Socialist internationalism met head-on. The traditional officer corps had been in no way prepared to deal with such an ideological confrontation, and it set upon a collision course with the new ideology that created a

Above left: Bismarck, chief minister of Prussia from 1862, Imperial Chancellor of the new German Empire from 1871 to 1890. Below: Prussian-built artillery: a Krupp steel breechloader of the 1870s, designed to fire 1000lb shells. Above far right: The field gun, the most widely used type of artillery in Prussia's wars. Above right: Prussian lancers.

seriously considered abdication. It was at this stage that Otto von Bismarck came upon the scene with his appointment as Prussian Prime Minister. Bismarck mastered the crisis, governing without the Diet and in opposition to it, and finding a dubious formula by which to appropriate monies until such time as the Crown and Parliament were 'in harmony' again. He had no great respect for generals, especially those who got themselves involved in politics, but for a time there were common interests between them. Bismarck, too, realized the need for the reforms. If Wilhelm I had resigned, the consequence would have been the extension of parliamentary control over the army, a development which Bismarck prevented. He restabilized the royal power of command over the army. In January 1863 he declared to the deputies in the Diet that the Prussian monarchy was not to be a cog within the mechanism of a parliamentary regime.

Nothing succeeds like success, and the wars of 1864 with Denmark and 1866 with Austria confirmed the efficiency of the Prussian Army. After Königgrätz, the decisive battle in 1866, most of the parliamentary opponents of Bismarck and the military party were won over and approved post factum the monetary appropriations which Bismarck had made without parliamentary consent between 1862 and 1866. He had avoided the extremes advocated by some of the generals, including the Chief of the Military Cabinet (head of an institution directly subordinate to the King and his advisor in military affairs) who had advocated a military coup d'état. Indeed, the King had already signed orders to this effect. But Prime Minister Bismarck usually respected the power of command vested in the King, except when it concerned decisions that entered the realm of foreign policy. Thus while the King and his generals would have been quite willing to march on to Vienna in 1866, it was

host of insoluble problems. In the center of the conflict between the armed forces and the new forces of democracy stood the question of the supreme command of the army and the extent of the royal powers. At the apex stood the King, followed by the Chief of the Military Cabinet and his Minister for War who alone was answerable to Parliament. Only matters within his competency were subject to parliamentary discussion. The result was a gradual reduction and erosion of the competencies of the Minister for War and an increase in the powers of the Military Cabinet and the General Staff, all of them beyond the reach of Parliament. This process had reached its full development by 1893. The Minister of War had become an administrator, not a policy maker. He had no powers of command. With that, the last segment of the reforms of 1807–1813 had been removed. The Chief of the Military Cabinet was independent of the Ministry of War and had direct access to the King and Emperor. Much the same applied to the General Staff – only Moltke was uninterested in direct access and kept on with the job at hand.

All this did not remove the conflict within the army caused by the intrusion of liberalism and social democracy. The army's main objective was to maintain a homogeneous and ideologically uniform officer corps, but as the wars of 1862, 1866 and 1870–71 had showed, the nobility was no longer numerically strong enough to command modern mass armies. Therefore access had to be provided for suitable candidates from the middle classes. This was achieved primarily via the institution of the *officer of the reserve.* Young men who had attended university or possessed university entrance qualifications could apply as candidates. They would have to apply to a particular regiment

in which the officers would subject each candidate to close scrutiny. Candidates of lowly social origin, like those whose fathers were shopkeepers, were thus excluded; so were those who held liberal or socialist opinions. In this way it was ensured that only solid conservative stock would enter the army as reserve officers. Although there was now a bridge between aristocracy and middle class, it carried only one-way traffic, and the new middle-class officers absorbed the pre-industrial feudal value system of the old officer corps.

In Prussia itself the absorption of the German middle class posed no major problems, because the divisions between aristocracy and middle class in Prussia were far less rigid than is commonly assumed. The greatest influx of new blood into the aristocratic elite had come from the middle class, whose representatives, within a few generations, were themselves part of the elite. The magnetism of the Prussian state and its nobility had been and was strong enough to attract the most talented members of the widespread middle class in Germany. Generally speaking, the pattern of the rise of Prussia's middle class was slow and steady enough to produce in it attitudes not significantly different from those that shaped the aristocratic tradition, culture and way of life. A typical pattern of social advancement began at the level of the property-holding peasant or artisan and progressed via a profession like that of teacher or clergyman to administrator or military subaltern and finally to high administrative or military office. Well-known families who followed this pattern included those of Humboldt, Scharnhorst, Gneisenau, Clausewitz, Schrötter, Schön, Yorck, Boyen, Grolmann and Steuben. Moreover, the marriage conventions were far from exclusive; the mothers of Bismarck and Bülow were of

Top: The Oldenburg Dragoons engaged with French lancers,
recognizable by their distinctive helmets, at the Battle of Mars-la-Tour in
August 1870. Above: Prussian artillery hurries down a street during the
Battle of Wörth, which the Prussians and their allies won by weight of
numbers, despite a muddled leadership. Above center: German infantry
attacks at the Battle of Gravelotte; the French, in good positions and with
their *chassepot* rifles, inflicted enormous casualties, but finally withdrew.
Above right: German artillery in action against French guns at Gravelotte.
The nearest gun seems to have been hit.

middle-class origin, as were those of Moltke and Elder and
Hindenburg. By comparison with the aristocracy of other
German territories, the figure of slightly less than 30 percent of
Prussian Junker marriage being to members of the middle class
represents an extremely high proportion.

As has been pointed out, one of the major factors making for
an integrated state was that the middle-class marriage did not
necessarily mean a permanent deviation from the Junker stock.
The spouse might adopt the Junker code and viewpoint and the
children frequently returned to the Junker fold when their turn
came to marry. The marriage traffic did not go all one way; the
scions of wealthy rising middle-class families not infrequently
married daughters of the nobility. Of the Prussian generals who
had middle-class origins on the eve of World War I, 43 percent
had married into the nobility.

The proportion of top jobs in the Prussian bureaucracy during
the 19th century held by members of the middle class amounted

to 22 percent; 34 percent of all Ministers of the Interior were members of the middle class. Between 1871 and 1918 32 percent of the Prussian diplomatic service was middle class, as was 26 percent of the Imperial German diplomatic service. In the Prussian lower house, 78 percent of the members were of middle-class origin. As a comparative analysis of the political and military leadership in Austria and Prussia between 1804 and 1918 has demonstrated, Prussia provided the middle class with greater opportunities for personal advancement while its aristocracy made a greater contribution than its Austrian counterpart in all spheres of life even outside the army and politics, especially in the arts and the sciences. Consequently, when considering the growing links between a middle class and aristocracy united in an effort to maintain the existing social and political structure, it must be borne in mind that in spite of differences past and present, the necessary conditions for this process already existed in Germany, especially in Prussia.

The increasing economic vulnerability of the landed nobility as a result of the agrarian depression between the mid-1870s and early 1890s aided the rapprochement between the two classes. Nonetheless, it was the institution of the reserve officer that was

favor of a German Army based on conscription, the Socialists in the Reichstag violently attacked this principle, advocating a militia system on the Swiss pattern in its place. As far as the officer corps was concerned, political debates were taboo. This applied also to middle-class officers. The military academies, which had previously been renowned for the broad intellectual instruction they provided for officers-to-be, had their range of courses narrowed down to strictly military subjects. What was needed was the perfect technician and not the broadly educated man. Homogeneity of the officer corps had to be achieved at all costs and it was not to be an institution marked by individualism. A broadly based humanistic syllabus could lead the army into entirely different directions and introduce a markedly different spirit.

The Military Cabinet even tried to oppose the requirement that applicants for commissions have university entrance qualifications, in which it was not fully successful. However, in Prussian cadet institutes, if a cadet did fail his matriculation examination, there always existed 'the King's grace' which would allow the candidate to be commissioned nevertheless. Increasingly, the General Inspector for Military Education

the major contributor to the process whereby that part of the German middle class that owed its rise largely to the economic and industrial transformation of the country was assimilated into a pre-industrial social order and corresponding value system.

The Reichstag, as already mentioned, possessed the power of the purse, but as far as budget appropriations were concerned, these were not made on an annual basis at first, rather for three-year periods, since it was argued that one could not confine planning for the army to a period of twelve months. In 1887 Bismarck succeeded in getting a Reichstag majority to extend this term to seven years, the so-called *Septeniat*. But from 1871 onward it was no longer possible to keep the new social and political influences out of the army. In Bismarck's view, the enemies of the Reich, the *Reichsfeinde*, were not simply knocking on the door, they were already well inside it.

Although Friedrich Engels frequently expressed himself in

raised complaints about the declining standards among officers. The War Academy became an institution specializing in military aspects of education and nothing else, and it was removed from the General Inspectorate for Military Education and subjected directly to the General Staff.

Yet all of these developments did not produce a grand strategy for an army that excluded economic, political, social and psychological thinking. In fact, the officer corps knew more than ever about railways, modern communications and improved weapons systems. The army did its best to isolate itself from new social developments though. It held at bay new currents of thought and new political factors and deliberately narrowed its horizon to figures, comparative troop strengths and mobilization plans.

However, Moltke took account of foreign policy. Having to fight a war on two fronts had been a nightmare of the General Staff since the 1860s. The question of where to achieve a quick

resolution, in the East or the West, had different answers. Any future war was, for Moltke, the affair of a highly mobile army and not of a nation fully mobilized economically. After 1871 he expressed the opinion that in any future war Germany could not expect to defeat its enemy in a quick and decisive offensive without the intervention of other European powers. Therefore the idea of a preventive war gained greater dominance in his thinking and that of his successors. Only a preventive war would provide Germany with the power of decision. And the instrument for that, the army, would have to be in expertly trained hands to effect it. War was a matter for the military and not for the politicians, a clear contradiction of Clausewitz's views. War and politics were different *métiers*. If they were to be mixed, this would be at the expense of the army. This view was, of course, reflected in the structure of the entire German Army after 1871. It led to an 'autonomy of the technocrats' with disastrous consequences during World War I.

The most important problem after 1871 was the replacement of the officer corps and the maintenance of its homogeneity. Such reforms as had been introduced in 1808 were discarded. The institution of the officers of the reserve and the criteria for selecting them have already been mentioned, but even as late as 1879 Kaiser Wilhelm I stated that as far as he was concerned, he did not place any great weight on a much-enlarged officer corps. The quality and social cohesion which the young men would have because of their family connections would represent the foundation upon which the integrity of the officer corps rested, rather than recruitment from disparate social and political elements. Many officer applicants were turned down as unsuitable on the grounds that they did not have the spirit that had to be preserved in the army at all costs. Only toward the end of Bismarck's chancellorship, when it had become obvious that it was impossible to recruit enough officers from the families of officers and civil servants, did Kaiser Wilhelm II issue a

SEDAN.

FOR THE PIANO FORTE.
BY
W. F. TAYLOR.

Left: Street fighting in Bazeilles, an early phase of the Battle of Sedan. The Bavarians are in their blue uniforms. Right: An imaginative view of the Battle of Sedan, illustrating a sheet of music written in England to celebrate that battle. Below: Prussian troops take a break in a captured French town. Below right: The last shots at Sedan; the French infantry make a last stand. MacMahon's army, with Emperor Napoleon in attendance, was trapped near the French fortress of Sedan while moving to relieve besieged Metz. Explosive shells were probably the decisive factor in the French defeat; it was not the one-sided battle that some observers described. 20,000 French troops were killed, while the remaining three quarters of the army were taken prisoner, as was Napoleon. The battle marked the end of the Emperor's regime, for France was immediately proclaimed a republic by Frenchmen who were weary of their Emperor but wished to keep up the fight against the Germans.

directive according to which nobility of birth was no longer sufficient and nobility of mental attitude was equally important, thus opening the doors wide to commissions in the regular army for the middle class. The period of conscription would have to be maintained, because only over this period could the transformation of a socialist laborer into a soldier loyal to King, Emperor and Reich be ensured.

None of this could stop the rise of Social Democracy. Between the Reichstag elections of 1871 and 1890 the Social Democratic Party increased its vote from 3.2 to 19.7 percent. There was nothing the army could do about it. Gradually its recruits, who had previously come largely from the conservative peasantry, came more and more from the urban proletariat. Nor did Bismarck's anti-socialist laws, introduced in 1878, do much good either. In spite of the obstructions in their way, the Social Democrats continued to gain votes. In the army this was countered by careful political supervision down to the company

and platoon level. Mail was censored by the army authorities, the barracks were frequently searched for subversive material and blacklists of Socialist party members in the army were drawn up. Kaiser Wilhelm I recommended dispassionate treatment of all new recruits but harsh sanctions against political activists who were to be transferred to fortress battalions or to the sappers, where they would have to engage in heavy manual labor. Formations with sizable contingents of Social Democrats in their ranks should not be stationed in the vicinity of urban areas, but in isolated countryside locations. All this was without effect and the army faced the phenomenon with utter incomprehension. It seemed totally unaware of the social and economic changes which were taking place around it.

At least two factors operated in favor of the integration of Social Democracy, or some aspects of it, including the trade unions, into the Empire. One was Bismarck's social legislation, continued after his dismissal; the other was the rise of the

Left: The 1st Bavarian Corps rushes
a French-held house in Bazeilles.
Below left: The French surrender at
Sedan; Moltke and German officers
await reports from approaching
horsemen. The hillside above Sedan
provided a grandstand view of the
battle. Not only the King of Prussia
and Moltke were there, but also
Bismarck, Prussian foreign office
officials, British, American and
Russian military observers, several
princes of German states (many of
whom did not relish Prussia's
triumph), and the correspondent of
The Times, watching as the German
artillery slaughtered the French.
Right: The King of Prussia, soon
to be Emperor Wilhelm I, seen in
the distance as he visits the
battlefield at Sedan. Monarchs still
sometimes expected to be with their
fighting men.

revisionist movement starting in the mid-1890s. Bismarck's social reform legislation was without precedent in the world. It was not, as is commonly asserted, part of a stick-and-carrot policy toward Social Democracy. There is ample evidence that the alleviation of the concrete hardships suffered by the working class had concerned Bismarck for many decades, even before he became Prime Minister of Prussia, and that this concern had its roots in a specific brand of state socialism practiced in Prussia since the days of the 'soldier king,' Friedrich Wilhelm I. But it was, like all Prussian reform policy, reform from above and not from below. The best example of the extent to which Social Democracy had been integrated into the Empire by 1914 is seen in its patriotic response to the outbreak of war in that year and in the endurance and spirit of the army during more than four years of hard fighting.

Another way in which it was thought possible to counteract socialist influence was the mobilization of the masses through patriotism. From funeral associations emerged veterans' organizations which included reservists. One such group was the *Deutsche Kriegerbund* to which 241 local associations with a membership of 27,511 belonged in 1873. By 1890 this had increased to 4,728 local associations with a total membership of 404,276. In 1900 membership had reached the million mark, and this was but one of several such associations. The army viewed them as a strong defensive force against endeavors hostile to the state. It kept them under close scrutiny and ensured that retired officers and officers of the reserve played an active part in them. Commanding generals were appointed honorary chairmen. This development unfolded fully only after Bismarck had left the helm of state. But despite its benefits for the army, it sharpened divisions within the nation even further. Social and economic changes continued apace and were otherwise largely ignored by the army.

After Bismarck had retired to his estate in Friedrichsruh, there was little else for him to do but to write the occasional critical article on government policy under Wilhelm II. The young Kaiser himself proclaimed that he would adhere to the military traditions founded by Wilhelm I, which he considered his proudest legacy. To what extent the rule of Kaiser Wilhelm II

in his first decade was a personal rule is a matter of controversy. Certainly, Chancellor Caprivi's policies, especially in the economic sector, were precisely the opposite of what the Prussian conservatives expected, but as long as he enjoyed the Kaiser's support there was little they or anyone else could do about him. The Chancellor's position did not depend on the Reichstag's support but on that of the Kaiser.

One of the first measures of Wilhelm II was to combine the officers in his personal service and in his entourage into the 'Imperial Headquarters,' headed by a senior general. Wilhelm II hated new faces and he held on to the old ones as long as he could. Thus General von Plessen was the commander of the Imperial Headquarters from 1892 to 1918. He also ensured that the reports of military attachés at embassies abroad would come first to him, rather than to the Foreign Office. Caprivi still managed to contain the influence of the attachés within acceptable limits, but under his successor every form of constraint went by the board. One early issue over which Kaiser and Chancellor differed concerned the period of military service. Caprivi meant to reduce it to two years; the Kaiser, advised by his military entourage, insisted on maintaining the three-year period. In the end, the two-year period of service was introduced.

Caprivi also tried to reform certain aspects of the penal code and this included a reform of the Military Code of Punishment. While the penal reform in the civilian sector was easily implemented for the most part, that of the military sector was the subject of a tug-of-war for years, since any reform affected the role of the Kaiser as Supreme Commander. Military jurisdiction, whether applying to officers or enlisted men, had so far been carried out *in camera*. The new draft envisioned limited access for the public, a measure which also found the support of Caprivi's successor, Chancellor Prince Hohenlohe, not a Prussian but a Bavarian general and politician who had reformed Bavarian military law in a like manner. Wilhelm II, however, insisted that military jurisdiction in Prussia be carried out privately. The Kaiser was also opposed in this by the Prussian War Ministry.

The civilians endeavored to raise the whole issue to cabinet

Below: The 1st Bavarian Corps storms a railway embankment on the outskirts of Orleans, a few French infantrymen being flushed out from behind the bridge parapet. The Bavarians were Prussia's most substantial allies in the Franco–Prussian War, although other German states also made a contribution; the proclamation of a German Empire under Prussian leadership which came at the end of this war, meant that states like Bavaria would be closely tied to Berlin. Orleans is many miles from the main front of the war; in the closing stages German units ranged far to the west of Paris, so weak was the French army after the Battle of Sedan.

level in order to restrain or contain the Kaiser's functions. Hohenlohe actually succeeded in persuading the Kaiser to constitute a supreme military court and to give up his power of ultimate sanction or dismissal of any judgment it made. Still the final draft of the law submitted to the Reichstag in 1897 contained provisions which seriously limited the public character of the proceedings, and in this form it was accepted by the Reichstag. However, the subsequent executive orders relating to this law emptied the Kaiser's concessions of their substance. The Kaiser, the Imperial Headquarters and the Military Cabinet had triumphed. They all held the view that the reform infringed the exclusivity of the officer corps.

Another development of this period was the *de jure* emancipation of the Military Cabinet from the Ministry for War, which had already been achieved in practice under Wilhelm I. The General Staff was also now completely free from interference from the one institution still answerable to the Reichstag. Officers of the General Staff enjoyed preferential treatment in the matter of promotion. This further increased and extended the Kaiser's power of command. Subsequent Ministers for War were content with the competencies they held. Inevitably, the increased powers of command of the Kaiser as the Supreme War Lord were at the expense of the central military administration, which was all the more serious in that the Kaiser did not have the military and political expertise required by his institutionalized military position. This lack was soon to be demonstrated in the

Left: Prussian troops skirmishing in the woods before Metz in September 1870. It was only in October that this beseiged French fortress city was surrendered. Below: Prussian troops bring out French wounded from the ruins of a town on the Paris outskirts, the scene of French sorties from the beleaguered capital in December 1870. Above right: Prussian uhlans (lancers) capture French guns at Loigny, a typical role for cavalry. Right: Lances against bayonets; Prussian uhlans charge French zouaves on the outskirts of Metz. Metz, on France's eastern frontier, was a key fortress.

early months of World War I, which led to the Kaiser's gradual withdrawal from positions he had formerly claimed to assume the role of a mere spectator.

The gains of the Social Democrats in the elections of 1890 produced the renewed specter of the 'red danger.' While the Kaiser refused to have the anti-Socialist laws renewed on the one hand, on the other he backed increased supervision of political life within the army and preparations to be made for dealing with the Socialists in case of a national emergency. It became obligatory for military commanders to keep an eye on the Socialist organizations and leaders and agitators in their garrison area and to keep the Ministry of War fully informed about them. A Prussian law concerning the stage of siege, dating back to 1851, contained a provision by which any military commander of a district or province could, if he saw fit, proclaim a state of siege. In non-Prussian territories the Kaiser's sanction was required for this. Once a state of siege had been proclaimed, the executive power of the civil authorities was transferred to the military commander and his troops were under orders to fire if necessary. Fortunately, the occasion never arose. Troops were used to carrying out police functions during various industrial disputes, but it never came to a collision between the army and the civilians.

Within this context the War Historical Department of the General Staff produced a study in 1907 on the use of troops in cities dominated by insurgents. In cases of unrest the early proclamation of siege was recommended and a precondition for the army's success against any insurgents was that the military commander and his immediate subordinates were intimately acquainted with political developments in their area. The new guidelines also envisioned the arrest of members of the Reichstag in spite of the fact that they enjoyed parliamentary immunity. Once this became publicly known, pressure in the Reichstag became so great that this provision had to be withdrawn. But in all cases it was the duty of the police to deal first with unrest while the army should provide a backup. Only in case of extreme confrontations should the army intervene directly.

This was how the army prepared for civil war, and the measures devised were in fact applied, not in the lifetime of the Empire, but during the early phase of the Weimar Republic under a government headed by Socialists. Here again, it was not the regular army that executed government policy, but the right-wing *Freikorps* recruited by the Republic. Some generals during Wilhelm II's reign were advocates of a radical course against workers and Social Democrats. They issued a great many memoranda that went so far as to advocate a military coup, but these notes remained in the file and were never resorted to. The army as such was very careful not to allow itself to be provoked. On the whole, the military leadership recognized that a coup provided no workable alternative to the parliamentary system.

As already mentioned, the main problem besetting the German Army of this time was the shortage of officers, which reached serious proportions especially for the infantry and the artillery. The middle class had to be more strongly involved, not only in the reserves but also in the regulars. In 1865 the Prussian officer corps still had 65 percent of its members coming from the nobility, but by 1913 this proportion had declined to 30 percent. One consequence was that the nobility concentrated itself in a few regiments, notably the Guards formations, while the other regiments had a predominantly bourgeois officer corps. There is an interesting contrast between the officer corps of the army and that of the Imperial Navy, which was on the road to expansion under Admiral von Tirpitz from 1897 onward. The naval officer corps had a reputation for more open-mindedness toward the new social, economic and technical developments than the army. Indeed, Tirpitz worked to expand his navy on the basis of a broad popular consensus. He lobbied the Reichstag and mobilized mass opinion to get the necessary support. There was a touch of liberalism in the navy sadly lacking in the army. It is by no means an overstatement to say that the navy was Kaiser Wilhelm II's preferred branch of the service, yet it is a paradox that it was so much more liberal than the army. Only a very few sons of the old Prussian nobility served at sea. In 1910 48 percent of the naval officer corps came from the families of academics. And its intake of volunteers came mainly from areas of Germany outside Prussia, notably from Bavaria. By 1914 over 90 percent of the naval officer corps was qualified for university or had taken a degree.

With the appointment of increasing numbers of officers

Above left: A captured French courier is searched and interrogated by the Prussians. Above: In the Bois de Boulogne; Prussian troops take a stroll among an apparently unconcerned local population. This is 1871, when many Parisians already regard the occupying troops as safeguarding law and order; the middle classes in particular had been alarmed by the left-wing Paris Commune which had sought to fill the power vacuum left by the war. Above right: The local population studies an unconcerned member of the German occupying army. Right: A German military band plays to a sparse audience in St. Quentin's main square in 1871. Relations between the French and the occupying army were not always quite as friendly as these pictures suggest, although not as baleful as in later wars.

originating in the middle class, the educational standards of the army officer corps again increased. The concept of the elite was no longer based on noble descent but on educational standards. However, the middle-class officers continued to adopt the value system of the Prussian officer corps.

Within the corps of the non-commissioned officers there were similar developments. In the 1890s there was a serious shortage of NCOs, so financial incentives were created to encourage them to enlist for a minimum service of 12 years. Furthermore, a policy introduced by King Friedrich Wilhelm I was revived, namely that the economic status of an NCO should be secured after his retirement by taking him into the civil service. Some of the ministries raised serious complaints, arguing that the

former NCOs were not up to civil service standards and that there were not enough openings there for them. These complaints were of no avail, and in the postal administration alone the number of former NCOs increased from 8,715 in 1900 to 19,324 in 1914. It should come as no surprise, therefore, that the atmosphere in the lower echelons of the civil service was rather military even until the 1960s. Of course, the NCOs at all levels of civilian administration – Reich, Land, provincial or municipal – tended to counteract the influence of the forces of Social Democracy.

In the recruitment of the army a different pattern developed. In the case of voluntary enlistment, it was reported in 1905 that in Bavaria, for example, the greatest number of volunteers with

a Social Democratic background came from rural areas, while the smallest number came from urban areas. This reflected the decline of agriculture on the one hand and the growing prosperity that could be found in urban industries on the other. From then on, volunteers of Social Democratic background were reported to the military authorities only if they had been active 'in word and letter' on behalf of the Social Democratic Party. The state, the Empire, its constituent parts and the army in particular were no longer in a position to control or to contain the existing political and economic upheavals, but to every traditional officer's surprise, the Social Democrats proved themselves to be highly efficient soldiers.

While the Emperor and the military establishment had originally insisted on the three-year conscription period as a way of transforming the recruits into loyal subjects of Crown and country, the period was reduced to two years in 1893. We have already seen that as a result the military leadership adopted the policy of cutting the recruits off as much as possible from Social Democratic influences – be they brochures, leaflets, or any other kind of alien influence. In addition, intensive new indoctrination courses were introduced in the training of the rank and file.

Socialist publications were banned from the garrisons, but excluding all such influences from urban areas was difficult if not impossible. A further step was taken by prohibiting soldiers from visiting taverns. Then the Ministry of War found itself swamped by a wave of protests from the tavern owners which forced a compromise solution. Only on certain days of the week were the soldiers prohibited from visiting a bar. The compromise, considering the objective behind it, made no sense at all, except that the taverns' incomes no longer suffered seriously.

In the elections of 1912 the Social Democratic Party became the strongest single party in the Reichstag and in 1913 it introduced a resolution to abolish all the existing military proscriptions, which was backed by the majority of the Reichstag. Although the resolution was passed, there was nothing in the constitution which compelled the government to act in accordance with it.

Ideological indoctrination was carried out by lecture courses pointing out to the soldiers the virtues of the monarchy, its traditions and achievements. Military ceremonial played as strong a role as did regimental history. What operated here to the army's disadvantage was the essentially non-political character and education of its officer corps. The majority of officers were simply not equipped for a task which in essence amounted to political indoctrination. Some attempts to remedy this were made before World War I, but they were unavailing. Some exceptional officers who went so far as to discuss with their men the substance of the Social Democratic program incurred the disfavor of their superiors. From January 1907 onward, the discussion of social and political questions was forbidden. This was the end of the program of ideological indoctrination.

This was also accompanied by a slow, at first almost imperceptible, change in the attitude of social democracy toward the

Left: Pre-Dreadnought battleships of the German High Seas Fleet in about 1910, when all warships still burned coal. Below left: German cavalry in Warsaw, admired by young locals, in 1915. Having ejected the disliked Russians, the Germans were not yet subjected to Polish hostility. Below: A German heavy gun in action on the Western Front in spring 1918. The crew protects its eardrums in the time-honored manner; it will be decades before ear-protectors are provided as a standard item. Below right: Chief of the German General Staff, Hindenburg (left) with his Quartermaster General, Ludendorff, both looking optimistic at the time of the 1918 spring offensive. By this time they controlled German policy, both civil and military; Kaiser Wilhelm was merely a figurehead.

military action against subversive elements were seriously considered.

Two events of 1913 are worthy of notice. One was the Army Bill of that year. The General Staff had an obsession that Germany was short of the kind of manpower required to fight a war on two fronts and to carry out successfully a vast maneuver such as the Schlieffen Plan, especially in the modified form devised by Moltke the Younger, Chief of the General Staff from 1905 to 1914. The army needed to be enlarged considerably. This, in turn, would require a greater number of officers who were not immediately available. The Military Cabinet feared that the vast increase would further dilute the homogeneity and therefore the quality of the German officer corps. The fear was expressed that politically unreliable elements, if not socialists, then at least liberals, would have to be admitted. The military establishment was not prepared to risk this and preferred to settle for a smaller increase in the army than was actually required, despite the problems this would cause in the conduct of military operations.

The second noteworthy event took place in a small town in the formerly French territory of Alsace. Since 1871 Alsace had been a *Reichsland*, not a state or a province in its own right as were the other constituent parts of the Empire. It was directly administered by the Empire. But in 1911 it had been given a constitution which was in many respects an advance over the constitutions of the other German Lands, especially Prussia. Its Diet was based on a universal franchise without any property

armed forces and national defense in general. Gustav Noske, the Social Democrats' spokesmen for military affairs, became a well-received visitor in military establishments, especially those of the navy. This change was no doubt conditioned by the darkening political horizons around Germany, and was equally a result of the ascendancy of revisionist currents within the Social Democratic Party – the recognition that change could not be achieved by revolution but by evolution from within the existing system.

The change could already be seen in 1908 with the publication in London of the Kaiser's ill-fated 'Daily Telegraph interview,' which caused a storm of protest in the Reichstag and after which the Kaiser moved more and more into the background politically and kept a strict rein on his all-too-quotable and disastrous extemporaneous remarks and pronouncements. Although the army refused to admit it, it had failed in its policy of screening off the troops from the politics of the day. It continued to lend strong support to the veterans' and reservists' organizations and partly resumed the course by which plans of

qualifications. Unlike the Prussian electoral system, Alsace did not have the three-class franchise.

Battalions of the 99th Infantry Regiment were stationed in the small town of Zabern. A young lieutenant, Günther Freiherr von Förstner, who was not even of age, instructed his recruits on 28 October 1913 that if they were ever attacked when on town leave, they should make use of their weapons. If in the course of such an action a 'Wacke' should come to grief it would not matter; indeed, he would pay the soldier concerned ten gold marks. 'Wacke' was a derogatory term for the people of Alsace. The lieutenant's statement was published in the liberal *Zaberner Anzeiger* and in the *Elsässer*, a paper of the Center Party. In fact, the use of the expression 'Wacke' had been expressly forbidden by a regimental order of 1903, but apparently Förstner used it frequently.

The story caused an uproar in Alsace. The German press was united in the demand that Förstner should be transferred to another garrison. The regimental commander, General von Reuter, could not ignore the incident, but he tried to play it down. Higher authority at XV Army Corps at Strasbourg took a similar attitude. Förstner became the joke of Zabern whenever he appeared in public, so he began to go out accompanied by a guard. More rumors emerged about what he was supposed to have said to recruits. These were denied by his superiors and three Alsatian recruits who had allegedly spread these rumors were arrested. Förstner himself was sentenced to a six-day arrest of which the public was not informed. The *Statthalter* of Alsace, Count von Wedel, also recommended to the commanding general at Strasbourg that Förstner be transferred. This too was kept from the public and the uproar in Zabern increased.

The matter was raised in the Reichstag and the Minister for War, General von Falkenhayn, gave a brief and inconclusive explanation while Chancellor Bethmann Hollweg announced that he would make a statement on the incident on 3 December 1913. Meanwhile, matters deteriorated in Zabern. The military demanded the proclamation of a state of siege but were overruled by the civil authorities. There was a public demonstration against which three platoons of infantry issued with live ammunition were sent. Thirty persons were allegedly arrested indiscriminately and released after a night in the cells of the garrison. Even before Bethmann Hollweg could make his statement, Förstner had created a new incident by using his saber to knock down a cobbler who was resisting arrest. In his statement to the Reichstag, Bethmann Hollweg described Förstner's behavior as unbecoming but, identifying himself with the cause of the army, emphasized that 'the king's uniform must be respected under all circumstances.' The Minister for War blamed the agitation on the press and ultimately took refuge behind the Imperial power of supreme command. Now the Reichstag was in an uproar. On 4 December 1913 the Reichstag passed a vote of no confidence in the government, carried by a vote of 293 against 54 with four abstentions.

A vote of no confidence mattered little, since the government was not dependent on the Reichstag but upon the Emperor. Nevertheless, both Förstner and his commander, Reuter, had to face a court martial which duly acquitted them, to the disgust of most of the German press. In January 1914 the Alsatian Diet unanimously condemned the incidents caused by the military. All the officers involved had to resign except the *Statthalter*, Count von Wedel. Conservative generals like von Wrochem warned of the 'terrible danger, for if the mob of all classes was seen to be victorious, the status and strength of the royal army would be damaged.'

The three Alsatian recruits who had informed the papers of the incident in the first place were sentenced to three to six weeks' arrest. Because of the incident in which he had used his saber, Förstner was sentenced to 43 days of imprisonment by the Strasbourg military tribunal. He appealed for a new trial, which subsequently acquitted him. The primacy of the military had prevailed, even in an affair which was purely local in its origins and could have been settled on the spot without much fuss if the advice of the civil authorities had been followed.

The slogan was raised that the army was in danger, and that in a country encircled by a host of enemies every sign of weakness, even in such a minor affair as this, was bound to debilitate the entire army. What those who took this line overlooked was that the assertion of the primacy of the military had showed up the fundamental weakness of the German political structure.

At a much more important level, the same was to be demonstrated during the July Crisis in 1914 which led to World War I and during the course of the war itself. Admittedly, given Germany's geographic position, the Schlieffen Plan was probably the only formula for victory, provided one had sufficient forces to carry it out. Once Russia had mobilized,

Top: German infantrymen advance on the Western Front; as was customary, their large packs have been left behind, to be brought up after the fighting. Above: On the Somme in spring 1918; advancing German troops take a rest. By this stage of the war motor transport was more in evidence, but footslogging infantry and horse transport still predominated. Right: Men of the *Freikorps* are proudly photographed at Riga, Latvia, where they were fighting the Russian Bolsheviks in 1919. The *Freikorps*, recruited largely from former soldiers embittered by Germany's defeat, was originally intended to maintain order in German cities and to oppose Polish incursions; but it soon rejected civilian authority, which it despised, and degenerated into a savage militarism exemplified by the murder of prominent pacifists.

there was no alternative but to set the plan based on railroad timetables into motion. The real failing of the German military establishment lies in the conduct of World War I, in which the politicians played only a secondary role and the Kaiser none at all. Once the Schlieffen Plan miscarried and a war of attrition began, the politicians exercised no influence whatsoever. After the Miracle of the Marne, the Allied victory that saved Paris, Moltke resigned and was replaced by Falkenhayn, who could think of very little except to try to bleed the French to the point of exhaustion. He tried to put this strategy into effect in the Battle of Verdun, but after early successes the Germans bled just as heavily.

Falkenhayn, in turn, was replaced by the Hindenburg/Ludendorff combination and they became Germany's secret dictators, to whom Bethmann-Hollweg had to give way. All subsequent chancellors until Prince Max of Baden were no more than the marionettes of the *Oberste Heeresleitung* (OHL) – the German Supreme Command. The army introduced total mobilization and succeeded in implementing it to a considerable extent, but they had no political alternatives to offer. Even if they had, it is doubtful whether the allies would ever have considered them, especially after the US joined the war. The Allied aim was the destruction of the German Empire. Even Ludendorff recognized that Germany was at the end of its resources in August 1918, but he kept up the propaganda that victory was just around the corner. The public, destitute and starving as a result of the effectiveness of the British blockade – the victims of total warfare – held on until the news of Germany's request for an armistice. For Germans, the skies caved

in; the full parliamentarization ordered by Hindenburg and Ludendorff and carried out by Chancellor Prince Max of Baden was again a reform from above. It had come too late. Revolution broke out, the thrones toppled and what was left was the progeny of defeat – the Weimar Republic. Even that republic took well over a year to quell internal uprisings, not by means of the regular army but rather by the use of irregular troops, the *Freikorps*, without whose aid the republic would not have lasted even that one year.

The army soon found its footing again, but it had yet to find its proper position within the new state. During the days of the Empire it had been a professional elite, as well as a political and social elite, in terms of its officer corps. Such changes as growing industrialization and the impact of new technologies upon warfare had left their mark. Military requirements involved the economy and society as a whole, necessitating that technical precision, mass production and all social resources be put at the disposal of a nation at war. Whether or not the officer corps liked it, the distinctions between army and society had become increasingly blurred.

This development affected all armies, but in Germany it confronted an officer corps which was still oriented along pre-industrial lines. Furthermore, industrial and technical changes endangered the exclusivity of the officer corps all the more, since the entire society had to be involved in the conduct of total war – a society which we have seen did not possess a commonly accepted value system. The professional military expert was no longer the only man essential to the conduct of war.

The results of this development had begun to show in the 19th century within the army itself, in the division between the officers of the General Staff and the troop officers. In the navy there was a distinction between deck officers, who had general duties and could rise to command positions, and the engineer officers. All this pointed toward the disintegration of a once distinct warrior class. World War I had accelerated this problem. The death toll in the traditional officer corps was so great that commissions had to be awarded to people whom the army would never have looked at before, even to Social Democrats. New ranks emerged to make up for the deficiencies in the number of officers, such as the sergeant lieutenant or officer deputy, who led units as large as companies in the field.

After the defeat of 1918 the army continued to represent the continuity of German history, to hold on to essential elements of its historical existence. It did not at first transform itself from a social and political elite into a purely professional elite. This

Above far left: Hindenburg and Hitler in front of the Potsdam garrison church, March 1933. Hindenburg, on the basis of his military reputation, had been elected President in 1925, and he reluctantly accepted Hitler as Chancellor in January 1933, even though general elections had indicated that the Nazis' support was waning. One reason for Hitler's success was that his private army, the storm troopers, was believed capable of resisting the regular army should the latter be summoned to suppress the Nazis. Above left: Von Fritsch, army commander, and Beck, Chief of the General Staff, in 1937. Above: Armored cars parade before Hitler at the Nuremberg Nazi Party rally of 1934. Left: General von Seeckt and Hitler in conversation. Below left: Hitler with his generals; Keitel is on his right, von Leeb on his left, as all three discuss a tactical problem.

became clear only in the course of time. The army was briefly preoccupied with the revolutionary situation and its aftermath. In the course of this period, three types of men emerged in the officer corps. The first were the dyed-in-the-wool monarchists advocating a policy of restoration, but they made their bid in the Kapp-Lüttwitz Putsch in March 1920 and failed abysmally, being excluded thereafter from the new army, the Reichswehr. The second group were national revolutionaries aiming at a German socialism modeled on the socialism of the trenches, but they were too divided among themselves to present a coherent front and disintegrated as the republic found its feet, wandering off to the various paramilitary organizations on the right. The third group, under General von Seeckt, did not love the republic, but considered it the least of a number of evils. Therefore they backed it. As members of the small hundred-thousand-man army which was all the Treaty of Versailles allowed, they could shut themselves off from the rest of society very much as the French Army had done between 1871 and 1898.

In the fluctuations of day-to-day domestic politics they represented the only stable and continuing factor. In spite of all the changes that had taken place around them, they claimed to be a professional elite and cherished the belief, however unreal, that they would become a social and political elite as well. This fond hope was not dissipated until after 30 January 1933 when Hitler came to power. True, there were currents pointing to a

renewal of the old attitudes and traditions of the officer corps. Between 1880 and 1913 the percentage of officers' sons joining the army declined from 30 to 28 percent. Between 1926 and 1930 it rose from 44 to 55 percent. Most of their fathers came from certain regiments, notably from the guards, and with rare exceptions they had been General Staff members. Their aim was the restoration of Germany as a great power with a minimum of risk. Using the Reichswehr offensively was not ruled out as long as the risks seemed manageable.

Under the command of Seeckt and his successors, the army remained a largely nonpolitical instrument at the service of the state. It meddled in politics only insofar as its own interests were involved. The single exception was the last head of the Reichswehr, General von Schleicher, who first tried to split the National Socialists and build a new basis not only for his position but also for the new German state. He next tried, unsuccessfully, to win trade union and Social Democratic support. However, the Nazis were not to be persuaded to part with their Führer and the trade unions refused their cooperation. The only alternative now was a military dictatorship under Schleicher which would have had to govern against the majority vote of the country.

This course of action was curtailed by President Hindenburg's appointment of Adolf Hitler as Reich Chancellor. His coalition was the only solution (a Social Democratic-Communist coalition would not have had a majority and was in any case obviated by the Communist preoccupation with fighting the 'Social Fascists') which could provide the government with a majority in the Reichstag. Thus ended the state of affairs existing since 1930, in which government was carried on by emergency decrees signed by the President – a situation which the aged Hindenburg had hated and a burden of which he was relieved by his appointment of Hitler, however reluctant. The army had nothing to do with putting Hitler into the saddle. It has been said that it did not prevent his appointment by military force, but then this accusation is raised by the very same historians who say that the German Army meddled too much in politics up to 1918. One cannot have it both ways.

In the early period, Hitler based his government on an entente – not an alliance – between the traditional elites and the NSDAP, the Nazi Party. He did not even have the opportunity to appoint his own Army Minister. Hindenburg, in order to

Left: So-called volunteers from the regular German Forces, forming the Condor Air Legion, leave for home after fighting for the victorious Nationalists in the Spanish Civil War. Below left: Hitler receives Condor Air Legion officers to hand them Spanish war decorations. Germany also sent land and sea forces to help Franco. Italy too, sent help, while Soviet forces were sent to aid the Republicans. All three countries gained valuable experience with modern weapons in this war, although the USSR wasted much of this knowledge by executing or incarcerating Soviet officers returned from Spain. Right: German tank crews attend to their vehicles, topping up fuel tanks, as they wait at a river crossing during the May 1940 *blitzkrieg* on France.

keep the army out of Hitler's reach, had appointed General von Blomberg to this post before swearing in the whole cabinet. But Blomberg, unforeseen by Hindenburg, subscribed to Hitler's theory that the new state was to be based on two pillars, the army and the NSDAP. It seemed as though the army was about to regain its position as a social and political elite. Within the army the existing differences were of a purely tactical nature. The army Commander in Chief, General von Fritsch, was essentially a conservative, insisting on the maintenance of traditional values. Only these would cement the army's autonomous position within the new state. Blomberg, and the head of his personal staff Colonel (later General and Field Marshal) von Reichenau, were not so much concerned with the maintenance of old values as they were with direct participation in the decision-making process, which in their opinion provided the only guarantee that the military elite would have a controlling voice.

On the initiative of Blomberg and Reichenau, National Socialist emblems like the swastika were introduced into the army. No such initiative was taken by Hitler or the NSDAP. Nor did Hitler demand the application of new anti-Semitic laws to the army. It was Blomberg and Reichenau who instigated this. One danger for the army arose in the form of the Nazi Party storm troopers, the SA, when the head of the SA, Ernst Röhm, demanded its inclusion in the army with the aim of creating a National Socialist army dominated by the SA. Hitler promised Blomberg that the army would be the only armed organization of the state and he kept this promise. However, Reichenau deliberately escalated the conflict between army and SA. He did not hesitate to manufacture fictitious reports about SA mobilizations which he fed to Hitler. This provocation culminated in the purge of 30 June 1934, the Blood Purge or Night of the Long Knives, in which the army provided transport and weapons to the SS to carry out the dirty business. In the course of this purge a number of old scores were also settled. General von Schleicher and his wife and General von Bredow were killed.

The army leadership refused to raise any protest about this murder of two members of its officer corps. When the President,

Field Marshal von Hindenburg, died in August 1934, and Hitler fused the offices of Reich Chancellor and President into the position of Führer, it was again solely at the initiative of the army leadership that all members of the armed forces swore loyalty to Hitler. The ties that had once existed between the army and the King and Emperor seemed to have been reestablished. However, between 1933 and 1934 the German Army had stepped onto a slippery slope which, in reality, removed it more and more from the exercise of political power. Hitler had promised Blomberg a predominant position for the army within German society, provided it stood quietly by while he carried out his internal revolution. The army did so, but very much at the expense of its own position. Some members of the army realized this, such as the Commander in Chief, General von Fritsch, who stated that Hitler had succeeded in nationalizing the working class, precisely that class to which the army had had no access in the days of the Empire and the republic. The army had conceded so much that it was no longer a political force.

The watershed of this development was reached in 1938 when Blomberg was sacked after he had married a lady of dubious repute. General von Fritsch was also dismissed on a trumped-up charge of homosexuality. The Reichswehr Ministry, which after the renunciation of the military clauses of the Treaty of Versailles had been renamed the War Ministry, disappeared. Hitler, who had also become Supreme Commander of the German Armed Forces when he merged the offices of presidency and chancellorship, now took over direct command. His instrument was the *Oberkommando der Wehrmacht* or OKW, the Supreme Command of the Armed Forces, subordinate to which were the OKH, OKL and OKM, the high commands for the army, air force and navy, respectively. General Keitel became Chief of OKW and also, at least nominally, exercised the functions of Minister for War. The coalition between the army and Hitler after 30 January 1933 did not provide the traditional military elite with a broad political base among the German people. Hitler had integrated the German nation at the expense of the old elites. For the first time in the history of the Prusso-German Army, it became a pure instrument of the state executive. The primacy of politics had been established.

If one subjects the war plans of the belligerent powers of Europe on the eve of World War I to close scrutiny, the conclusion soon reached is that the image of war, the *Kriegsbild* of the various general staffs, was one based on a short war. The dogma of the battle of annihilation prevailed, the belief in the single decisive battle such as Hannibal's at Cannae. What they failed to take into account was that while Hannibal had won the Battle of Cannae, in the end, of course, he had lost the war. The only important disagreement came from Lord Kitchener, who became Great Britain's Minister of War. He believed that the war would be of rather longer duration. He was not endowed with any greater vision or knowledge than his counterparts on the European mainland, but he realized that the mobilization of Great Britain's manpower resources would take considerably longer than those of the continental countries with their conscript armies. The lessons learned by the generals of 1914 had been those of the Danish War of 1862, the Austro-Prussian War of 1866 and the Franco-Prussian War of 1870–71. More recent confirmation of the belief in a short war had apparently been provided by the Balkan Wars of 1912–13. The fact that in the 19th and 20th centuries there had been wars which seemed to contradict this traditional view was ignored. In fact, all official European observers who had been sent to America to study the American Civil War concluded that it had little relevance for war in the future and especially for war in Europe. The Boer War and the Russo-Japanese War were often similarly ignored. Each of these wars will be examined in turn.

Slavery in the southern states is often given as the reason for the war between the North and South, in spite of the fact that President Abraham Lincoln had promised not to interfere with slavery in those states where it already existed. The extension of slavery into the territories of the United States which had not yet entered the Union and were about to do so provides another reason, but this reason was devoid of practical substance because there were territories such as Kansas and Nebraska in which cotton could not be grown and slavery would have been unprofitable. Indeed, there were hardly any slaves in either of these states, but this did not dampen the ardor with which the issue was debated.

Economic differences between North and South were an additional reason. A dynamically industrializing North was confronting the stagnant agricultural system of the South, but there is no reason to assume that, on economic grounds alone, the North would not have welcomed the secession of the South as removing a political and economic burden. The insistence upon states' rights is another reason put forward, and here we have perhaps something of more substance. The question of states' rights had already preoccupied the writers of the US Constitution. Whereas Thomas Jefferson had always been concerned about a reintroduction of a monarchic system, his close friend and collaborator, James Madison, was more concerned about the protection of a minority from a dominant majority. This was precisely the situation into which the southern states were moving from the 1820s onward. Not only did their economy remain stagnant – one has only to look at the railroad system of the United States in 1860, which shows a dense network linking the northeast and the midwest while the railroad network in the South was sparse.

The acquisition of new territories, and in due course new states, affected the equilibrium between North and South which thus far had been held in balance in both Houses of Congress. Inevitably and irrevocably the South moved into the position of the permanent minority, the danger which James Madison had already described eloquently in the *Federalist Papers*. Once the equilibrium was lost, from a southern point of

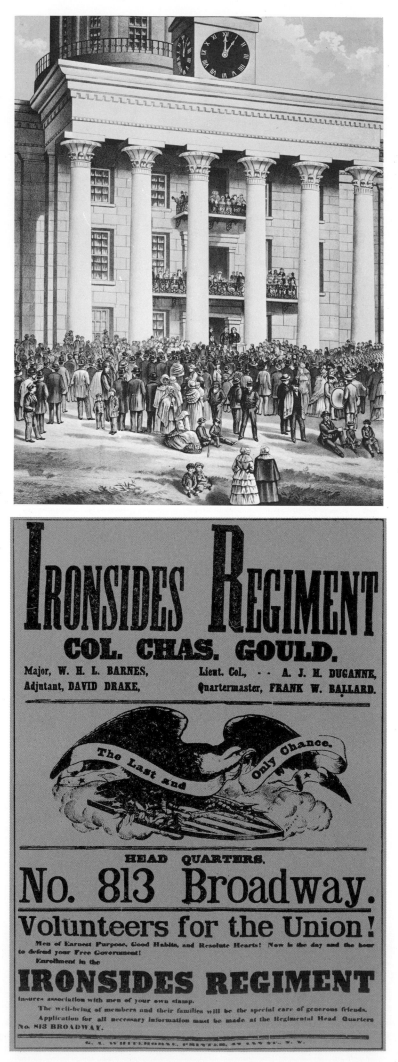

Previous page: A company of the Sumter Light Guards of Georgia on parade in 1861. Left: The inauguration of the Confederates' President, Jefferson Davis (standing, to right of Senate President, who is introducing him); this is from an 1861 photograph. Below left: A Civil War recruiting poster addressed to New Yorkers. Right: The bombardment of Fort Sumter (Charleston) in 1861. Below: Robert E. Lee, the best-known Confederate general. Below right: New military technology; an observation balloon in the Civil War.

view it could be restored only by insisting on states' rights or by an altogether different conception of the Union.

Irrespective of its real importance, slavery was the great public issue. It was the ideal instrument of propaganda because as an institution it most offended man's moral sense. Yet it is hardly likely that the South would have rallied solely to the defense of its 'peculiar institution.' More than 76 percent of all Southerners were not slaveowners. Less than 10 percent of the population owned plantations with more than 50 slaves, 6 percent held up to 50 slaves and 8 percent had only one or two. Consequently, if the defense of slavery was the cause for the South entering into war with the North, over three quarters of the population did so without having any stake in slavery whatsoever.

Between 1820 and 1860 the population of the United States had increased from 9.6 to 31.3 million. Of these 31.3 million, about 22 million lived in the North and only slightly more than

9 million in the South, of whom fewer than two fifths were blacks. Industrially, the North was vastly superior. Manufacturing industries important in the production of war materials favored the North by a ratio of three and one-half to one. For every six factory workers in the North there was only one in the South. The South's economic base was its agriculture, which was about double the value of that of the North. As far as cotton was concerned, the South had an overwhelming share of world trade. The economic and communications structure had made it inevitable that the South was primarily export-oriented while the North protected its nascent industries with high tariffs. The South, for its part, largely supported free trade.

Of decisive significance for the war was the fact that the United States Navy was almost exclusively in the hands of the North, while the merchant fleet, because of the South's agricultural exports, was concentrated there where it was of little use except for blockade running.

Far left: The Siege of Vicksburg took place May–July 1863. Its fall gave Union forces control of the Mississippi Valley. The officer lower right with spyglass is Ulysses S Grant.
Right: The fall of Petersburg, 2 April 1865.
Far right: General Gouverneur Warren, Chief Engineer of the Army of the Potomac looks out from a signal post on Little Round Top hill during the Battle of Gettysburg.
Below: Confederate General Longstreet's attack on Fort Sanders on 29 November 1863 failed in part because of the wire entanglements – a portent of the use of barbed wire on the Western Front.

Left: A street in Richmond after its abandonment by the Confederates in 1865. With nearby Petersburg, Richmond occupied a key situation close to Washington and was long an objective of the Union forces. It was not until the closing stages of the war that it was taken, and its loss led directly to the Confederate surrender. Below: Map of the Civil War campaigns, demonstrating the wide extent of territory in the war zone which made the railroad a key element in this war. Right: Abraham Lincoln. Below right: Ulysses S. Grant, who after victories in the western campaign became commander of the Union armies. He is portrayed bareheaded here, in a picture designed to inspire more than instruct. Grant subsequently became US President.

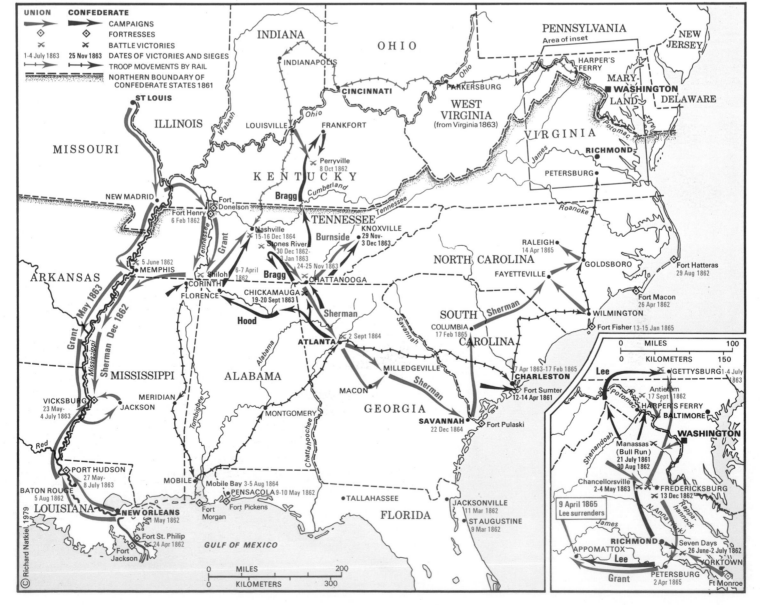

UNION CONFEDERATE
CAMPAIGNS
FORTRESSES
BATTLE VICTORIES
1-4 July 1863   25 Nov 1863   DATES OF VICTORIES AND SIEGES
TROOP MOVEMENTS BY RAIL
NORTHERN BOUNDARY OF CONFEDERATE STATES 1861

After President Lincoln's election, the South established the Confederacy under President Jefferson Davis. Ironically, both Lincoln and Davis had been born in the same border state of Kentucky. The war was formally opened by the South firing upon Fort Sumter, a step into which, according to some relatively recent studies, the South was maneuvered by President Lincoln.

Until the outbreak of war, the Army of the United States consisted of 16,000 regulars whose task, in the main, was to secure the advancing western frontier from the opposition put up by the Indians. Indeed, the settlement of the West and even the building of the transcontinental railroad was continued throughout the war. Even in peacetime there had been neither time nor opportunity to train the army to operate in large formations. Frontier Indian warfare was conducted by sizeable raiding parties but not by the large forces of all arms that were necessary in a European theater of war. In point of fact, commanding large formations effectively was one of the problems with which, at the early stages of the Civil War, American generals had the greatest difficulty.

At the outbreak of war, the Union Army was at first supplemented by volunteers from the militia who served for a period of 90 days and afterward simply left for home. Initially, they also elected their own officers. Much the same military system prevailed in the South. But dire need and experience soon necessitated a change in these methods. There were nothing like enough volunteers to cover the actual needs of the armies, especially since cases of mass desertion were frequent. Desertion was in fact a problem throughout the war. This in no way detracts from the bravery and readiness for sacrifice of most of the troops in the field. The fatal casualties of 360,000 men for the North and 258,000 men for the South speak for themselves.

It was the South that first introduced conscription in 1862. The North, as a first step, increased the period of service in the armed forces to three years and in 1863 it also introduced com-

pulsory military service for every single male. It was possible to evade conscription in return for a certain sum of money and the provision of a substitute. Also, people were hired into the army in return for a fee which was to increase with the length of service. The North did not refrain from impressing immigrants into the ranks, particularly Germans, who made up about 30 percent, and Irish, who made up 39 percent of the Union Army. Only after they had completed their military service could they become naturalized American citizens. Both conscription and impressment evoked considerable public protest, culminating in New York, where the Civil War was highly unpopular anyway, in anti-draft riots.

By European standards, the discipline of both Northern and Southern armies was very slack. Only bitter experience taught the soldiers not to throw away their equipment once it became too heavy on the march or in battle. This lack of discipline also seriously affected the civilian population, which was frequently molested by gangs of marauding soldiers. Another adverse feature, especially in the North, was that the press often undermined discipline by publishing political and strategic arguments for all soldiers to read.

Abraham Lincoln was a member of the Republican Party, while his first Commander in Chief, General McClellan, was a Democrat. Indeed, McClellan stood as a Democratic candidate for the presidency. At the time it was often suspected that Lincoln's fellow party members did not wish McClellan any great victories, in case this should affect the Republicans adversely.

For the Confederacy, once the war had broken out the primary objective was to protect its agricultural areas to ensure the continued supply of foodstuffs for the populace and the army. Then, if possible, it aimed at taking the industrialized areas of northern Pennsylvania and Maryland and at capturing Washington. In that way the Union could be hit decisively. This, at least, was the view of General Beauregard, the commander of the Confederate forces. All resources were to be mobilized and concentrated with this aim in mind, a policy that he argued would justify the temporary sacrifice of the South's harbor cities. The plan found little support among the population and President Jefferson Davis put forward an alternative war plan by which the Confederate Army was to withdraw into the interior before an invading Union army, then concentrate its forces and defeat the enemy wherever he appeared. Beaure-

Above: Confederate soldiers case their colors for the last time after Lee's surrender.
Left: The Wagon Box Fight, 2 August 1867. Men of the 9th Infantry hold off a Sioux attack. The long experience of Indian fighting did little to prepare the forces of either side for the demands of the Civil War.
Right: A Union soldier using the Beardslee telegraph. Fifteen words per minute could be transmitted on this machine.
Below right: A Union signal station in 1861. One of a number of flag signal posts established along the Potomac.

gard found little that appealed to him in this plan and viewed it as the overture to a long drawn-out campaign of attrition that was bound to reduce the South's resources to the point where it would be forced to yield to the North. This prediction proved to be correct.

It was first shown at the Battle of Bull Run in 1861. Though the Southern forces were victorious, they still failed to defeat McClellan decisively. The Confederate Army then encamped at Manassas and left the initiative to the Union Army, which became active again in March 1862. Time and again, the Confederate Army managed to win battles, but never decisively enough to exploit these victories strategically.

The Union Army, after it had failed in its early efforts to take the Confederate capital, Richmond, Virginia, adopted the policy of a war of attrition, as advocated primarily by General Ulysses S Grant. An army was to advance along the Mississippi via Memphis, Vicksburg and Port Hudson, all important military and supply bases for the Confederacy, and finally take New Orleans. In this it succeeded, New Orleans being taken by 1 May 1862, while Vicksburg capitulated in July of that year. Thus the Confederacy had been cut off from its supply bases in

Above: 'An August Morning with Farragut' lithograph from a painting by Overerd of the Battle of Mobile Bay, 5 August 1864. Above left: The painting 'First at Vicksburg' showing the attack made by the 13th Infantry on the Confederate lines on 19 May 1863. Left: Union troops charge a Confederate barricade.

Tennessee, Louisiana and Texas.

The Union Navy blockaded the entire Atlantic coast and Southern harbors in the Gulf of Mexico. Successful blockade runners with arms and ammunition from Great Britain and France were the exception rather than the rule. For a short time the blockade was threatened by an event which was to revolutionize the whole conduct of naval warfare. The South built an ironclad warship, originally laid down as the *Merrimack*, but renamed the CSS *Virginia*. She was launched from Norfolk, Virginia and soon sank two wooden frigates of the Union Navy at the mouth of the James River. All cannon shells were repelled by the iron plates of the *Virginia*. This single vessel could have threatened the entire Union Navy blockade. It might even have been able to bombard Washington and New York. But the very next day, 9 March 1862, an 'armed chesebox on a raft' appeared. Like the *Virginia*, it was a fully armor-plated ship, but built with a very low profile. This was the Union's *Monitor*, which was armed with two guns mounted in a revolving armored turret. The two ships fought two inconclusive actions, but the Confederacy's ability to break the blockade was destroyed. From then on armored vessels were to dominate naval warfare.

In the meantime, the Union Army endeavored to take possession of the east-west communications of the South, the Cumberland and Tennessee Rivers, and the important railroad line running from Atlanta to Chattanooga to Nashville. Once this railroad link was in the Union's hands, all the other sub-

sidiary lines would fall of themselves and the Union Army could advance upon Savannah, Georgia and deliver the *coup de grace* to the Army of the Confederacy. This plan was actually carried out in 1864 by General Sherman's 'March through Georgia,' which was accompanied by an orgy of destruction the like of which North America had never before experienced. In a war of attrition the civilian population was as much a strategic target as were the armies in the field. This example of ruthlessness, one of many which manifested themselves on both sides during the Civil War, showed that war was no longer the exclusive province of the professionals, but that the entire nation was seen as a legitimate object of warfare.

In Virginia, however, the Union Armies were determined to remain on the defensive in order to protect Washington, Pennsylvania and Maryland. The Battle of Gettysburg, 1–4 July 1863, effectively destroyed the offensive capacity of the Confederate Army. The tide had definitely turned; the North could move to the offensive, but it preferred to stay put and starve out the Confederates. It remained in this position until the South evacuated Richmond in March 1865. The superb defender of this sector was General Robert E Lee, but he was ultimately compelled to capitulate in April 1865 to General Ulysses S Grant at Appomattox Court House.

A war of attrition of this kind included the destruction of all foodstuffs and raw materials wherever the Union Armies found them. General Sheridan had devastated the Shenandoah Valley in 1864, as well as the entire area of Vicksburg and Port Hudson. When he was sent as an observer to the German Military Headquarters during the Franco-Prussian war of 1870–71, he expressed astonishment at the Germans' humane conduct of war. According to his views, the enemy ought to be left nothing except a handkerchief in which to shed his tears for having ever gone to war. For the Northern strategy, it was more important

Left: 'Sheridan's Ride.' Union cavalry commander Philip Sheridan led his forces through the Shenandoah Valley of Virginia in the fall of 1864 causing such destruction that 'a crow flying over it would have to bring his own rations.' Above: An engagement between shore batteries and a river squadron. The Union victory in the Civil War was made more certain by control of the Mississippi.

to deprive the South of its depots, supply bases and railways, to seize the logistical apparatus, than to actually defeat the army in the field.

General Lee acquired military preeminence among the armies of the South because he insisted on bold and ruthless military strokes, while at the same time, once pushed onto the defensive, he conducted it with a skill that was not to be seen in Europe until the latter part of 1914. Lee displayed genius on the offensive as well as the defensive, but victory was denied him.

Grant, too, was aggressive on the offensive and certainly not inferior in spirit and boldness to Lee. He found a strategy by which a tactically inferior army could nevertheless beat an enemy by numerical and industrial superiority. This was the essentially new feature which the American Civil War displayed and which should have been a warning, especially to the German General Staff in both World Wars. Today even the best army cannot beat an enemy who is technically and industrially superior. Added to this must be the will and determination to continue the war until the opponent is totally exhausted. All of Europe ignored this important lesson, but the signs of total war were first seen in the American Civil War.

The strategy of attrition as first practiced in the Civil War has often been argued to be much the same as the strategy of attrition in previous centuries. Nothing could be further from the truth. In the 17th and 18th centuries the objective of this strategy was to force the opponent to give in by weakening his army short of his utter destruction, while husbanding one's own forces as much as possible. The purpose of Grant's strategy of attrition was to force the enemy to capitulate and accept unconditional surrender (a phrase invented in the American Civil War) and to impose his own will upon him. In this Grant succeeded to the fullest extent. He is therefore entitled to be counted among the greatest strategists of military history.

Of course one must not forget that only a protagonist who has the advantage of exterior lines can conduct a strategy of attrition as understood by Grant. It is possible to conduct it from interior lines only if there are inexhaustible supplies of the foodstuffs and raw materials necessary for the conduct of war which cannot be destroyed and if industry itself is secure from attack. This invulnerability does not exist anywhere in the world today.

Another important element in the American Civil War was that of propaganda. It was the first modern crusade, as much as America's war against Spain in 1898 was termed a crusade. To the public at large, it was a crusade for human rights and against slavery. Karl Marx was one of the first to comment upon this aspect of the Civil War, although he interpreted it as a victory for the working class against a slaveholding society. His friend and collaborator, Friedrich Engels, saw it in much the same way, but he also clearly recognized the importance of railways for the operational conduct of a war, especially in the campaigns against Tennessee and Georgia.

The second of the forgotten wars was the Boer War. At the beginning of the Boer War, the armies of the Transvaal and the Orange Free State consisted of armed farmers. It was truly a people's army, numbering about 50,000 men who had been hardened in the continuous conflicts with the natives. As hunters for their daily supplies, they had developed considerable skills as individual fighters, but they found it difficult to operate in large formations. The tactical unit was the *Kirchspiel*, or parish, led by a local man, a field cornet, who was elected every three years. In peacetime he was responsible for administration and jurisdiction. Lieutenants and corporals, also elected, supported him in his task. Several *Kirchspiele* in a district formed a commando, at whose apex stood the elected commandant who held his office in peace and war. The strength of his forces varied according to the number of *Kirchspiele* and ranged from 300 to 3000 men. Generals were selected to command the larger formations, but they had no formal rank distinctions. The discipline of this militia army was on a voluntary basis and showed serious shortcomings. Time and again, individual units simply rode home or intervened in a battle whenever it suited them.

It comes as no surprise that as a result of these conditions the British had great difficulty in assessing correctly the actual strength of their opponents. Although the government supplied rifles, other equipment was usually provided by the Boers themselves; only the poor were equipped by the *Kirchspiel*. The Boers fought as mobile infantry, with mobility being provided by their horses. In many respects they were the forerunners of the modern motorized infantry. Both of the Boer Republics had a mobile artillery and telegraph communication force, patterned on the German example. Service in this force was for three years. There were also some reservists and long-serving volunteers whose training and discipline were good. The total artillery strength available to the Boers was 87 guns served by 1200 men.

The greatest problems were encountered in the leadership of the Boer Army. There was no General Staff, not even any adjutants to aid the generals who, like most officers, habitually wore black tailcoats and top hats. Orders were issued through a war council participated in by all ranks down to corporal. Since these men were all dependent on election by their subordinates, they inevitably supported the majority view. The ultimate results of these proceedings were largely negative.

The Boer Army was nonetheless one of the greatest cavalry armies in history. It boasted a mobility that could initially compensate for its numerical inferiority. In an area about the size of western Europe, this mobility was of considerable importance. By comparison, the British Army, like all European armies since 1859, was dependent on the few existing rail lines along which most of the major engagements took place.

The Boers' standard weapon was the German Mauser rifle bolt-operated with a magazine holding five rounds of ammunition, a type of rifle which had been introduced into most armies by that time. However, lack of fire discipline often caused the Boers to waste much of their ammunition. The rifle could be fired effectively from a distance of 700 yards, but the greatest accuracy was obtained at 300 yards. The Boer War also demonstrated for the first time in history the devastating effect of machine guns, with which both British and Boers were equipped. It was in the nature of things that the British suffered most because they were usually on the attack and, like the Germans during the initial phase of the Franco-Prussian War, they often attacked at first in company columns, thus making an ideal target for the defenders, especially when they were equipped with machine guns.

Above left: A British periodical's engraving of two Boer sentinels
standing guard at an outpost during the so-called First Boer War, then
known as the Transvaal Rising. Top: The Gloucester Regiment charges
the Boer guns at the Battle of Paardeberg Drift. This 1900 engagement
resulted in surrender by the Boer General Cronje, and demonstrated that
the Boers were unlikely to win set-piece battles against the growing British
forces. Left: In the early stages of the Boer War, the British public was
comforted by dramatized description of the sturdy defense of a few key
towns as its forces retreated. This picture shows the defense of Mafeking.
Above: The disreputable Jameson Raid; Jameson makes a last stand. He
was later imprisoned by the British but received a baronetcy in 1911.

Below: A German painting showing the destruction of the British artillery at the Battle of Colenso in 1899. Thanks largely to the impetuosity of some subordinate officers, this became a humiliating defeat for the British, many of whose infantry fled. However, casualties were not heavy and the commander in chief, Buller, soon restored morale. Inset, far left: Colonel Baden-Powell, who conducted the successful defense of Mafeking against the Boers, became a British hero, and later founded the Boy Scout movement on the inspiration of his South African experiences. Left, inset: General Buller in 1900. Buller was blamed for the early British reverses in South Africa and was replaced; later commentators have suggested that he was not incompetent, but was a victim of poorly selected and poorly trained subordinates.

Left: The winning of a Victoria Cross; Captain Towse in a heroic stance as British troops defend themselves against advancing Boers. Right: Map of the Boer War campaigns, showing campaign and supply routes. The importance of sea supply routes can be discerned. Railroads were also important in this war, and raids upon them by Boer cavalry were quite frequent, despite the armored trains which patrolled them. The British command, especially after the appointment of Kitchener as commander in chief, usually sent its troops on foot and its supplies by rail. Below: Lord Methuen is pictured rallying his broken forces at Tweebosch. This was one of the most humiliating defeats suffered by the British in the Boer War. It came when the main Boer forces faced defeat and peace seemed in prospect. The Boers had developed their 'commando' forces, fast well-disciplined horsemen who struck at times and places of their own choosing. The most successful of these was that commanded by De la Rey, and Kitchener sent mobile columns to destroy it. Lord Methuen's column was crushed by De la Rey at Tweebosch, the Boers capturing not only Methuen but his field guns as well. Only at the very end of the war did this commando force meet its heroic end, trapped by superior forces.

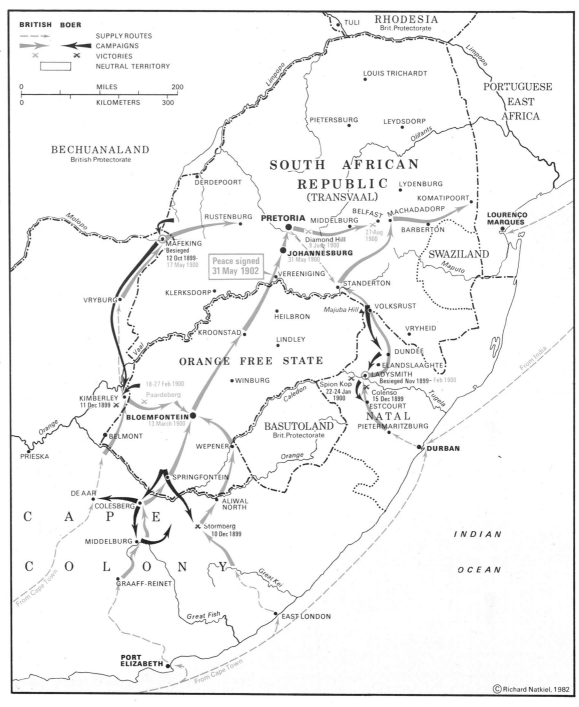

The forerunner of the modern machine gun was the French *mitrailleuse*, which had been used to deadly effect against the German cavalry in 1870–71. It had a high rate of fire, but reloading was time consuming. In 1884 an American, Hiram Maxim, patented a recoil-operated weapon, a true machine gun which could fire several hundred rounds per minute.

The British had tested the machine gun some years before the Boer War, adopting it for army use in 1889. In 1893, at the Zambezi River, 50 British soldiers had defended themselves successfully against an attack by over 5,000 natives with the aid of a single Hotchkiss machine gun. Similar successes were achieved by the British during the Afghan Campaign of 1895, a feat to be repeated in the Sudan Campaign of 1898 when the numerically inferior British forces with 20 machine guns and 38 pieces of artillery, supported by gun boats on the Nile, routed the Dervishes who left behind 12,000 dead and 16,000 wounded.

The Boer War was the first in which soldiers fought one another with these modern weapons. The conclusion drawn from all this by the European armies was that the infantry should advance in a dispersed formation as soon as defensive fire was received. But they still adhered to the principle that the first

objective of an attacking infantry unit would be to gain supremacy of fire-power, which could only be achieved in closed formation, a conclusion soon to be outdated and abandoned during World War I.

The artillery force of the Boers was small, but it was highly mobile. Also, for the first time in the annals of military history, the Boers prepared alternative artillery positions into which the artillery could be moved quickly during combat. Moreover, the quality of their equipment was superior to that available to the British Army. The Boer artillery consisted mostly of 120mm Krupp guns and 155mm French Creusot guns with a range of approximately four and one-half to five miles. The reverse side of this superiority was a lack of Boer resilience when under the fire of the British artillery.

As with all militia-type forces in military history, the greatest strength of the Boer Army lay in its defense, while its attacking power left much to be desired. The Boers were past-masters in guerrilla-type tactics and in small engagements, as they had already shown at Majuba Hill in 1886 during the first Anglo-Boer War. Creeping upon their opponents unnoticed, they opened their well-aimed fusillade to devastating effect, but because of their lack of offensive power they rarely achieved more than local tactical victories. Knowing their territory, they could exploit the terrain to the utmost. They preferred to take their positions behind the ridges or in the bushes of the veld. They used trenches extensively; later on, they had each man dig his own hole. Once they had established their defensive position, it was immensely difficult to dislodge them. When the British, in spite of the odds, did succeed, more often than not it was due to lack of discipline among the Boers. Once they believed that they could not resist a British attack, many simply left their holes without being ordered to do so. European army observers held the opinion that combat from firm entrenchments was a form of warfare which could not be transferred to Europe because of the different terrain there and the character of European armies – another fundamental error.

To the Boers' superior mobility one must add the advantages of their knowledge of the country and their ability to adapt to the prevailing climate. Unlike the British, they knew all the

water holes. Their personal requirements were few and whatever supplies they needed could be carried in a train of ox-drawn carts. As the siege of Kimberley showed, this changed once the Boers were joined by their womenfolk and children, forming a large siege camp or *laager*. In February 1900 at Paardeberg the practice of families joining their men in the field presented a serious disadvantage, because although the Boer Army had achieved a clear defensive victory, it could not move on account of the many dependents. Stationary and devoid of supplies, it ultimately had to surrender. Much the same situation arose at Polar Grove shortly thereafter, but the Boers were already so demoralized by the capitulation at Paardeberg that after the first rounds of artillery fire, they ran to their carts and wagons, which contained all their belongings, and fled helter-skelter. Although the Battle of Driefontein was the last of the large engagements fought by the Boer Armies against the British, it did not put an end to the war as such. The armies of the Boers had been defeated by the British, but for another two years the guerrilla war – the 'little war,' as Clausewitz called it – was to continue.

Mounted Boer commandos interrupted the British lines of communication. The reaction of Lord Kitchener, by then commander of the British forces in South Africa, was swift and ruthless. He demonstrated that organization was more important than the tactical and operational aspects in this kind of war. First of all, he initiated what in our day we have called 'search and destroy missions.' He had the farms and villages of the Boers burned down to deprive them of their supplies. Women and children were imprisoned in concentration camps (the first use of this term) in which by mismanagement rather than deliberate mistreatment over 5000 perished. Thus deprived of their dependents, the Boers at first seemed to have regained their mobility, but when news of the starvation, disease and deaths in the concentration camps leaked out, it seriously undermined their morale.

Another measure introduced by Kitchener seriously hampered the Boers' maneuverability. He established a system of blockhouses along the rail lines which he then extended into the open country. These were secured by barbed wire and fences built several miles apart. Each blockhouse was manned by an NCO and six men. Patrols moved between the blockhouses continuously and penetrated the areas beyond. The crews in the blockhouses, on their own initiative, fortified them even more for maximum protection against artillery attack. Dogs and booby traps warned the occupants of any Boer approach. At first the Boers penetrated time and again, but the defense system became so closely meshed that ultimately the Boers did not venture near a railway line and were confined to smaller and more and more exactly defined areas.

The British also copied Boer tactics by creating raiding parties on horseback who chased the Boers where they found them and destroyed them. Since the Spanish rising of 1808 against Napoleon's invasion, no European troops had fought an extensive anti-partisan campaign except against ill-armed tribesmen. Partisan terror and counterterror became an established feature of the last phase of the Boer War. Europe was still to experience the renewal of this kind of warfare.

However, it was a war that the Boers could not win, any more than they could defeat any fully professional army. Although truly a people's war from the Boer point of view, they were lacking in professional leadership, had no real war plan or any other plan of operations and, above all, were short of supplies. Their only railway line, which the British cut, ran through Mozambique, and the Royal Navy also established a kind of unofficial blockade off the East African coast by which,

Left: A drawing of 1847, when British artists were favorably disposed towards the Boers; Boer women load their menfolk's guns as the latter beat off a spear attack. Right: The reproduction in a British publication of a 1900 German illustration showing how the British in South Africa encouraged the black locals to drive white Boer women from their homes as the latter were put to the torch. British actions against the Boers were strongly criticized in continental Europe, especially in Germany; many Britons were also uneasy.

with methods previously considered illegal, they intervened in international sea traffic, searching any ship they suspected of carrying supplies for the Boers. Among the people of the European powers, the fight of the Boers was immensely popular, but this did not produce any decisive intervention by any of their governments on the Boer side.

Although the defeat of the Boers was a foregone conclusion, the British Army encountered considerable difficulties in bringing the guerrilla war to an end. European armies were not trained for it, and even experience with the Indian Army on the Northwest Frontier with Afghanistan was of only limited value. Nevertheless, due to their superiority in numbers, equipment and efficient communications systems, the British Army prevailed while the Boers, scattered and short of ammunition and food, had to give up.

The British Army operating in the Boer Republics was about 28,000 men strong at the beginning of the war, only about half the size of the Boer armed forces. It was a professional army of volunteers, as yet too small to operate in the vast territory of South Africa. Reserves and reinforcements coming from Great Britain took three to four weeks to arrive, those coming from India two to three weeks. Initial reinforcements were recruited from volunteers in South Africa. In Great Britain, volunteers from the yeomanry of the counties (the Militia cavalry) rushed to serve in South Africa, but the main weight of the fighting rested on the regular army. Great Britain's standing army was not yet permanently organized into divisions and corps; this was to take place only during the course of the war. Four battalions of infantry formed a brigade to which were attached formations of artillery, engineers and cavalry. The initial inferiority of British artillery was soon corrected and by the half-way point of the war proved equal, perhaps even superior, to the artillery of the Boers. Although the training of the infantry was badly dated, the British quickly adapted to the new tactic of attacking in dispersed formations.

The first uniforms adapted to the existing environment had been introduced by the British Army in India in 1857. After experience in the Sudan in 1898 it was decided to make khaki the color of the service uniforms of all British Army units although the troops in South Africa at the start of the war still had the old red and blue uniforms. This example was followed by Austria-Hungary in 1909; Germany introduced field-gray in 1910 and in the same year Russia clad its army in green uniforms. France took until 1915 to introduce the 'horizon blue'

service uniforms.

In the early phase of the Boer War the British still adhered to a belief held in all European armies that it was possible to achieve fire power supremacy with infantry weapons. In time they changed these tactics and shifted their emphasis to holding down the enemy by concentrated artillery fire while the infantry attacked. However, inexperienced as they were in this, the British artillery frequently fired into its own advancing infantry. Artillery observers, to guide the fire of the artillery from a position in the front line, did not exist; this development, too, was a product of World War I.

To match the Boers, the British Army had to attain an equal standard of mobility, which was a problem. Unlike the Boers, the regular British Army was not accustomed to the prevailing temperatures, which ranged from 40 to 50 degrees Centigrade during the day to night temperatures so low as to cause snow showers. Tents were essential but difficult to transport. Considering this single problem and adding to it all the other supplies needed by an army on the march, it seems natural that the British kept as close as possible to the existing railroads. However, the British also introduced more mobile, mounted infantry units. In each battalion one company was mounted.

How the supply train was to be organized was another question which Kitchener solved. He had had little experience in modern warfare; as a young subaltern he had served in Egypt and later, in 1898, he made his military reputation there and in the Sudan by building up an army to beat the Mahdi. He proved a brilliant organizer and solved the supply-train problem in South Africa in two ways. First he divided it into two contingents. The first was an army train based, like the Boers', on ox-drawn carts; the second was the train for individual units in the field, in which supplies were carried by mules. The ox-drawn train had the advantage that the animals knew the country and could traverse every kind of territory, but they had the disadvantage of being able to graze only by day, and of course they were slow. Mules, on the other hand, were faster and could graze day and night. Therefore British forces on the march, once they adapted to their environment, could be on the move at any time of day and thus achieve a mobility which made them largely independent of the railroads. They became more than a match for the Boers, who could no longer rely on the vastness of their territory. Once equal or superior mobility had been achieved by the British Army, the outcome of the war became a foregone conclusion.

The third of the forgotten wars before 1914 was the Russo-Japanese war. Among the great powers of Europe the Czarist Empire was the most backward in military affairs. Nonetheless, ever since the days of Peter the Great, the Czarist Empire had wanted warm water ports, on the Black Sea with rights of access to the Mediterranean through the Dardanelles, and on the Pacific. In the 19th century this drive led to territorial expansion toward the Balkans in Europe, Persia and Afghanistan in the Near East and Sinkiang, Mongolia, the Amur Provinces and Sakhalin in the Far East. This inevitably produced a conflict of interest between Russia and the Hapsburg Empire concerning the Balkans on the one hand and between Russia and Great Britain over the Near East on the other. In the Far East Russia founded the Amur Province and in 1860 the coastal province that included the harbor of Vladivostok, a word that translates into 'Ruler of the East' and gives a clear enough indication of Russia's ambitions. In 1875 Russia handed over the Kurile Islands to Japan in return for Sakhalin. In 1896 it intervened on behalf of China against Japan, backed by both France and Germany. In return Russia received from China railroad concessions in Manchuria. Prior to this, in 1894, it had leased Port Arthur and the peninsula of Liaotung from China. Russia also used the Boxer Rising in China in 1900 as a pretext for reinforcing its military presence in Manchuria with the ultimate objective of penetrating into Korea.

Japan, whose geographic position *vis-à-vis* the Asian mainland is not entirely dissimilar to that occupied by Great Britain *vis-à-vis* the European mainland, could not, in the interest of its own military security, tolerate the establishment of a major European power dominating the disintegrating Chinese Manchu Empire. This led to the war between Russia and Japan in 1904.

In 1874 Russia had introduced conscription with a six-year period of military service, but whereas compulsory military service was backed by the whole population of the other European powers, this was not the case in Russia. Serfdom had been formally abolished in 1861, but this did not mean that in practice the Russian peasants – the vast multitude of the population – were no longer in a state of servitude. Social tensions continued and even increased. Land reforms that had been introduced proved ineffective. The peasantry had to pay the landlords for every piece of land they acquired, increasing their debts. The rising load of taxation rested mainly on the peasants. Nevertheless, the Czar, being not merely an Emperor but the head of the Orthodox Church, still retained his aura of sanctity among the peasant population. His faults and shortcomings were laid at the door of the vast bureaucracy which had spread its tentacles across the entire Empire. Russia's intelligentsia adopted a different and more revolutionary attitude. Three main currents coexisted. One comprised the Narodniks, that is, the Populists, who believed that Russia had suffered by contact with the degenerate West. They advocated strict separation from the West and the rejuvenation and modernization of Russian society from its own moral and economic strength. Then there were Nihilists and Socialists, most of them very remote from the majority of the population. It was not until later years that peasants and workers joined the revolutionary movement in large numbers. Like many representatives of the intelligentsia in Europe and the United States, most Russian intellectuals argued that patriotism was an outmoded concept and that war was a crime, or at least an anachronism. Military virtues to them were nothing but an obstacle to progress.

During the Russo-Japanese War, tendencies were apparent which, vastly enlarged and amplified, were to come to the fore during World War I: attempts by the intelligentsia to demoralize the forces, to cause unrest among the ranks, to carry out acts

Top: Manchuria in 1904. A Russian observation post awaits the Japanese. An Austrian military observer, one of many attachés sent to the Russo-Japanese War by the great powers, has his back to the camera. Above: The Russian cruiser *Varyag* sinks in the harbor at Chelmulpo (Inchon) after her hopeless battle against a Japanese squadron. Above right: Japanese battleships and cruisers were built in Britain. Here the new battleship *Hatsuse* is eased down the Tyne, her topmasts lowered to clear the rail bridges of Newcastle. Right: The Russian commander in Manchuria, Kuropatkin, greets his officers.

of sabotage were some of them. At that time this did not affect the Russian Army in any serious way. By contrast, however, the Japanese population backed its forces to the hilt.

Russia's internal condition was bound to be reflected to some degree in its army. The education of the officers was meager, to say the least. Promotion came only very slowly and not usually on the basis of merit but of social connections. There was an enormous chasm between the Guards officers serving in St Petersburg and the officers serving with the line regiments. Promotion was quicker if an officer managed to have himself transferred to one of the staffs or to the administration. The Russians also had reserve officers, but considering the low social status of the average Russian officer, there was not such a rush to become one as was the case in Germany. Hence they were in very short supply.

162

Below: As soon as the Japanese captured a hill overlooking Port Arthur, the Russian Pacific Squadron was doomed to succumb to artillery fire. At the left is the cruiser *Pallada*, and at the right the battleship *Pobieda* ('*Victory*'), lying on the bottom of the harbor. A sister of *Pallada* and survivor of Tsushima, *Avrora*, is preserved at Leningrad. Opposite page, top left: General Kuropatkin. Not an incompetent general, Kuropatkin was good at organization and administration, but his bureaucratic qualities did not fit him for the direction of rapidly-moving events. His strategy of a fighting retreat until his forces were overwhelmingly superior to the Japanese was basically correct, but too unpalatable for his government. Opposite page, right: The well-equipped Japanese infantryman. This page, left: Russian artillery horses en route to the Manchurian front. In the top lefthand corner of the boxcar is the celebrated inscription '40 men or 8 horses'.

Top: A British artist's impression of the Russian garrison leaving Port Arthur as the smart Japanese troops move in. Above left: En route to his defeat at Tsushima, the Russian Admiral Rozhestvensky comes ashore at Tangiers. On leaving, his ships' anchors broke the cable connection with Europe. Above right: A Russian coastal gun at Port Arthur. Left: Japanese heavy howitzers bombarded Port Arthur, with decisive results.

To be an officer was more of a job than a calling motivated by traditions of service. The Russian General Staff and the Russian Military Academy also reflected the prevailing situation. There was a premium placed on formal training, not on individual initiative. Wargames were a rarity. In contrast to the German concept of the *Auftragstaktik*, the Russians adhered to the strict execution of orders issued by the staff, carried out to the letter right down to the last private in the army. A French military observer who inspected the Russian Army commented that it had not learned a single lesson from its past campaigns.

Russian military staffs were over-manned. Also, a great many civilian advisors were attached to them. Although the Russian Army was well-fed in normal times, the staffs lived in extreme luxury, and this caused resentment among the troops. The generally favorable condition of Russian Army supplies was largely the achievement of the Minister for War and future commander of the Russian Army in Manchuria, Kuropatkin. Though a brilliant organizer, he was, however, a mediocre general. Like every Russian general, he commanded troops who were largely illiterate. Although they hardly knew what a war was about, particularly the Russo-Japanese War, they excelled in steadfastness and stubbornness as long as their officers were with them. Once these had been killed, they soon gave up all resistance. Since the officers never had even the

vaguest outline of the situation as a whole, they were vulnerable to panic. The Czarist Empire was multi-national, and among the soldiers recruited from national minorities, morale was considerably lower than among pure Russian troops.

In the field the Russian Army was divided into corps, each with two divisions. An engineer battalion was attached to each corps. A standard infantry division included four infantry regiments, each with under 3000 combat troops, as well as cavalry detachments used for raids or for reconnaissance. By the end of August 1904 Kuropatkin had seven army corps, four divisions of Cossacks, 590 pieces of artillery, but only 16 machine guns. Artillery tactics were still influenced by the maxims of the late 18th and early 19th centuries. The Russian artillery was always stationed on the tops of hills or along ridges. They had no high-explosive shells – only shrapnel. The telegraphic system

cannot be described except by saying that it was utterly inadequate.

This was the army which met an enemy whose forces had been structured and equipped according to the most modern standards. While the Japanese Navy had been trained by the British, the army had been trained by the Germans. The only shortage of the Japanese Army was in its number of trained officers and NCOs. It was structured into armies whose size actually corresponded more closely to that of European corps. Three divisions formed an army. The infantry divisions consisted of four regiments, each with three battalions. Three squadrons of cavalry, an artillery regiment with three batteries of six guns each, an engineer battalion and a telegraph communication detachment were attached to each division.

The structure of the Japanese Army was more flexible than that of the Russian and the 224-man infantry company was a tactical unit superior to the smaller Russian formation. The Japanese placed great emphasis upon fire tactics while the Russian Army was still conducting its attack *en masse* by a bayonet charge. Moreover, each Japanese company had one heavy machine gun. The regular Japanese Army numbered 270,000 men with 870 pieces of artillery, to which must be added 530,000 men from the reserves.

In Manchuria the Russian Army had 83,000 men at first with 196 pieces of artillery. The portion of the Trans-Siberia Railroad bypassing Lake Baykal was still incomplete and initially only three trains per day could be sent with reinforcements. In the course of the war this was increased to 12 trains per day and once the Trans-Siberian Railroad around Lake Baykal had been completed in September 1904, a rate of 18 trains per day was achieved. In total the Russians transported 800,000 men, 150,000 horses and 1500 guns as well as supplies to the front during the war.

The Japanese forces had, of course, to be carried across the sea. Japanese supply vessels could not transport more than three divisions and equipment from Japan at any one time. The process of embarkation took three days, disembarkation five days. Only from the late summer of 1904 was the problem of food supplies solved when, because of a good harvest, the Japanese could live off the land.

The success of the Japanese depended on supremacy at sea. The Japanese Navy comprised 29 modern ships including six battleships and over 90 older vessels. Japanese docks were capable of repairing ships but not of undertaking new construction. The Russian Pacific Squadron consisted of 72 vessels, some of which were based at Vladivostok and some at Port Arthur.

To prevent interference with the movement of their army, the Japanese plan of war envisioned the achievement of absolute naval dominance in the Yellow Sea, to allow the land forces to aim at a final decision in Manchuria. Therefore, while Russo-Japanese negotiations were still in progress and without a declaration of war, Admiral Togo, the Japanese naval leader, was sent to attack the Russian naval units stationed in Port Arthur on 8 February 1904. The enterprise was a complete success for the Japanese and established their supremacy at sea.

Thereupon, in March 1904, the Japanese landed an army half-way up the Korean Peninsula which made its way to the Yalu River, while a second army landed northeast of Port Arthur, the bulk of which turned toward Kuropatkin's forces at Liaoyang while the rest turned toward Port Arthur, which was still held by Russian forces.

The Russian war plan envisioned holding a defensive line, backed by the Harbin-Mukden-Port Arthur railroad until sufficient reinforcements had arrived to allow a move to the offensive. However, the position of the Russian Armies

Left: The only modern Russian battleship to survive Tsushima, *Orel*, after surrender to the Japanese. The fractured barrel of one of her four 12-inch guns can be seen. A Japanese sailor stands on guard. The *Orel* was only a year old, having been built in Russia to an essentially French design. Below: Togo's flagship *Mikasa*, the only pre-Dreadnought battleship to be preserved to the present day. The inscription is in Togo's handwriting, and is his signal to his ships as they joined action at Tsushima. The Japanese officers' Nelsonian background is clear from this signal, 'The Empire's fate depends on the result of this battle . . . Let every man do his utmost duty'. At the end of the war *Mikasa* accidentally blew up in harbor, but was later salvaged. Right: Togo in his later years, when he was a national hero and something of an elder statesman too. Far right: Signed, sealed and soon to be delivered; the Treaty of Portsmouth. The Russians signed in Latin script, not Cyrillic. Because Japan, though victorious, had reached the end of her resources, the Russian negotiator Witte was able to secure an agreement which many Japanese found distasteful. A Tokyo anti-peace riot was the result.

depended largely on what was happening at sea. The Japanese largely preserved their naval dominance and used it to capture harbors which would give them better access to Port Arthur. There was a temporary setback when Russian naval forces coming from Vladivostok managed to sink the vessels carrying the siege train for Port Arthur.

Russian attempts to keep open the land route to Port Arthur failed. The Japanese forces at Liaoyang linked up with the forces crossing the Yalu and forced the Russians to withdraw. Time and again the Russians counterattacked in vain. Frontal attack having failed, they tried to get around the flanks of the Japanese, but their forces were too weak to do so successfully. They continued to withdraw and to dig in. The war of movement turned into a war of fixed positions, trenches and field fortifications, very much like the one waged near Richmond in the American Civil War. For months Russian and Japanese forces confronted each other without much activity. The fact that European observers failed to draw any decisive lessons from this is shown by the report of the German General Freytag-Loringhoven, who wrote: 'A highly cultured country increases the mobility of the armies, so that the attacker does not have to halt before the fortified positions of the defenders as in East Asia, where war forms a continuous engagement of defensive fire, because in East Asia the mountains in the east and the desert in the west confine operations to a relatively small area.'

In many respects, though not in all, the siege of Port Arthur foreshadowed Verdun. The Japanese attacks were extremely costly in manpower. Fifteen thousand Japanese were killed in the process of capturing the outer ring of the fortifications. The harbor and docks were subjected to the fire of 280mm howitzers, but Port Arthur itself still held out against the Japanese onslaught. A whole network of Japanese trenches surrounded the fortress. Mortars, dynamite hand grenades and wire-cutting equipment became standard weapons and tools for the Japanese. The first artillery barrage of the type with which we have been familiar since World War I was opened upon Port Arthur without seriously denting the Russian defense. Engineers became more important than the infantry; only with their aid could the important fortifications overlooking Port Arthur be taken by December 1904. Finally, on 3 January 1905, Port Arthur capitulated.

In the north, General Kuropatkin still held his defensive line at Mukden and there the most important battle of the war raged from 23 February to 10 March 1905. In numbers, the Russians and Japanese were about equal, each side having about 300,000 men. The battle ended with a Russian withdrawal along the rail line to Harbin. Again the Russians dug in, reinforced by troops who had come via the Trans-Siberian Railway. In spite of their victories, signs of exhaustion could be seen in the Japanese Army. Operations on both sides were impeded by the thaw which put the road communications out of commission.

After the defeat of the Pacific Squadron Russian hopes rested upon regaining naval supremacy in the Yellow Sea, which was to be achieved by Russia's Baltic Fleet which made the long round-the-world trip to join the fighting. These hopes came to nought when the Japanese Navy defeated the Baltic Fleet on 27–28 May 1905, sending 30 of the 47 vessels to the bottom. To all intents and purposes, the outcome of the war had been decided, even though Russia still had large forces with which to continue the war on land. But the Czarist Empire and its army were debilitated, and mediation by President Theodore Roosevelt and the German Empire led to the conclusion of hostilities. For the first time in modern history, a European power had been defeated by an Asian army. The process of decolonization in Asia dates from that moment.

The Russo-Japanese conflict carried many lessons for the armies of all countries. It had caused a change in infantry tactics; the effective fire of modern rifles and machine guns entrenched in the first line should have put an end to the attack by company columns. Even the reserves no longer moved in compact bodies but spread out to avoid becoming an easy target for the artillery. Attacks were carried out by short rushes in dispersed formations, taking advantage of any temporary lulls in the defensive artillery fire. Companies no longer attacked as a body but in dispersed platoon formations. If losses increased seriously, the spade became the most important weapon beside the rifle, since the men would dig in. Once a firm line was established, the opposing forces fought for fire supremacy and, once this was achieved, the final attack was mounted. But as in the Boer War, the artillery was rarely used to prepare an infantry attack. Unfortunately, most of these and other lessons taught by the American Civil War, the Boer War and the Russo-Japanese War were ignored in 1914 – to be learned again only after an immense toll of life had been taken.

7. World War I

It is not our task to investigate the causes of World War I. But we have to ask the question, would any of the belligerent powers have been prepared to pay the price which the preservation of peace would have involved? The answer to this must be an emphatic *No*. Russia was not prepared, for domestic as well as for foreign policy reasons, to give up its claim to dominance in the Balkans. Austria-Hungary, already showing signs of internal weakness, could not afford any further strengthening of the Serb position. Germany could not afford to be moved into a position of utter isolation – the consequence if it had forsaken its ally, nor could it view with complacency the strengthening of Russia to a point where Russia could overrun Germany (a view also held by the British Ambassador Buchanan in St Petersburg and Sir Henry Wilson, the Chief of Great Britain's Imperial General Staff). France was unable to accept the risk of isolation on the European mainland if it left its Russian ally unsupported. And Great Britain, its resources already strained, could not risk the security of its imperial position which it had obtained first through the Anglo-French entente of 1904, and later through the Anglo-Russian entente of 1907. Nor could it ignore the potential threat posed to Great Britain's sea power by the growing German battle fleet.

The lessons which the general staffs of the European armies had learned went back to 1859, 1866 and 1870–71, as well as to the Balkan Wars of 1912–13. What was totally ignored at both the tactical and operational levels was the immense fire power of modern infantry weapons, especially the machine gun. With the exception of the British Army until 1916, the armies of the European powers were mass conscript armies. The generals therefore believed in the virtue of mass, and in the infantry as the main force for bringing about a decision.

According to staff calculations, the frontage of a division in an attack should amount to little more than three miles. A German infantry regiment consisted of 12 companies and a machine-gun company which was to provide covering fire from the rear and not accompany the attacking line. Attacks were carried out initially in slightly dispersed company columns, still too tightly bunched and providing an ideal target for the defense. The cavalry was to carry out reconnaissance tasks. But Zeppelins, as well as aircraft themselves, had begun to take over that task from the cavalry. Balloons had already been used as platforms for observers directing the fire of the artillery. Trucks and tractors were already widely used for tactical movements. Telegraph communications connected the General Staff with lower-level staffs. Railroad regiments were essential for the reliable functioning of the communications network, which was still based on rail, with motor vehicles taking second place. As a rule, military forces on the advance could move only about 75 miles from their rail head. The engineers and railroad troops had to move the rail heads forward as quickly as possible. This reliance on the rail system during World War I made it impossible to carry out large pincer movements like those commonly employed in World War II, when the road network was utilized to the same extent as were the railroads. Frontal penetration was therefore limited by both space and time.

The Allies had at their disposal some 250 divisions, against which the Central Powers could bring approximately 160 divisions. The Allied supremacy was even greater at sea, the oceans being dominated by the Royal Navy. But most important, the Allies enjoyed an unquantifiable superiority in the supply of raw materials. The markets of the world were open to them – naval supremacy ensured that – while they were closed to the Central Powers. This superiority was demonstrated with a vengeance when the Allies carried out the long-range blockade of Germany, showing that fighting from the interior line without sufficient raw materials and foodstuffs was hopeless against adversaries with unlimited access to all that they needed. *Ersatz* (artificial) materials including food, as developed by Germany's chemical industries, could alleviate the situation in some sectors but could not solve the problem.

The Central Powers had neither a combined supreme command nor a common and concerted war plan. There were a number of agreements made between individual members of the respective General Staffs, such as that Austria should hold the Russians at bay until the Schlieffen Plan had been carried out and the German forces could turn east. The German Eighth Army with its weak formations was to hold East Prussia. But the Schlieffen Plan was no longer the plan conceived by its originator.

Russia intended to move with four armies against the Austrians in Galicia and with two armies against East Prussia. The French planned to break through the German front in the area of Metz, but in their blue coats, red trousers and red kepis they became an ideal target for German machine guns. The British Expeditionary Force was to bolster the French left wing while the Belgian Army envisioned fighting only for the neutrality of its country.

As in most wars, unforeseen events necessitated the modification or complete alteration of the original plans. Besides tactical and strategic errors, and underestimation of the effectiveness of defensive fire power, stockpiles of ammunition, especially artillery shells and other military hardware, were consumed far more quickly than expected and the physical resources of the men actually carrying out the operations were overestimated.

Previous page: On the Western Front during the Final Allied offensive; British troops with German prisoners during the attack on the so-called Hindenburg Line near Bellicourt in September 1918. Right: A map of the European alliances on the eve of World War 1. The Central Powers clearly have the advantage of internal lines of communication, but are subject to attack from several directions; the vulnerability of Russian Poland is also evident. Below: Belgian troops on the march during a sortie from Antwerp in September 1914. Below right: French infantry of 1914, occupying a shallow trench.

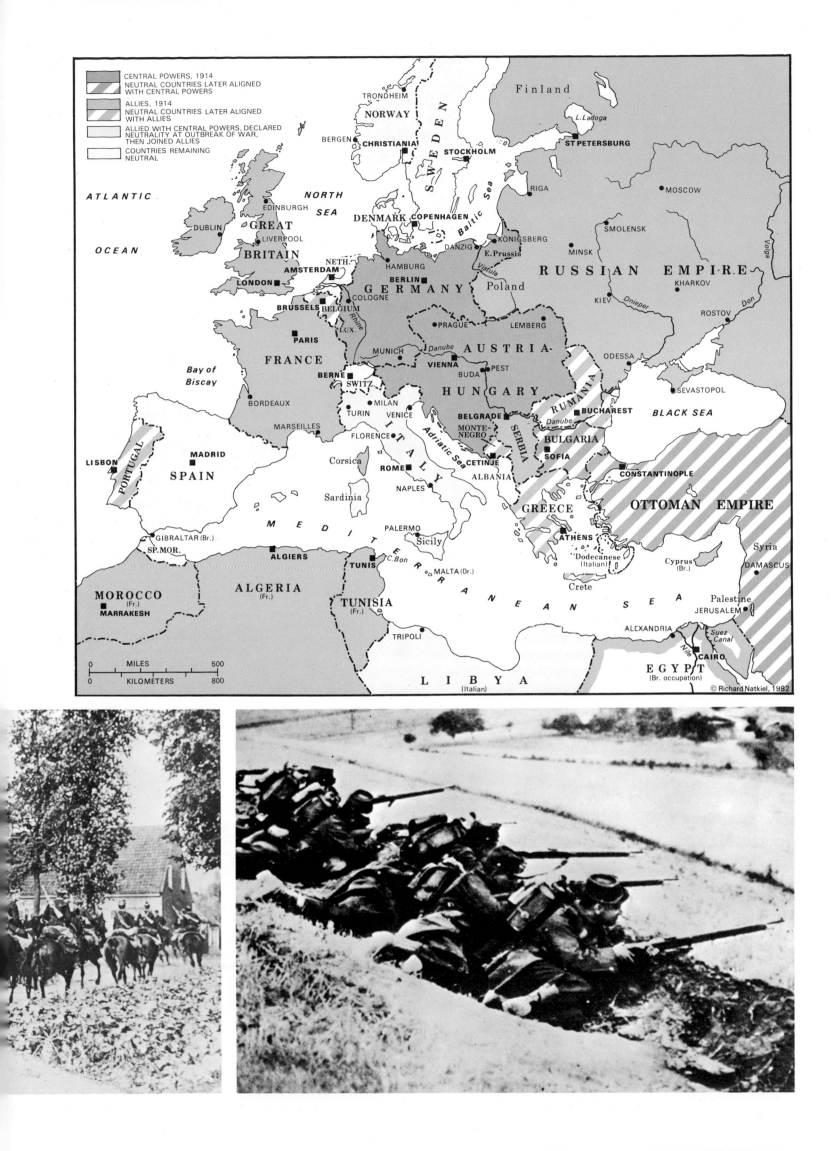

CENTRAL POWERS, 1914
NEUTRAL COUNTRIES LATER ALIGNED WITH CENTRAL POWERS

ALLIES, 1914
NEUTRAL COUNTRIES LATER ALIGNED WITH ALLIES

ALLIED WITH CENTRAL POWERS, DECLARED NEUTRALITY AT OUTBREAK OF WAR, THEN JOINED ALLIES

COUNTRIES REMAINING NEUTRAL

ATLANTIC

OCEAN

Finland

TRONDHEIM

NORWAY

L. Ladoga

ST PETERSBURG

BERGEN   CHRISTIANIA

STOCKHOLM

MOSCOW

NORTH
SEA

EDINBURGH

RIGA

DUBLIN   GREAT

LIVERPOOL   BRITAIN

DENMARK   COPENHAGEN

Baltic Sea

KONIGSBERG

SMOLENSK

DANZIG   E.Prussia

RUSSIAN EMPIRE

MINSK

NETH.   HAMBURG   Vistula

AMSTERDAM

LONDON   GERMANY   Poland   KHARKOV

BERLIN

KIEV   Dnieper

BRUSSELS   COLOGNE   ROSTOV   Don

BELGIUM   PRAGUE   LEMBERG

LUX.   Rhine

PARIS   MUNICH   Danube   AUSTRIA-   ODESSA

FRANCE   VIENNA

BERNE   PEST   SEVASTOPOL

Bay of   SWITZ.   BUDA

Biscay   HUNGARY

BORDEAUX   TURIN   MILAN   RUMANIA   BLACK SEA

VENICE   BUCHAREST

MARSEILLES   BELGRADE   Danube

FLORENCE   MONTE-   SERBIA   BULGARIA

LISBON   MADRID   NEGRO   SOFIA   CONSTANTINOPLE

Corsica   ROME   CETINJE

SPAIN   ALBANIA   OTTOMAN EMPIRE

Sardinia   GREECE   Syria

GIBRALTAR (Br.)   NAPLES   DAMASCUS

SP.MOR.   M E D   PALERMO   ATHENS   Cyprus

ALGIERS   Sicily   Dodecanese   (Br.)

MOROCCO   TUNIS   C.Bon   (Italian)   Crete   Palestine

(Fr.)   ALGERIA   MALTA(Br.)   JERUSALEM

MARRAKESH   (Fr.)   TUNISIA   ALEXANDRIA

TRIPOLI   (Fr.)   Nile   Suez

CAIRO   Canal

0   MILES   500   L I B Y A   EGYPT

0   KILOMETERS   800   (Italian)   (Br. occupation)

The Schlieffen Plan failed because, as already mentioned, Moltke the Younger, the Chief of the General Staff, had converted it into a double pincer movement, intending to launch an offensive in the north and south and thereby depleting the manpower of his right wing. The Russian forces penetrated into East Prussia much more quickly than had been expected, which required a further reduction of the German right wing in France when much of it was shipped to the east. The German armies had to swing around east of Paris, instead of west as planned by Schlieffen. The French Supreme Commander, General Joffre, recognized the German weakness and partly by commandeering all vehicles on wheels in Paris, transported all available troops and threw them against the exposed German right wing. Kluck, the commander of the German First Army, had allowed a gap to appear in his front into which British and French forces pushed. During this crisis the commander of the German Second Army, Bülow, advocated withdrawal while Kluck wanted to continue the attack. Moltke sent a staff officer to Kluck and Bülow with authority to adjudicate the dispute and he ordered a withdrawal. This was the 'Miracle of the Marne.' Moltke, beset by doubts, suffered a collapse and was replaced by General von Falkenhayn. Now the battle in the west turned into a race for the opponent's northern flank. This failed, and instead the Allied and German armies reached the Channel coast. Mobility ceased, replaced by trench warfare from the Channel to the Swiss frontier. With hindsight we can see that the outcome of the war was now decided. It became a war of attrition in which the Central Powers were burdened by disadvantages which nothing in the world could reduce.

Left: The Russian General Samsonov, who committed suicide after his army was shattered in the Battle of Tannenberg, having blundered into an encirclement planned by Ludendorff's talented chief of staff. The Russians' failure, which brought to an end their prompt invasion of East Prussia, might have been avoided if their cavalry, commanded by Rennenkampf, had been more active. But Rennenkampf and Samsonov were on bad terms, having come literally to blows in the Russo-Japanese War.

Below left: Russian infantrymen in their trenches. Their bayonet was a fearsome four-sided blade which, when attached to the rifle, formed a weapon five and a half feet long. Top right: Russian infantry on the march to the front in 1914; as in World War II, they carried a rolled blanket around their shoulders. Center right: German infantry rests in a cornfield during the Battle of the Marne. By invading at harvest time, the Germans were able to live off the land to an unexpected extent; this compensated for defective supply arrangements, caused by the advance outpacing the provision of transport. Below: Russian infantrymen attack through the barbed wire entanglements of the East Prussian front. Entanglements covered by machine guns were a murderous obstacle.

Left: French infantry set up barbed wire over a communication trench. A front line trench would be deeper and provided with dugouts and traverses to make defense easier. Below: Men of the 59th Field Company, Royal Engineers, prepare to leave their bivouac at Bavai on 22nd August 1914 just before the Battle of Mons.

In East Prussia General Paul von Hindenburg, pulled out of retirement, and his Chief of Staff, Erich Ludendorff, put an end to the Russian invasion of East Prussia at the Battle of Tannenberg between 26 and 30 August 1914. Two Russian armies were virtually destroyed. The Battle of Tannenberg showed the immense advantages of the principle of *Auftragstaktik*, since most commanders in the field, like General von François, had to act independently of the main headquarters. They had no more than directives and were sometimes willing to set aside these directives if the prevailing situation made it necessary. The Battle of Tannenberg was also fought over a relatively small area, whereas the German campaign in France covered a much wider area and was conducted by forces clearly under-strength for this kind of operation.

In the East the war was more mobile and, Tannenberg apart, the main actions took place largely in Galicia. There the Russians tried to inflict a serious defeat on the Austro-Hungarian forces and to open the road to Budapest and Vienna. Although the Austro-Hungarian forces were clearly inferior in numbers, the Chief of the Austro-Hungarian General Staff, Conrad von Hötzendorf, met the Russian attack offensively and achieved important victories at Krasnic and Komerov. The Russian Army was checked, and its attempt to cut Hötzendorf's lines of communication failed. But on the flank near Lvov the Russians created a situation which Hötzendorf could meet only by withdrawing part of his forces to the lower San River. Here it was a question of keeping vital lines of communication in the hands of

the Central Powers. Nonetheless, the initiative remained with the Austro-Hungarian forces. In December 1914, at the Battles of Limanova and Lapanov, the Russian threat to the important industrial region of Upper Silesia was eliminated. In the east, time and again the belligerents made attempts to encircle the enemy – attempts in most cases unsuccessful because of bad road conditions and lack of transport. The shortage of materials which afflicted the Austro-Hungarian Army was balanced by the Russian lack of flexibility in their operations. But at the level of the rank and file, the firepower of modern infantry weapons caused serious losses on both sides, especially among the regular officers and NCOs. The Austro-Hungarian Army was also much inferior to the Russian in artillery. Thus, as in the West, the Eastern fronts hardened into seemingly impenetrable lines of trenches and fortifications, from the Russian frontier in East Prussia, to Lowicz at the Bzura River, across Poland to the Carpathian Mountains.

Movement came only with the onset of spring when the Russians attempted again to make their way into the Hungarian plain but were brought to a standstill by the forces of the Hapsburg Empire. Their effectiveness was surprising, considering that it was an army of national minorities, which, with a few exceptions, kept intact until the fall of 1918.

Neither in the East nor in the West did the trench warfare produce any decision. The French mounted offensives in the Arras and Champagne areas in 1915, but failed to achieve a breakthrough. The German trench system (although it had not yet acquired any great depth) and German machine gunners brought the French attacks to a halt. The French attempt in March 1915 was followed by a German attack in April in the Ypres sector which made some territorial gains but failed to achieve its true aim, which was to break through and restore mobility to the campaign in the West. For the first time the Germans made extensive use of poison gas, which came as a surprise to the defenders, but the Germans lacked the reserves with which to exploit the initial surprise they achieved.

The problem of how to restore mobility to warfare was not tackled, as one might expect, at staff level, but in the front line and the solution was the *Stosstrupp*, the shocktroop, with which the first experiments were made in the Argonne. They were formed in groups of three and were to spearhead any attack. The leader of the party carried no rifle but had a pick and the shield of a machine gun for his protection. On each side of him was an expert handgrenade thrower loaded with shoulder-slung sacks of hand-grenades. For hand-to-hand combat they used bayonets or sharpened trench spades.

Left: The first winter of the war; German troops facing the Russians in East Prussia. Right: General Galliéni, military governor of Paris, whose advice to Joffre led to the Allied victory at the Marne in 1914 and the failure of the Schlieffen Plan.
Below: A map of the 'Battle of the Frontiers', August-September 1914.

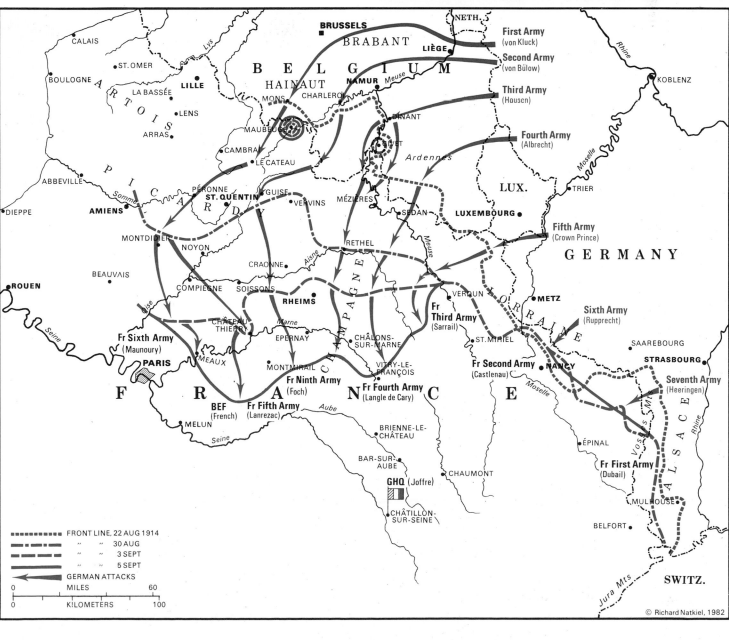

© Richard Natkiel, 1982

Below: Serbian artillery on the banks of the Danube attempts to hold off the Austrian advance. Far left: Sir John French, commander of the British Expeditionary Force in France for the first year of the war. Left: General d'Espérey, one of the best of French World War I generals.

Once the attack had been carried into the enemy's trench, one problem was how to protect the flanks, a task usually given to the artillery. But their positions were often too far in the rear to allow precisely aimed fire. At first it was believed that the shock-troops would be able to use some of their own lighter artillery, but all types tested proved too cumbersome; instead, they used the trench mortar. This added more men to the unit, while dealing with enemy fortifications required engineers as well. In this way the shocktroops became the first mixed formation.

An attack was usually launched by the small groups of expert hand-grenade throwers and engineers experienced in the handling of explosives, plus a team of wire cutters and flame throwers. They were followed by machine gunners and mortar crews to protect their flanks. Once the first trench had been reached, close combat was the rule with all the weapons available, even those of the enemy.

The principle of the *Stosstrupp*, based on a mixed formation, would have been of little use had there not been men brave enough to carry the attack forward. They would be followed by the bulk of the infantry attacking through the breaches opened by the stormtroops. Naturally, the *Stosstruppen* considered themselves a warrior elite. They had to be in top physical condition and their training was carried out with the use of live ammunition. This type of soldier has been best described in Ernst Jünger's book *Storm of Steel*.

The relationship between officers and men was rather different to that existing in the regiments of the line. It was based on comradeship, rooted in the knowledge that everyone depended upon everyone else. Ranks were considered functional, devoid of any social connotations. Stormtroop training did not include the barrack square drill, still prevalent among the troops in the rear areas. Loyalty to one another was the guiding principle.

Regular officers were extremely rare in stormtroop units. They were commanded mainly by officers of the reserve or those who had become officers only in the course of the war. For a long time the *Stosstruppen* were used mainly in raids to gather intelligence. Their great hour came in the March offensive of 1918 when shocktroop formations, attacking in platoon size, spearheaded the German attacks.

In May 1915 Italy entered the war on the side of the Allies. Besides its other war aims, Italy strove to capture the South Tyrol from the Austrians and establish a new frontier at the Brenner Pass. General Cadorna, Chief of the Italian General Staff, believed he would be able to achieve this by a push across the Isonzo River in the direction of Ljubljana, and via Toblach toward Villach. The Austro-Hungarian forces on the southern frontier were weak, but in spite of this weakness they managed to halt all the Italian attacks in the four Isonzo battles of 1915. In the western Trentino sector, the Italians cherished the belief that it was important to occupy the summits of the peaks before risking the push through the valleys. It was a fundamental error. The war on the summits and glaciers came to the same end as the fighting near the Isonzo. For many months, Italians and Austro-Hungarians fought at heights often over 10,000 feet without much gain for either side.

Below: HMS *Majestic* sinks off Gallipoli after being torpedoed by the German submarine U21. The Dardanelles operation, designed to take the pressure off Russia, is now seen to have been strategically justified but abysmally planned. However, unlike the troop losses, the sinking of several Allied battleships was not a result of muddle but an inevitable and expected price. *Majestic* was an elderly Pre-Dreadnought, as were the other sacrificed battleships; such losses were not critical although they had a depressing effect on naval morale. *Majestic* was U21's second victim, for two days earlier another Pre-Dreadnought, *Triumph*, had been sunk by the same craft.

The success of the German battlecruiser *Goeben* in evading the British in the Mediterranean and its entry into the Dardanelles was instrumental in bringing Turkey into the war on the side of the Central Powers. The Turks' task was now to close the Dardanelles to any supplies destined for Russia, a task they carried out successfully throughout the war. Winston Churchill, then First Lord of the Admiralty, successfully argued for mounting an attack to open the Dardanelles. The operation began with naval bombardments of the forts guarding the Straits. This was followed in April 1915 by the landing of Allied troops at Gallipoli. A total of 75,000 men reached the beaches. Opposing them were 80,000 Turks commanded by the German General Liman von Sanders. However, the Allies failed to take early opportunities to reach the commanding heights. Early in August they landed additional forces at Suvla Bay, but there, too, chances of success were wasted and the Turkish resistance was so ferocious that they dominated the heights overlooking the bay and contained three British and two French divisions on the beaches. Between December 1915 and January 1916 the Allies found themselves compelled to evacuate their forces and ship them back. The first great modern amphibious enterprise thus came to an end.

In 1914 Great Britain and the German Empire had the strongest battle fleets in the world. The British had 32 modern capital ships, most with the Home Fleet, soon renamed the Grand Fleet, while Germany had 17 modern vessels, 14 of an older type and four battlecruisers (plus *Goeben* in the Mediterranean). Taking into account all ships of the respective fleets, the ratio was five to two in favor of the navy of Great Britain.

The establishment of the long-distance blockade by the Royal Navy ultimately led to an attempt by the German Admiralty, after initial caution, to break it. Vice-Admiral Scheer, who took command of the German High Seas Fleet in January 1916, tried to bring about a decisive battle. The Battle of Jutland on 31 May 1916 was the only great sea battle fought in World War I. Although the Royal Navy under Admiral Jellicoe was almost twice the size of the German Navy, the battle ended in a tactical victory for the Germans. The British lost three battlecruisers, three armored cruisers and several destroyers, while the Germans lost one battlecruiser, one old battleship, four small cruisers and five torpedo boats. In terms of manpower, the British lost over 6,000, the Germans 2,500 men. In spite of its tactical success, it was not the desired strategic victory that would have achieved the lifting of the blockade.

In the Baltic the German Navy, on the whole, fulfilled its tasks, maintaining the transport of iron ore vital to Germany's war economy from Sweden to Germany and securing the flanks of the German forces advancing through the Baltic countries.

At the outbreak of war a number of German naval units operated overseas, such as the East Asia Squadron under Admiral von Spee. Spee managed to inflict a serious defeat on British naval units at Coronel, only to be blasted from the surface of the ocean by the Royal Navy at the Falkland Islands a few weeks later. A small number of individual raiders carried on cruiser warfare against British commerce, but slowly, one by one, they too disappeared from the high seas. Now the German Admiralty

placed its hopes on the U-Boats, one of which had sunk three British armored cruisers in a couple of hours one day in September 1914. On 2 November 1914 the British government had declared the entire North Sea a war zone, to which the Germans replied by opening unrestricted submarine warfare in February 1915. The U-Boat was considered by the old established naval powers to be a barbaric weapon, typical of the 'Hun.' But the German U-Boats could not afford to surface to warn passengers and crew, since most British merchantmen were soon armed and the U-Boats of that time were still so fragile that even a burst of machine-gun fire could destroy their diving tanks.

The sinking of the British liner *Lusitania* in 1915 with over one hundred Americans on board had caused a violent American protest. The Germans were alleged to have struck a medal to commemorate this event. Such a medal had indeed been struck – but in Great Britain for the purpose of propaganda. Finally, mainly as a result of pressure exerted by President Wilson, the Germans abandoned unrestricted submarine warfare in September 1915. But when the war escalated, when it became blatantly obvious that the United States supplied Great Britain and France with arms, raw materials and foodstuffs, the Germans resumed unrestricted submarine warfare in February 1917. The submarines available, however, were too few to achieve a decisive success. On the contrary, this policy caused the United

Left: A British howitzer bombards Turkish positions at Gallipoli. The
rocky, hilly terrain provided good protection for the defenders; even
British naval guns had little effect against the Turkish positions. Top right:
A German flamethrower in use on the Western Front.
Above: French soldiers in a casemate of the Douamont fortress, one of the
key strongpoints of the Verdun defenses which was captured by the
Germans, then recaptured by the French.

States to enter the war in April 1917. Still, the German submarine arm posed a major danger, sinking in total over 8
million tons of shipping.

In the meantime, the war on land continued, but in spite of
intensive artillery preparation, often lasting for days, once the
attackers went over the top they met the deadly hail of machine-
gun bullets. No weapon had been found to overcome the stalemate. Neither party could outflank the other; only a breakthrough could achieve that. In the face of this situation, the
Central Powers shifted their attention to the Eastern Theater of
war. In May 1915 German and Austro-Hungarian formations
opened an offensive in the Gorlice-Tarnowe area. Circumstances

favored the Central Powers; they could rely on an excellent rail
network. After a four-hour intensive artillery preparation, the
German Eleventh Army with four German and one Austro-
Hungarian Corps attacked across a front of little more than 20
miles. While the artillery continued its bombardment, Germans
and Austrians advanced close behind the artillery screen. The
Russians were utterly surprised and unable to throw in reserves.
The first major breakthrough during World War I had been
achieved. But even that was not decisive, for the Germans and
Austrians lacked the ability to exploit the operational freedom
which they had achieved. The Austro-German lines advanced
to the Bug and Dniestr, where, once again, they dug in.

Left: A German picture of the interior of the Douamont casemate. This fortress, mostly built in the 19th century, included a concrete stronghold about 200 yards long and containing numerous chambers and tunnels. There was accommodation for at least 500 defenders but, almost by oversight, there were only 60 elderly artillery reservists holding it when the Germans captured it in 1916. In October its recapture by the French was not so bloodless, but was an important step forward in the relief of Verdun, which was achieved by December; much of the German strength had been diverted to meet the Allies' Somme offensive. Below left: Another Verdun fortress, Vaux, whose defenders fought bravely against gas, flamethrowers and grenades and surrendered only when their water was exhausted. Above: French camouflage screens.

Gorlice-Tarnowe could not be compared to the battles of *matériel* raging on the Western Front. Early in 1916 the German High Command transferred its emphasis back to the West. There, from February 1916 until July of that year, General von Falkenhayn tried to cripple the French Army in the Battle of Verdun. In spite of initial German successes, French resistance was such that no victory could be gained. It was Grant's concept of the war of attrition; Falkenhayn hoped to bleed the French Army white. It was a completely abortive venture. Verdun, and for that matter most battles of World War I, reflected the inability of the generals and the politicians to find alternative solutions. The fact that these battles demonstrated heights of bravery and self-sacrifice by all the troops involved in them does not balance the failure at the military and political level.

While the Battle of Verdun still raged, the British launched their offensive at the Somme, starting with an artillery barrage that lasted seven days and nights. Then 20 British and 11 French divisions, supported by three divisions of cavalry, attacked a line held initially by only 11 German divisions on a 25-mile front. After the seven-day bombardment by 3000 guns the British did not expect any defenders to have survived. They managed in places to overrun the first trench, but the German defense, which by then was exceptionally strong, quickly threw in the reserves necessary to prevent any further penetration by the Allies. The traditional methods to which the armies of Europe had become accustomed and the technical limits of their weapons made it impossible to overcome lines of defense constructed in depth.

One weapon that provided an answer to this problem was the tank, developed by the British and first used in September 1916 on the Somme front. These tanks penetrated the German lines until they were put out of action at point-blank range by the German artillery. The new weapon helped restore mobility to warfare, but its significance in World War I must not be overestimated. At first it had a high psychological impact, but once the German Infantry had become used to the tanks, they also knew how to deal with them. Apart from that, the tanks of World War I still had too many technical shortcomings. Their range was under 20 miles and they could hardly be used for extensive raids. So the stalemate in the west remained unbroken.

The year of 1917 brought no change; the senseless slaughter continued. The Allies failed to achieve a breakthrough either in the west or on the Isonzo front. However, the Battle of Verdun had shaken the confidence of the German soldier in his leadership for the first time. Doubts began to increase, and in Germany the first voices were raised demanding an end to the bloodletting. For the French, however, Verdun for some time became the symbol of the invincibility of the French Army. But later, after the bloody failure of the Nivelle offensive in the spring of 1917, the French Army entered a period of uncertainty caused by the immense losses it had sustained and by news of the March revolution in Russia. Whole contingents of the army mutinied and court martials had to be used to restore discipline. General Pétain succeeded in overcoming the crisis and restoring confidence within the army. This crisis, which raged for a number of weeks, went unnoticed by the German leadership, but whether it could have been exploited to the benefit of the Central Powers is doubtful. In view of the overall situation at the fronts, they would have been unable to muster the reserves necessary for a vital push.

By the summer of 1917 it was clear to all that the Central Powers had not been adequately prepared for this kind of war, neither politically, militarily, nor economically. Time was working on the side of the Allies with their inexhaustible supplies of raw materials and their reserves of manpower, while the Central Powers could not so readily replace the men they had lost. Knowing this, the Allies could afford to reject any attempt at a negotiated peace.

Profound changes had taken place among the forces in the field. The belief that the infantry was the queen of battles had vanished. Defensive fire made any attack carried out without overwhelming artillery support a certain failure. Only the combined action of artillery and infantry could yield results. In defense, the artillery supported the infantry by holding down the enemy. Dugouts with various exits gave the infantry shelter and the chance to rest. The infantry needed the support of the engineers in building these positions, especially in terrain where it was difficult to establish them, such as in the Alps. The rifle line of 1914 had been transformed by 1917 into a battle zone crisscrossed with trenches, dugouts, pillboxes and bunkers. Taking the first trench in an attack was no longer decisive because reserves could be brought forward through the trench system leading far to the rear to expel the enemy from his position. Behind this network of trenches were the artillery positions, but the backbone of the entire defensive system was the system of machine-gun posts. The whole network was protected by vast barbed-wire entanglements. Such a system made it possible to survive the heaviest artillery bombardment, and every attack following it met with an energetic counterattack in which in many cases hand-to-hand fighting took place, largely with bayonets, spades and hand grenades, not over the top but within the trenches themselves. In short, the machine gun carried the main burden of the infantry fire.

The cavalry had been demoted to a minor role in the west. The last, and in terms of human lives, most costly major cavalry attack had been mounted in 1870. Cavalry was of limited use even in the plains of Russia and the Baltic countries, so it de-

Below: British battleships in action at the Battle of Jutland. The ships are of the improved Dreadnought type. The heavy tripod masts were designed to support the fire-control platforms even if one of the legs were shot away. In fact the British gunnery control system was inferior to that of the Germans, partly because an excellent British system had been rejected by the Admiralty in favor of one designed by an influential officer. Because the British lost more ships than the Germans, this battle was regarded as a defeat, although the flight of the German High Seas Fleet to its ports suggested that the defeat was only tactical, not strategic. Left: Two German submarines meet in the Mediterranean in spring 1917; by this time the U-boats were wide-ranging and a real threat to Britain's command of the sea. Right: Haig, British commander in France from 1915.

Left: A Russian howitzer crew in their firing position. Above left: The succession of battles fought in the Belgian mud around Ypres resulted in enormous casualties for very little movement. Artillery, used by attackers to disrupt the enemy's positions and by the defenders to shatter attacking formations, played a role even more massive than in previous battles. In this picture German soldiers pick their way between flooded shell craters. Above right: The first US troops disembark at St Nazaire in western France. To distribute troops and supplies the Americans operated their own trains over the French railroads. Above far right: Wounded are brought to a Russian field hospital. There were numerous volunteer nurses on the Russian front.

generated into mounted infantry, riding at great speed to the defensive line, dismounting and then doing duty like every infantry unit. Only in reconnaissance did it still play a role, less so in the west but more so in the East and the Balkans.

Among the Central Powers the artillery managed to play its role effectively on the Western front and at the Isonzo. What gave cause for serious alarm was the shortage of ammunition. The British and French adhered to the belief that they could achieve success by artillery bombardment lasting for several days, living by the rule that artillery conquers and infantry occupies. According to this rule, they calculated how much ammunition would have to be spent per square yard to destroy the enemy. The calculations looked good on paper, and there were ample stocks of ammunition, but in practice it was found time and again that many defenders had survived and sufficient machine guns were still intact to repel any attack and gain time to bring up reserves from the rear.

On the German side, artillery tactics changed. Colonel Bruchmüller, in charge of artillery at the German Army's Supreme Command, realized that the duration of artillery fire mattered less than its strength and intensity. He therefore abandoned the introductory ranging fire, beginning the concentrated artillery barrage suddenly and continuing it for several hours – a method that had proved its effectiveness in the east during 1917. Thus German artillery opened up with and maintained a high rate of fire, followed closely by the attacking infantry. This, of course, required an artillery observer to be with the advancing forces to guide and extend the range of fire. Mine throwers became more useful, as did light infantry guns.

The Western Allies based their hopes on the tank eliminating the machine-gun nests, but this required close cooperation between tanks and infantry. The Battle of Cambrai in November 1917 saw the dawning of a new age in warfare. At Cambrai, after a short artillery bombardment, hundreds of British tanks attacked and broke through the German defense system. Only when face-to-face with the artillery did they sustain serious

losses, and the lack of infantry reserves did not allow them to exploit the breakthrough. A few days later a German counter-attack regained most of the lost territory. The tank was useful only at the tactical level; as noted earlier, it was still technically deficient for extended operations.

Like all the armies of the Central Powers, the German Army lacked the means to build tanks in adequate numbers. They suffered from an endemic shortage of raw materials. Priorities had to be placed on the production of guns, aircraft, mine throwers and U-Boats. Experience showed these priorities to be correct. What the German Army did not do was develop an effective antitank weapon which could have supported the infantry in their forward positions.

Aircraft went through rapid development during World War I. In the beginning, the aircraft of the belligerent nations were mainly unarmed and used for observation, but technical progress made such immense strides that fighter planes with machine guns mounted to fire through the propeller arc could clear the skies of observer balloons, while tactical aircraft could intervene in the ground fighting and bombers could seriously impede the enemy's supplies by destroying roads and bridges. Essentially the task of the air forces was of a tactical nature. Strategic warfare from the air was introduced by German Zeppelin raids on London. War had become more total; even the civilian population was no longer safe. But the Zeppelins proved too cumbersome and too easy a target for the enemy. Their effect, and in this sense the effect of strategic bombing, was, for the time being, short-lived.

For the staffs of all the armies, the problem of supplying forces firmly entrenched was one more of organization than of tactics. The troops had to be provided at all times with the necessities of everyday life. Among the Central Powers, suffering heavily from the blockade after mid-1916, food supply priority was given to the army at the expense of the civilian population. This seemed appropriate enough, but when soldiers came home on leave to find their families starving it was not likely to improve their morale.

Hindenburg, as Chief of the General Staff, and his General Quartermaster Ludendorff had taken over from Falkenhayn in August 1916. Falkenhayn's reputation had been destroyed by the abortive Verdun venture. Generally the people of the Central Powers acclaimed the rise of Hindenburg and Ludendorff, the victors of Tannenberg, and expected them to win the

war for Germany. The Hindenburg program initiated a new policy domestically and economically. With one mighty effort it strove to mobilize all men able to carry arms and send them to the front while increasing the production of armaments. Beginning in the fall of 1916, German women entered the factories to make weapons and ammunition. There was no opposition from the trade unions who on the whole loyally supported the government. Some strikes took place, but the front-line soldier naturally showed little understanding of them.

In every country the civilian population was drawn into the vortex of war. Not only did armies fight one another – scientific research and development and industrial production vied with one another in the opposing countries. World War I was well on the way to becoming a total war. From 1916 on, Ludendorff, although nominally subordinate, was the real leader and in part practiced what he finally set down in his book *Total War*. Together with Hindenburg, he not only led the German Armies but also the country's policy. After Bethmann Hollweg's fall, subsequent chancellors received their directives from the Supreme Army Command. It amounted to a total reversal of Clausewitz's teachings. This was to reap a bitter harvest, because neither Hindenburg nor Ludendorff possessed the political training necessary to the roles they assumed. They were military specialists, nothing more. Among the Allies, Clemenceau and Lloyd George had come to the fore, with almost dictatorial powers, but they were clever enough to avoid getting mixed up in military matters. They could, however, deploy the political weapons available to them, particularly the propaganda weapon, which they wielded with a virtuosity hitherto unknown. Graphic accounts not only of mutilated Belgian children, but of the raped women and the crucified Tommy in the Belgian barn became the stock-in-trade for a gullible public ready to believe anything since the rise of sensationalist journalism at the end of the 19th century. Given the state of the public mood in the Allied countries, a negotiated peace became an impossibility. The peace resolution passed by the German Reichstag was taken by the Allies as a sign of the weakening of German moral fiber.

Allied war aims corresponded to their propaganda: Germany was to be destroyed forever as a military power. The Austro-Hungarian Empire was to be divided up, while France was to recover Alsace-Lorraine and control the left bank of the Rhine. German war aims fluctuated according to the fortunes of war,

Right: An aerial dogfight of the type that so caught popular imagination. Below: The first downing of a Zeppelin over England by a conventional fighter attack; this marked the end of the period in which Zeppelins could bomb England and return home with little risk. Below right, inset: Tsar Nicholas II, who lost his throne and his life as a consequence of the war.

but as far as Europe was concerned, the military aimed at creating large buffer zones to the west and east of Germany to make her secure from future attacks and envisioned a possible Central European Customs Federation under the aegis of the German Empire. At no time during the war, however, were these nonnegotiable aims that stood in the way of making peace. Indeed, the Central Powers' war aims had never been coordinated, and in fact the political cooperation between the two powers left much to be desired. This lack of coordinated planning carried over into the military sphere: there was no joint supreme command. The Allies, for their part, appointed General Foch as supreme commander of their forces in the west only after serious reverses in early 1918.

The consequences of the lack of joint military command between the Central Powers had shown up during the Brusilov Offensive of 1916. The Austro-Hungarian front ran from Czernowicz via Jastowiec and Sapanov along the Styr to Pinsk. The forces of the Hapsburg Empire were well dug in but the front was quiet and discipline was lax. Brusilov dug trenches stretching forward toward the Austrian positions until they were about 200 paces away. The Austrian shortage of artillery prevented them from seriously interrupting these preparations. Russian artillery preparation was to be short but concentrated. When the Brusilov Offensive began on 4 June 1916 the Austro-Hungarian forces were completely surprised, and within a week the Russians captured an area 50 miles wide and 30 miles deep. By 7 July the Russians had reached the Hungarian frontier in the Carpathians. Only with the greatest difficulty could the Russian offensive be halted, and the Austrians had lost 475,000 men – among them over 226,000 prisoners. It encouraged Rumania foolishly to enter the war on the side of the Allies. The Austro-German campaign in Rumania which ensued was the only one of World War I which was characterized by mobility. Attacks, outflanking movements and pocket battles followed rapidly upon one another. By the end of the campaign the 23 Rumanian divisions had been reduced to six. A campaign such as this was only possible in a relatively confined geographic area, the superior leadership and better-trained forces of the Central Powers quite apart.

By 1917 war weariness was apparent in all the belligerent countries. The French mutinies have already been mentioned. In Great Britain, voices rose demanding an end to the slaughter, but worst was the crisis in Russia where the war weariness culminated in the Revolution of March 1917. Contrary to the expectations of the people, the Russian Provisional Government did not entertain the idea of making a separate peace with Germany. Instead it hoped to fight more efficiently than before

on the side of the Allies. The grievances about the war had first been directed against the Czarist regime, but during the course of the year they turned against the Provisional Government and thus produced the October Revolution and the victory of the Bolsheviks under Lenin. Backed by the organizer of the Red Army, Leon Trotsky, Lenin decided to end the war, cost what it might. They were sure that the revolution would spread to central and western Europe and secured their peace by the Treaty of Brest-Litovsk.

In the words of George F Kennan, the American diplomat and historian:

'The Brest-Litovsk Treaty has usually been regarded as an extremely onerous settlement – a prize example, in fact, of the ruthless brutality of the German mailed fist. I think this assertion deserves some modifications. In comparison with the settlements the western allies themselves imposed, on the basis of unconditional surrender, after two world wars, the Brest-Litovsk Treaty does not strike me as inordinately severe. No reparations were originally demanded in the treaty itself. The territories of which the Bolsheviks were deprived were ones the peoples of which had no desire for Russian rule, least of all Russian Communist rule. The Bolsheviks themselves had never at any time had authority over these territories. It was a hope rather than a reality of which they were deprived by the terms of the treaty. The settlement accepted by the Allies at the end of the Russian Civil War – the arrangement, that is, that prevailed from 1920 to 1939 – was considerably less favorable to Russia, territorially, in the Baltic-Polish region than that which the Germans imposed on Russia in 1918.'

While the war in the west was still stalemated during 1917, fluctuating in terms of territory gained or lost by a few miles either way, in Italy, Austro-Hungarian and German forces went over to the offensive in the Twelfth Isonzo Battle, also known as the Battle of Caparetto. Seven German and five Austro-Hungarian divisions commanded by General von Bülow attacked in the last days of October 1917, broke out from the Tolmino area southwesterly and took the Italians on the Isonzo from the flank and the rear. It made the position of the Second and Third Italian Armies untenable. Circumventing the Monte-Nero massif, the forces of the Central Powers moved toward Saga, then Stolrücken and the valley of the Natisone. The Italian withdrawal quickly turned into a rout which did not stop even at the River Tagliamento. Only at the Piave River, which was deep, did the Italians stop, and there with the aid of British, French and their own reserves, they managed to establish a defensive line. Numerical weakness now forced the Central Powers to abandon any out-flanking movement, but the success was still considerable. The Italians had lost all the territorial gains of the last two years, as well as 40,000 dead,

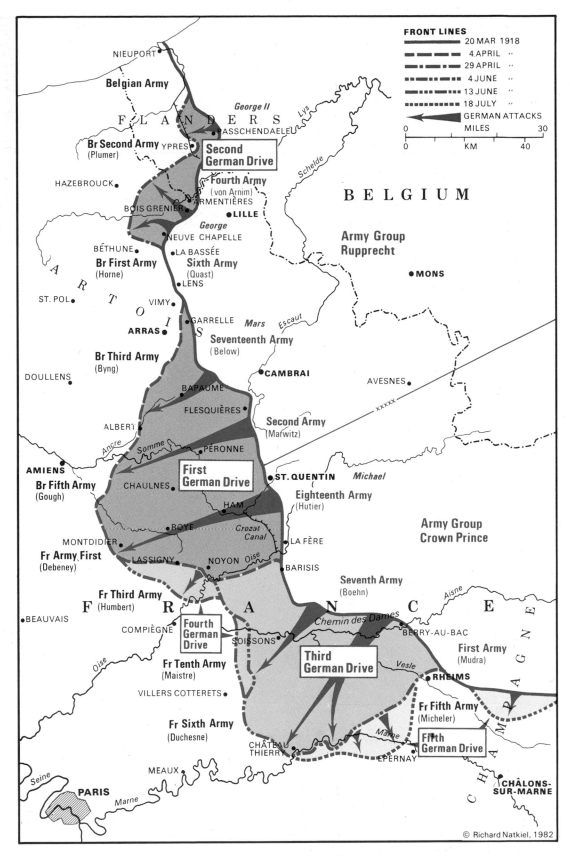

Above left: German infantry
assembled in their trenches,
presumably waiting for the signal
to begin an attack, or to proceed to
the main trenches. The depth of
this trench and the absence of firing
positions suggests that it is a
communications trench, used for
providing a covered approach to
the main trenches, or sometimes to
assemble men for an action. Above:
The German offensive of spring
1918; British prisoners of war under
German escort pass eastwards
through a French town. The
German drive, Ludendorff's last
throw, was initially directed against
the British-held sector of the
Western Front. Thanks partly to
shorter but very intensive
preliminary bombardment, and
partly to the undermanned and
unrepaired situation of the British
line, the German offensive gained
considerable ground in the first
days. As the situation worsened
Haig called for French
reinforcements, but the latter
were small. The appointment of
Foch as supreme commander then
brought better coordination.
Right: A map of this campaign.

265,000 prisoners, 3000 guns and much other war materiel.

The method of attack as originally devised by Colonel Bruchmüller, which had proven its value in the east and in Italy, was
to be applied by Hindenburg and Ludendorff in the offensives of
March–July 1918. In all cases a breakthrough was achieved, but
none of them could be exploited decisively. Fighting on foot,
the army could not sustain the impetus of the original attack.
The German Army in the west was short of men and had no
genuinely motorized infantry, which alone would have given
the German forces operational liberty. Initially, the German
offensives caused trouble. Paris was in danger once again, but it
did not affect Foch's belief in ultimate victory. Since 1917 fresh

American troops had been arriving in France, first divided up
over the various Allied contingents and ultimately formed into
an American Expeditionary Force under the command of
General Pershing. The production of tanks, aircraft, guns and
trucks outdistanced anything the Central Powers could produce.

In July 1918, under General Foch, the Allies moved into the
counteroffensive which culminated in the 'Black Day,' 8
August 1918, for the German Army. The tide had finally turned.
The German Army withdrew beyond the Siegfried Line and
by 14 August 1918 the German military leaders had to admit to
themselves that the continuation of war to German victory was
an impossibility.

Above left: A North Atlantic convoy, consisting mainly of American vessels. The convoy system was to be the best defense against the German U-boat campaign. Although in itself it did not guarantee an increase in the number of submarines sunk, it made it harder for the U-boat to find worthwhile and attainable targets; in other words, it reduced the monthly tonnage of Allied shipping sunk by submarine action. Despite the dangerously high losses being incurred by Britain, the Admiralty was for long reluctant to introduce convoys; although the role of the prime minister, Lloyd George, has been exaggerated, it was his pressure which caused the admirals to change their minds. The ships in this picture carry 'dazzle paint' an effective device for breaking up the form of a ship, as viewed from a submarine. Left: A painting of the Battle of Soissons, an engagement in the third German drive of 1918. French tanks were important in turning back the Germans here; tank support can be seen in the background. Above: An American machine gun post in France.

In September 1918, when the Central Powers' ally, Bulgaria, collapsed and asked for an immediate peace, Austria-Hungary was directly threatened and Ludendorff demanded an immediate armistice from the German politicians on the basis of Wilson's Fourteen Points, which the American President had proclaimed the previous spring. Thus the primacy of politics was restored. Upon the orders of the German High Command, full parliamentarization was introduced in Germany and the three-class franchise in Prussia abolished. However, when the German Navy planned one last sortie against the British at the risk of its own utter annihilation, the crews of the German High Seas Fleet mutinied. The torch of revolution had been lit and spread rapidly throughout Germany and Austria. On 9 November revolution broke out in Berlin, and on 11 November the Germans signed the armistice at Compiègne. World War I had ended; the Kaiser and all the German monarchs and princes had abdicated. But the blockade of Germany was not lifted and the peace that followed laid the groundwork of yet another war.

Strategically, World War I had demonstrated that continental powers can be contained by powers enjoying naval supremacy. The Central Powers had become a fortress under siege, militarily and economically inferior to the Allied powers. This was underlined once the United States had joined the war. But even while still neutral, it could supply the Allies with all the essentials. Allied naval supremacy ensured that the Central Powers would be cut off from their traditional sources of raw materials and foodstuffs. The unrestricted German submarine warfare was waged with too few resources and, above all, came too late. For the Allies, it was only a question of starving out the fortress of the Central Powers.

It has been argued that before the United States entered the war, the Central Powers enjoyed the advantage of operating from interior lines. This is misleading. The British Empire and the French Colonial Empire could tap resources closed to the Central Powers; whatever was lacking was already being provided by the United States between 1914 and 1917. Even before the United States entered the war, the Central Powers did not have economic self-sufficiency, the necessary condition for successful conduct of a war on interior lines. At a different level, it was a serious disadvantage that the Central Powers did not possess a joint political and military policy or command.

At the operational level it was shown that modern infantry weapons were so devastating that a breakthrough was virtually impossible or involved losses no army could afford. If an attack succeeded, the farther the distance between the attacker and his point of departure, the slower his movement, so his effectiveness was reduced. Mobility was what was required, and it did not yet exist. What emerged for all to see clearly was the primacy of defense, although this had already been foreshadowed in the 'Forgotten Wars.' The defender was closer to his supply bases, and as long as he still had reserves of manpower, foodstuffs, arms and ammunition, he could bring the offensive to a halt. Even in such an area as France, it had become impossible to carry out large encirclements because of the lack of mobility. No attacking force could afford to move more than about 80 miles from its rail heads. Only the Twelfth Isonzo Battle and the Battle of Cambrai pointed toward new forms of attack, but both fell short of their aims due to lack of the reserves that could have been thrown into battle by means of motorized transport.

Some of the lessons that had been learned were expressed in the armistice conditions and the political demands of peace treaties. Naval supremacy had to be ensured. Therefore, the disposition of the German High Seas Fleet, interned in Scapa Flow, was a potential difficulty solved only when the German crews scuttled their ships. More important was the prohibition denying submarines to Germany. The armies of the defeated powers were reduced to a minimum size which restricted their role virtually to that of a police force. Furthermore, no reserves of any size could be built up. The Allies gave their support wholly to the successor states of the Hapsburg Empire, thus ensuring the Balkanization of Eastern Central Europe and the disruption of what had once been a viable unified economy. No doubt these demands were justified from the point of view of military expediency, but politically they were unwise, as the history of the next two decades was to demonstrate.

The lessons of World War I entered the manuals of the post-war armies. Opinion was unanimous on the point that the infantry alone would no longer decide the outcome of a war. Attacks *en masse* were discarded. Instead, attacks were to be carried out by units widely dispersed. The firepower of infantry weapons forced the soldiers to make the most of the ground they were covering, and they had to dig in. Infantry weapons were developed with a power to penetrate steel.

There was a great difference of opinion about how to deploy tanks and other armored vehicles. Both the French and British General Staffs adhered to the belief that the tank was primarily an infantry support weapon. Their thinking was still dominated by extensive field fortifications, trench systems and barbed wire. Only three people in Great Britain realized the full potential of armor, and they were Major General J F C Fuller, Captain B H Liddell Hart and General Sir Percy Hobart. General de Gaulle is usually added to this list. While he was certainly a 'tank enthusiast' in the 30s, ideas about independently operating armor are fully developed in his works only in their first English translation published in 1943. Fuller, Liddell Hart and Hobart recognized the true dimensions of the armored warfare of the future, but they were not taken seriously by their compatriots. Fuller dismissed the value of the horse in modern warfare and thus violated one of the sacred cows of the traditional British officer corps. In 1927, however, his pressure brought the intro-

Top: A US rail-mounted gun in action against German positions. This is a 14-inch piece, of naval origin, with an effective range of about 20 miles. Above: The German retreat of November 1918; a scene at a town on the Dutch-Belgian frontier. The variety of transport in use can be noted; the horse is still dominant and no motor vehicles are in sight, although good use is being made of steam tractors, pulling road-trains. Top right: American troops are welcomed in the Ardennes, relieved after four years of German occupation. Above right: Australian infantry in trenches near Bois de Crépy at the beginning of the 1918 Allied offensive.

duction of a mechanized brigade on a trial basis. In point of fact, it was an infantry brigade equipped with a few tanks. Fuller wanted to resign.

However, his vision was not without its faults. According to him, the time for mass conscript armies was past. The future, according to Fuller, would be determined by small, excellently equipped mechanized armies supported by a strong air force, which would push deep into the enemy's territory with lightning speed. Armor would replace infantry. Specialized tanks would have to take over the various tasks of the infantry, artillery and cavalry.

Liddell Hart was more correct in his assessment. He developed the theory of the 'Strategy of the Indirect Approach.' The attack was to be carried out at the enemy's weakest point and where least expected. Simultaneous attacks elsewhere would divert the enemy's attention from the point of impact of the main attack. Liddell Hart had learned the lessons of the German stormtroops. These attacks were then to be followed by armored formations whose function was to penetrate in depth, cut the enemy's supply routes, encircle him and annihilate his forces. The future land army should consist of mechanized infantry, armor and a tactical air force.

Far left: US infantrymen stroll into a captured settlement in their sector of the Western Front. Although inexperience led to many unnecessary American casualties, the arrival of US forces tipped the balance against the Germans, whose last throw, the offensive of spring 1918, was designed to grasp victory before the Americans were ready in full strength. Left: General John J. Pershing, commander in chief of the American Expeditionary Force. Pershing was a general of extensive active service. After graduating from West Point, he served against Spain in Cuba and the Philippines, became a brigadier general in 1906, and 10 years later commanded the US force which invaded Mexico in search of anti-American activists. As US commander in France, he opposed the 1918 Armistice because, having a brand-new army, he felt confident that the Germans could be forced to a complete surrender. Below: Allied infantry in pursuit. Right: US Marines capture a machine gun.

But the role of the air force was conceived differently by the Italian General Douhet, another important theorist, who advocated the strategic role of air forces whose task it would be, through intensive bombardment of the enemy's hinterland, to devastate his cities and thus demoralize him with much the same effect achieved by the British blockade of the Central Powers. At the outbreak of World War II, Great Britain was well on its way to creating a strategic air force – the Wellington bomber, introduced in the RAF in 1938, had a range that extended from the British east coast to Munich and back, as compared to the German Heinkel 111 which could not even cover the whole of Great Britain from its bases in France, Belgium and Holland.

Most of the European states maintained conscription as the basis for their recruitment. Only Great Britain had abandoned it at the end of World War I and returned to the concept of the small professional army. Conscription was only revived in Britain in 1939. Of course Germany's army was kept at 100,000 men until 1935, but under General von Seeckt as chief of the *Heeresleitung* the first steps were being taken to transform it into a cadre army readily expandable if and when the time came. Limited cooperation with the Red Army allowed the Reichswehr to train panzer drivers and aircraft pilots, while cooperation with Sweden and Spain ensured a limited opportunity for training submarine crews.

In the 1920s Europe experienced a serious erosion of the democratic process. Of the newly established democracies that existed when the Versailles Treaty came into force in 1920, all but one had disappeared 10 years later. All that remained was the multi-national state of Czechoslovakia, a democracy characterized by the Czech historian Boris Czelovsky as a democracy in which a lot of talking was done, but in which the Czechs ensured that they would always have the last word.

Previous pages: German refugees move west to escape the advancing Russians in 1945. Right: A German *Stuka* dive-bomber. Dive-bombing was less inaccurate than conventional bombing, and the *Stuka* destroyed many targets, including several British warships. Top: A German tank crew in France. The padded berets were for protection against concussion when moving over rough ground; other tank corps adopted similar measures. Below: German infantry takes a rest under cover during the 1940 campaign in France. Below right: A German Mark IV tank in France in 1940. Tanks like this, although of recent construction, were soon to become obsolete, being superseded by new designs with, among other improvements, longer guns.

The five years following the coming to power of Adolf Hitler on 30 January 1933 saw a considerable change in the map of Europe. Why should the Western powers have acquiesced to Germany's departure from the League of Nations at the end of 1933, to renunciation of the military clauses of the Versailles Treaty in 1935, the reoccupation of the demilitarized Rhineland zone of Germany in 1936, the *Anschluss* of Austria and the annexation of the Sudetenland in 1938? Any answer is bound to be complex. For brevity's sake, we can quote the British historian, the late Professor E H Carr:

'The mass of political opinion in Great Britain and Germany (and in most other countries) agreed for many years that a criterion of justice and injustice could properly be applied to the Versailles Treaty; and there was a surprisingly considerable, though far from complete, consensus of opinion about the parts of it which were just and unjust respectively. Unfortunately, Germany was almost wholly deficient for fifteen years after the war in that power which is a necessary motive force in political change; and this deficiency prevented effect being given, except on a minor scale, to the widespread consensus of opinion that parts of the Versailles Treaty ought to be modified. By the time Germany regained her power, she had become – not without reason – almost wholly disillusioned about the role of morality in international politics. There was not, even as late as 1936, any reasonable prospect of obtaining major modifications of the Versailles Treaty by peaceful negotiation unsupported by the ultimatum or the *fait accompli*. Even though she continued to base her claims on grounds of justice, Germany expressed them more and more in terms of naked force; and this reacted on the opinion of the *status quo* countries, which became more and more inclined to forget earlier admissions of the injustices of the Versailles Treaty and to consider the issue as exclusively one of power. There is no doubt that the easy acquiescence of the *status quo* powers in such actions as the denunciations of the military clauses, the reoccupation of the Rhineland or the annexation of Austria was due, not wholly to the fact that it was the line of least resistance, but in part also to a consensus of opinion that these changes were in themselves reasonable and just. Yet they were greeted in each case by official censures and remonstrances which inevitably created the impression that the remonstrating powers acquiesced merely because they were unable or unwilling to make the effort to resist. In March 1939, the British Prime Minister Neville Chamberlain admitted that in all the modifications of the Treaty down to and including the Munich Agreement there was "something to be said for the necessity of a change in the existing situation." If, in 1935 and 1936, this "something" had been clearly and decisively said, to the exclusion of scoldings and protests, by the official spokesmen of the *status quo* powers, it might not yet have been too late to bring further changes within the framework of peaceful negotiation. The tragedy by which successive removals of long-recognized injustices of the Versailles Treaty became a cause not of reconciliation, but of further estrangement, between Germany and the Versailles Powers, and destroyed instead of increasing the limited stock of common feeling which had formerly existed, is one for which the sole responsibility cannot be laid at Germany's door.

'The negotiations which led up to the Munich Agreement of 29 September 1938 were the nearest approach in recent years to the settlement of a major international issue by a procedure of peaceful change. The element of power was present. The element of morality was also present in the form of the common recognition by the Powers, who effectively decided the issue, of a criterion applicable to the dispute: the principle of national self-determination. The injustice of the incorporation into Czechoslovakia of three-and-one-quarter million protesting Germans had been attacked in the past by many British critics, including the Labour Party and Mr Lloyd George. Nor had the promises made by M. Benes [the Czech leader] at the Peace Conference regarding their treatment been fully carried out. The change in itself was one which corresponded both to a change in the European equilibrium of forces and to accepted canons of international morality.'

This, in a nutshell, sums up the background and the motives of the policy of appeasement toward Hitler and his regime pursued by the Western Powers. Obviously, Hitler could not pursue an active foreign policy without expanding his army. Officially it began in 1935, but with considerable difficulty, since there were serious shortages of officers and NCOs to command the new forces. Reserves were initially in short supply and consisted mainly of soldiers who had served in World War I. Equally difficult was rearmament, which was hampered by a shortage of raw materials that were obtainable on the international market but had to be paid for in gold, of which Germany was in very short supply. Rearmament was carried out to the accompaniment of a huge wave of propaganda. German economic recovery was not achieved by rearmament but by a policy of guns *and* butter, and Hitler's public statements on German rearmament were based largely on bluff and inflated figures. Nor was it in any way a coordinated policy of rearmament. The three branches of the services, Army, Navy and Air Force, competed with one another for the available raw materials. Each service developed armament plans which, if combined in 1939, would have required the establishment of fuel reserves in excess of the world's total oil production at that time.

Rearmament could not be carried out in depth. The only advantages possessed by the German armed forces were many excellently trained regular officers and NCOs and a concept of warfare which General Guderian had borrowed almost exclusively from Fuller and Liddell Hart. But Guderian had a very difficult stand *vis-à-vis* his Commander in Chief, General von Fritsch, who hated anything to do with engines and motors. Hitler, however, fully realized the potential of this new system of warfare and backed Guderian.

The rebuilding of the Luftwaffe concentrated on fighters and tactical aircraft. Until 1936, General Wever had advocated a strategic air force with four-engine strategic bombers – a policy that was ignored after he died in that year. It was difficult enough to provide the existing force with adequate fuel, let alone four-engine bombers.

The navy, like the other services with their extravagant plans, had not by 1939 even achieved the levels granted to her by the Versailles Treaty, much less built up the U-Boat force conceded by the Anglo-German Naval Treaty of 1935. At the outbreak of war only 25 U-Boats fit for Atlantic service were operational, as compared to the 75 which Germany was allowed to build under the Anglo-German agreement.

If one compares all the forces on the eve of war in 1939, there were a total of 2.9 million German soldiers confronting 4.07 million Polish, French and British forces. But the German troops were better trained for the type of war that would ensue. This ensured their superiority for the first two years of the war. In the west, German armor and that of the Western Allies was about evenly balanced in numbers, though German tanks had inferior guns and armor compared with some of their French and British counterparts. The margin in favor of the Allies was frittered away by deploying armor as infantry support weapons instead of freely and independently operating formations.

On the German side, the command structure was a source of serious weakness, with Hitler as Supreme Commander in Chief and under him the *Oberkommando der Wehrmacht* (OKW), the *Oberkommando des Heeres* (OKH), the *Oberkommando der Luftwaffe* (OKL) and the *Oberkommando der Marine* (OKM). The deficiencies of this setup were not realized until 1941, but until that time the supreme commands of Germany's opponents were not much better.

Concerning raw materials, Germany was as badly off as during World War I; only the Russo-German Non-Aggression Pact of 23 August 1939 alleviated the situation. Financial resources were equally inadequate. In 1939–40 Germany spent 63.5 thousand million marks while its official receipts amounted to only 61 thousand million marks. Germany's only chance was to conduct a short and limited war.

The campaign in Poland was just that. Poland had mobilized and concentrated its major forces in an offensive forward position in which they became an easy victim of the German attacking forces – 53 divisions in all, including all six panzer divisions. Only 30 low-grade divisions protected Germany's western frontier. Within the first three days of the campaign, from 1 to 3 September 1939, the Luftwaffe destroyed the Polish Air Force virtually on the ground. The German Army was divided into Army Groups North and South, each supported by panzer corps employed as operationally independent units. The panzers used were primarily the Mark I armed with two machine guns and the Mark II with a 20mm gun. The Mark III

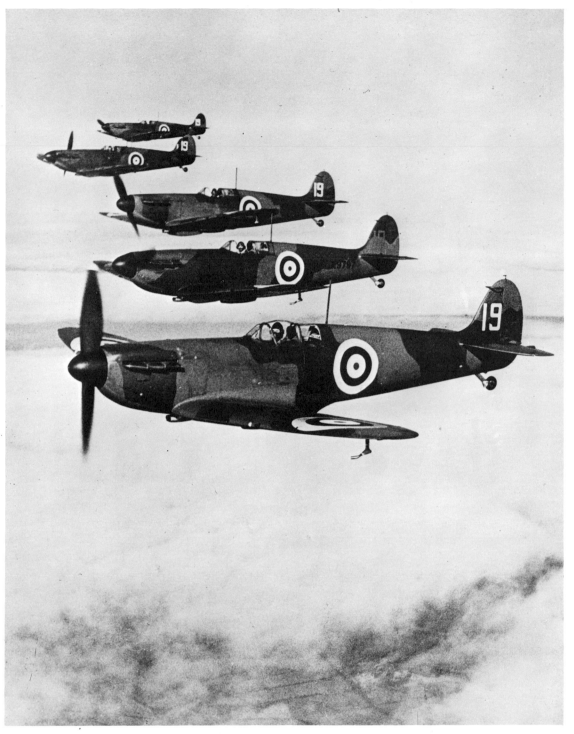

Above: After Dunkirk; the British Army's motor transport abandoned on the dunes. By no means all of the vehicles have been wrecked by their former users; ex-British Army motor trucks were to play a notable role in Germany's invasion of the Soviet Union a year later. Left: General de Gaulle, leader of the Free French, at work in Algiers. It was here that he gained recognition for his Liberation Committee by the Allies, enabling it to become the French Provisional Government. Right: A flight of five Spitfires. These aircraft won British supremacy in the Battle of Britain and, in successive improved versions, continued to serve the Royal Air Force in a first-line capacity throughout the war.

and Mark IV, with greater speed and heavier guns, were not yet available in large numbers. But coming from the south and the north, they cut the Polish forces into ribbons. When on 17 September 1939 Russia invaded the eastern part of Poland, conceded to her in the Russo-German Friendship Treaty, the war in Poland was at an end for all practical purposes. Only isolated pockets of the Polish Army still offered resistance. Warsaw also held out and was defended by the die hard Polish military leadership. German aircraft circled the city several times, dropping leaflets demanding surrender or the evacuation of the civilian population. No heed was paid to these warnings, and Warsaw was subjected to an intensive aerial bombardment, after which it finally surrendered.

Germany acquired the former territory of East Prussia and the Province of Posen, Russia the territories east of the Curzon Line. The rest of Poland was organized as the General Government which Hitler held on to until August 1940 as a bargaining tool in negotiations out of which a Polish satellite state could emerge. He abandoned this plan only in August 1940. Having

ended the campaign, he thought of making peace, but Allied hopes still rested on their knowledge of a military and civilian resistance movement inside Germany, with which they had been regularly in touch since 1937 and which assured the Allies that it would replace Hitler. However, nothing came of this fond hope. With no peace in sight, Hitler decided to attack in the west but the weather conditions in October and November 1939 proved unsuitable for such an undertaking.

Germany's supplies of foodstuffs and raw materials were now adequate; the Russians provided what the British Navy block-aded. This brought Germany into an ever-increasing depen-dence on Russia, which, as the following year would show, was potentially dangerous. Apart from Russian supplies, Germany's oil came mostly from Rumania and its iron ore from Sweden. After the outbreak of the Russo-Finnish War on 30 November 1939, the Allies believed that they would be able to use this conflict as a pretext to aid the Finns with the actual objective of cutting Germany off from its iron ore supplies from Sweden and its nickel supplies from Petsamo.

As signs of Allied intervention in Scandinavia increased, Hitler decided upon a preemptive strike there with the codename *Weserübung*. On 9 April 1940 the operation was launched, involving almost all the existing units of the German Navy. Denmark was occupied almost peacefully. There had, in fact, been previous feelers between the two governments. It was hoped that Norway could be occupied in much the same way. While Oslo was occupied peacefully, German bands already playing in Oslo's public squares on the first day, in the north Norwegian resistance began to build. In the Narvik region it was supported by British and French forces. Here the situation first became critical for the German forces, and only German supremacy in the air ensured that the mountain forces could hold on until events in France compelled the British and French to withdraw from Norway.

On the Western Front, on the eve of 10 May 1940, 137 German divisions confronted a roughly similar number of Allied divisions. In addition there were now 10 German panzer divisions, though the Allies had 3124 tanks as against 2580 for the Germans. However, as already stated, the Allied tanks were mainly deployed as infantry support weapons. In contrast, the German panzer formations could operate independently, break through in depth and encircle the Allied forces. As far as the air forces were concerned, 2979 planes of the Luftwaffe confronted 2513 Allied planes, but most of the French Air Force was hopelessly outdated. Only the RAF had aircraft on a par with those of the Germans. But such Allied air power as existed was also frittered away piecemeal, while the Luftwaffe was organized into *Luftflotten*, air fleets, to support the various sectors of the German advance.

When the initial planning for the campaign in the west had begun, all the OKH could offer to Hitler was a revamped version of the Schlieffen Plan in which the 'right hook' was to hit Holland as well as Belgium. Colonel (later Field Marshal) von

Manstein, chief of staff at one of the German army groups, offered an alternative solution in line with the strategy of the indirect approach – to place the main weight of the attack where the Allies expected it least. He advocated attacking through the Ardennes with panzer formations, pushing toward Sedan, crossing the Meuse and then moving on to the English Channel. This movement would cut off any British and French troops who advanced to help the Dutch and Belgians. These forces would also be confronted by the German forces advancing from their bases on the lower Rhine. Manstein's plan was at first dismissed by the General Staff, but Hitler's adjutant, Colonel Schmundt, drew the Führer's attention to it. Hitler convened a staff meeting to which Manstein was invited, and he was given the opportunity to state his case. Hitler was immediately convinced by Manstein's plan and adopted it.

In the plan, Army Group C was to hold the upper Rhine opposite the Maginot Line, while it was Army Group A's task to cut through the Ardennes with five panzer and three motorized divisions, push into the rear of the Allied forces to the north of them and continue to Abbeville. Army Group B was to invade Belgium and Holland, closing the pincers behind the Allies with Army Group A.

Thus the campaign in the west began in the early hours of 10 May 1940. The Dutch were the first to surrender, followed by Belgium by the end of May, while the British Expeditionary Force was finally contained in the Dunkirk area. It is not the place to enter into the controversy about Hitler's decision not to have his armored forces attack and annihilate the British. No doubt the German armor required rest and refitting after the race to the coast, especially as the German Army expected strong resistance from the remaining French forces at the Somme. In spite of intensive bombardment by the Luftwaffe, the bulk of the BEF and a French contingent managed to escape across the Channel, minus their heavy equipment.

Below: A German anti-tank gun in action. Until the development of specialized armor-piercing rockets, the gun was often the main defense against tanks, and was not always effective against thick armor. Far left: Soviet tanks bogged down in marshland and captured by the Germans. Huge expanses of western Russia are marshland, and in two wars have constituted a natural defense; but, as this picture shows, they could embarrass the Russians, too. Left inset: German paratroops (recognizable by their special helmets, with unbroken rim) take it easy in 1941. These airborne troops played a distinguished, probably decisive, role in the capture of Crete, the last foothold of the British troops who had been sent to help Greece.

The Italians, afraid of getting no share in the spoils of victory, entered the war at this point, but their advance was soon halted by the French. Now the time had come for the Germans to turn south, break through the Weygand Line and cut across France to the Spanish frontier in the south; to take Paris and to take the Maginot Line from the rear. The attack on the Maginot Line was coordinated with Army Group C which attacked across the Upper Rhine. France was defeated.

On 25 June 1940, France under Marshal Pétain accepted the German armistice conditions. The Germans occupied all of northern France, including Paris, and all coastal areas from Holland to the Spanish border. Alsace-Lorraine was occupied and a closed frontier introduced from the Atlantic to the Swiss border. Beyond that was the unoccupied part of France where Marshal Pétain established his government in the spa town of Vichy. The Germans had won another campaign, but not the war. From May until August 1940 Hitler remained optimistic, expecting a British peace offer at any time. He demobilized more than 10 divisions and ordered a halt to all weapon development that could not be completed by the end of 1940. In Germany the public mood was most enthusiastic, though at the back of many minds was the question of how the war should now continue.

Hitler introduced orders for the invasion of Great Britain, but unlike his previous military planning, he was rather half-hearted about this enterprise. Some of his entourage claimed that, in fact, he was totally uninterested in it. The precondition for any landing was the establishment of German dominance of the British air space. Göring promised that, but within two months it became apparent that the strength of the Luftwaffe was not up to this task. The bomber formations, so valuable as tactical weapons, showed their shortcomings when used in a strategic role. German losses could not be replaced by increased aircraft production, for in Germany on the whole a peacetime economy still prevailed. Women were not drafted into armaments factories, as in Great Britain, and the entire industry worked on the basis of a single shift per day. This raises an important question. Why did Hitler fail, until it was too late, to put the German economy on a total war footing, or for that matter, why did he not put the whole of Germany's industrial effort behind rearmament before 1939. The answer lies in the trauma of 1918 when the German domestic front collapsed, thus allowing the allies a free hand in formulating the Versailles Peace Treaty. Throughout 1919 the German government was concerned with internal disorders and would have been unable to fight even a purely defensive war until a more acceptable peace was forthcoming. That trauma lies very much at the core of Hitler's domestic policy in peace and war time. On the one hand were the concentration camps, initially established for the internment of active political dissidents, while on the other hand there was a consumer boom, maintained to a great degree also when war broke out. Hitler wanted to ensure the best possible conditions at home in order to prevent any internal upheaval. Hence productive capacities were not fully utilized. Albert Speer, who became Minister of Armaments in 1942, reversed this policy and by 1944, with no greater productive capacity than existed in 1941, German arms output was quadrupled. By that time it was too late. Allied advances on the ground and effects of the strategic bombing campaign meant that there was little fuel to power the tanks and aircraft which were now available. Hitler also gave orders early in the war that the development of new weapons was to be stopped. This also had serious consequences. What was to be the first operational jet fighter of World War II was already on the drawing board and its first engines were being tested. Willy Messerschmitt carried

Above: A British 6-pounder antitank gun comes under artillery fire in the Desert in 1942. The open spaces and clear air of North Africa added to the potential of both tanks and antitank weapons. The Germans were particularly skilled in drawing the British armored forces into attacking prepared antitank positions. The British were handicapped at first by being equipped with the rather ineffective 2-pounder gun but the 6-pounder and the later 17-pounder were far better. Right: Map of the initial stages of the German advance into the Soviet Union showing the three main axes of advance.

on the development on a small scale because he was under-financed. Tank development was cut back, which was a serious error, as shown by the events of 1941.

The invasion of Norway had been the German Navy's greatest hour, but the losses sustained, particularly to destroyers, were never fully made up during the war. Two battleships, the *Bismarck* and the *Tirpitz*, were not yet completed. The existing battlecruisers *Scharnhorst* and *Gneisenau* were prone to mechanical failures. So the main weight of the war at sea rested on the German U-Boats, which during 1940 were dogged by faulty torpedoes, insufficient numbers and the low output of U-Boat manufacturing shipyards.

Two problems preoccupied Hitler throughout 1940 – how either to end the war with Great Britain or bring her to her knees. Obviously, Britain was not willing to make peace, and the attempt to bring her to her knees by air had led to defeat in the Battle of Britain. The other problem arose out of the situation in the east where in June Russia had annexed Estonia, Latvia and Lithuania. Admittedly, these countries had been included in Russia's sphere of interest in the Russo-German Nonaggression Pact, but their occupation and annexation was another matter, especially since the uneasy peace prevailing between the Soviet Union and Finland since March 1940 seemed fragile and likely to rupture at any time.

In the face of this development, it was not Hitler but the Chief of the Army General Staff, General Halder, who issued the first orders to make a preliminary study for the invasion of Russia. Hitler himself, for the time being, kept his options open. Unable to cripple Great Britain, he set about trying to forge a continental league against her. His attempts to draw Spain and Vichy France into it failed, because for them the precondition of joining such a league would have been the prior defeat of Great Britain. As far as Russia was concerned, a new political settlement was the precondition.

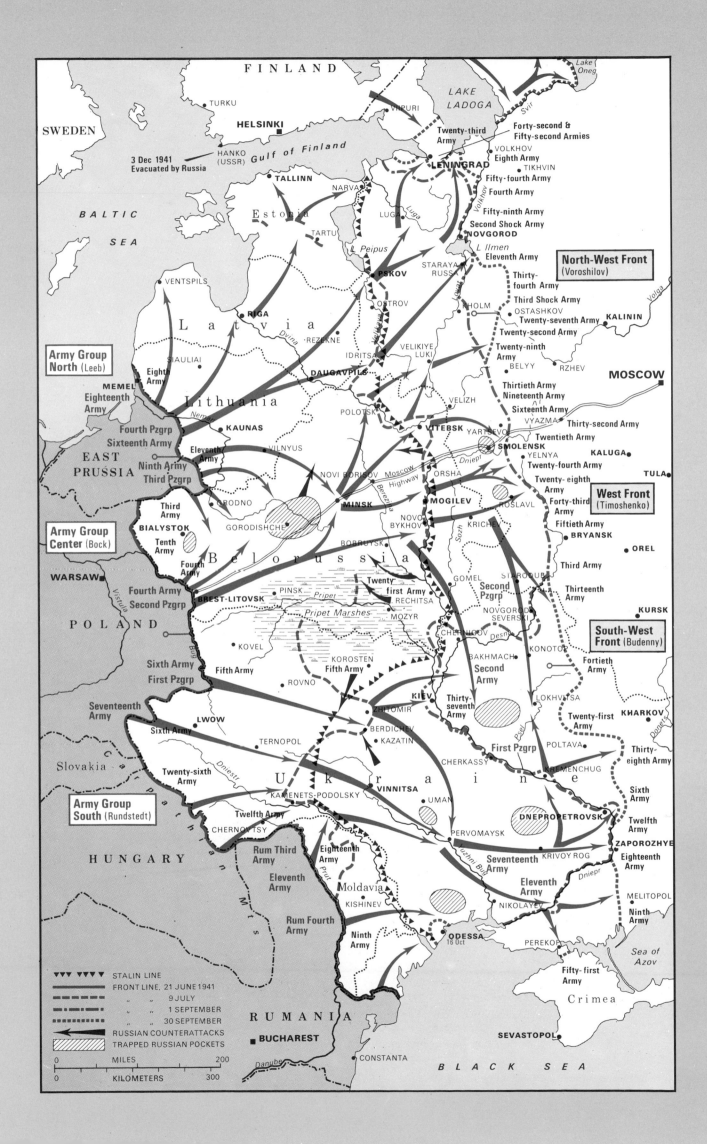

SWEDEN

FINLAND

TURKU

HELSINKI

HANKO
(USSR)
3 Dec 1941
Evacuated by Russia

Gulf of Finland

BALTIC
SEA

TALLINN

Estonia

VIIPURI

LAKE
LADOGA

Lake
Oneg

Svir

Twenty-third
Army

Forty-second &
Fifty-second Armies

VOLKHOV

Eighth Army

TIKHVIN

LENINGRAD

Fifty-fourth Army

Volkhov

Fourth Army

VENTSPILS

NARVA

L Peipus

TARTU

Luga

LUGA

Luga

Fifty-ninth Army

Second Shock Army

NOVGOROD

RIGA

PSKOV

L Ilmen

STARAYA
RUSSA

Lovat

Eleventh Army

North-West Front
(Voroshilov)

Latvia

Dvina

OSTROV

Thirty-
fourth
Army

SIAULIAI

REZEKNE

IDRITSA

Velikaya

VELIKIYE
LUKI

KHOLM

Third Shock Army

OSTASHKOV

Twenty-seventh Army

Twenty-second Army

KALININ

Volga

Army Group
North (Leeb)

Eighth
Army

DAUGAVPILS

Twenty-
ninth
Army

BELYY

RZHEV

MOSCOW

MEMEL

Lithuania

POLOTSK

VELIZH

Thirtieth Army

Nineteenth Army

Eighteenth
Army

Nemen

KAUNAS

VITEBSK

YARTSEVO

Sixteenth Army

VYAZMA

Thirty-second Army

Fourth Pzgrp
Sixteenth Army

EAST
PRUSSIA

VILNYUS

Eleventh
Army

NOVI BORISOV

Moscow
Highway

ORSHA

SMOLENSK

Twentieth Army

YELNYA

KALUGA

Ninth Army
Third Pzgrp

Dnepr

Twenty-fourth Army

TULA

Berezina

Third
Army

GRODNO

MOGILEV

Twenty- eighth
Army

West Front
(Timoshenko)

BIALYSTOK

MINSK

ROSLAVL

Forty-third
Army

Army Group
Center (Bock)

Tenth
Army

GORODISHCHE

NOVO-
BYKHOV

Fiftieth Army

WARSAW

Fourth
Army

Belorussia

BOBRUYSK

Sozh

KRICHEV

BRYANSK

OREL

Third Army

Fourth Army
Second Pzgrp

BREST-LITOVSK

PINSK

Pripet

Twenty-
first Army

GOMEL

Second
Pzgrp

STARODUB

Thirteenth
Army

KURSK

POLAND

Bug

Pripet Marshes

RECHITSA

MOZYR

NOVGOROD
SEVERSKI

Vistula

KOVEL

KOROSTEN

CHERNIGOV

Desna

Sixth Army
First Pzgrp

Fifth Army

Fifth Army

ROVNO

BAKHMACH

KONOTOP

South-West
Front (Budenny)

Seventeenth
Army

LWOW

ZHITOMIR

KIEV

Thirty-
seventh
Army

LOKHVITSA

Fortieth
Army

Twenty-first
Army

KHARKOV

Sixth Army

TERNOPOL

BERDICHEV

KAZATIN

Second
Army

Psel

Donets

Twenty-sixth
Army

Dniestr

VINNITSA

First Pzgrp

POLTAVA

Thirty-
eighth Army

Slovakia

KAMENETS-PODOLSKY

CHERKASSY

KREMENCHUG

Sixth
Army

Army Group
South (Rundstedt)

CHERNOVTSY

UMAN

Twelfth Army

DNEPROPETROVSK

Twelfth
Army

ZAPOROZHYE

HUNGARY

Rum Third
Army

Eighteenth
Army

Prut

PERVOMAYSK

Seventeenth
Army

KRIVOY ROG

Dniepr

Eighteenth
Army

Carpathian Mts

Eleventh
Army

Moldavia

Yuzhni Bug

Eleventh
Army

MELITOPOL

KISHINEV

NIKOLAYEV

Ninth
Army

Rum Fourth
Army

Ninth
Army

ODESSA
16 Oct

PEREKOP

Sea of
Azov

RUMANIA

Fifty-first
Army

Crimea

SEVASTOPOL

BUCHAREST

CONSTANTA

BLACK   SEA

Danube

▼▼▼ ▼▼▼▼ STALIN LINE

FRONT LINE, 21 JUNE 1941

"   "   9 JULY

"   "   1 SEPTEMBER

"   "   30 SEPTEMBER

RUSSIAN COUNTERATTACKS

TRAPPED RUSSIAN POCKETS

0   MILES   200

0   300
KILOMETERS

Below: The US cruiser *Savannah* at Algiers in July 1943. North Africa had been the objective of a big Allied combined operation in 1942, Operation Torch. Algiers then became one of the ports used for supporting the invasion of Sicily and in the summer of 1943 was the object of a U-boat campaign against Allied shipping in its waters. In this picture two 'Liberty' ships can be seen burning. Above: Fighters on the deck of a US escort carrier during Operation Torch. Escort carriers, small aircraft carriers converted from merchant ship or cruiser hulls, were one of the most successful innovations of the war, enabling fighter and air reconnaissance cover to be abundantly provided for convoys at sea. Above right: General George Marshall, a great American general who later won a Nobel Peace Prize for his post-war Marshall Plan. Above far right: US paratroopers in North Africa.

Left: Soviet tanks on the outskirts of Stalingrad. The steppes of southern Russia were regarded by both sides as perfect tank country, and the world's greatest tank battles were fought there. In these the Germans were usually out-numbered, but this was not the only reason for the Soviet successes in the latter part of the war. Below: Soviet infantry in street fighting. Although obviously a carefully posed photograph, it is not at all unrealistic. Stubborn street fighting was a frequent role of the Red Army, and the techniques, for example, enabled Stalingrad to be held until reinforcements could be assembled. In the foreground is one of the celebrated Degtyarev light machine guns.

Russia was also increasingly exercising its influence in the Balkans. Bessarabia had also been included in Russia's sphere of influence, and it was occupied in the summer of 1941. Now Russia also claimed the Dobruja from Rumania, which Hitler opposed because it would have brought the Russians too near the oilfields of Ploesti on which Germany depended so heavily. True, the manufacture of synthetic fuel in Germany had begun before the war, but it proved inordinately expensive and the output did not match the requirements. Further Russian offensive steps included the occupation of vital islands in the mouth of the Danube, which established Russian control of this entrance to the Black Sea.

Hitler believed that there was still a possibility of a political settlement with Russia, and to this end Molotov was invited to Berlin on 12 November 1940. Hitler's and Ribbentrop's attempts to divert the Soviet Union away from southeastern and northeastern Europe toward Persia and Asia failed. When Hitler asked how Molotov envisioned the solution to the Finnish problem, Molotov blandly replied that the solution would be similar to that carried out in the Baltic countries. Ribbentrop produced a draft treaty for Russia's adherence to the Tripartite Pact (which had been signed between Germany, Japan and Italy the previous summer) which Molotov took with him when he returned to Moscow. Stalin's reply contained conditions that seriously affected German interests in southeastern and north-eastern Europe. Hitler did not bother to reply. Now the planning for 'Operation Barbarossa,' the invasion of Russia, went ahead.

Germany's ally Italy, meanwhile, had precipitated the very action which Hitler had meant to avoid at all costs. Late in October 1940 Italian forces from Albania had attacked Greece, and although they were quickly stopped by the Greeks, the danger that the Balkans would be set aflame became a reality. Germany was compelled to assist its ally because the Italian action provided the British, who had just chased the Italians out of Cyrenaica in North Africa, with the possibility of landing in Greece to lend support to the Greek forces. The offshoot of this was Germany's 'Operation Marita,' the German invasion of Greece via Bulgaria. Furthermore, it was necessary to send support to Italy's forces in North Africa, and Rommel arrived with a small force during the middle of February 1941. In addition, Yugoslavia, which under Prince Regent Paul had joined the Axis Powers, was rent asunder by a popular revolution against the government. As a result, an invasion of Yugoslavia was launched simultaneously with Operation Marita which began on 6 April 1941.

Many of the armored and motorized formations of the German armies intended for Barbarossa had to be detached and transferred to the Balkans. The German operation against Yugoslavia and Greece was successfully concluded by 23 April 1941. Once again, armor and motorized formations and air supremacy had been decisive. However, as far as Yugoslavia was concerned, the operations had been conducted along the main arteries of communications, ignoring the barely accessible mountainous territory – the very area in which Tito's Partisan movement was to develop. The success also obscured difficulties due to the absence of a joint combined command of the German-Italian forces, even though the British were expelled from Greece, as they were shortly afterward from Crete in May 1941, by German airborne forces.

Rommel, in the meantime, achieved unexpected successes in Africa. Even when driven back, he was always resourceful enough to turn the operations to his own advantage again. He was dependent on supplies reaching him across the sea, but the British generally had naval supremacy in the Mediterranean. The Italian naval forces, though strong, avoided major engagements as much as possible. With Gibraltar, Malta and Alexandria in British possession, the British position remained intact, although twice, in 1941 and 1942, Rommel knocked at the gates of Egypt. In many respects, the warfare in the desert reintroduced many devices already in use during World War I. Extensive barbed wire entanglements and the mining of substantial areas were used by both sides. At El Alamein, hopelessly outmanned and outgunned by Montgomery's Eighth Army, Rommel had to give way, though Montgomery failed to achieve his objective of destroying the German Afrika Korps. Defensive line after defensive line had to be overcome until the Germans had been pushed back to Tunisia.

In the meantime, in November 1942 Allied forces had landed in Morocco and Algeria under the command of General Dwight D Eisenhower. Pushing east, despite several reverses inflicted by Rommel, the Americans and British contained the remaining Axis forces in a bridgehead around Tunis where some 250,000 German and Italian soldiers capitulated in May 1943. After the disastrous reconnaissance in force carried out by largely Canadian forces on the French coast at Dieppe in August 1942, the landings in Algeria and Morocco were the first successful major Allied amphibious operation in the war. The subsequent landing in Sicily and the invasion of Italy once again established a two-front war for Germany.

The Americans had acquired much experience in amphibious operations from 1942 onward in the Far East, where Japan had entered the war on the side of the Axis in December 1941. The period 1941–43 also contained the height of the German submarine offensive – the Battle of the Atlantic. However, by increasing aerial surveillance of the Atlantic convoy routes, and by the introduction of highly sensitive radar equipment, the Allies were in a position to decide that battle in their favor. From May 1943 the U-Boats were fighting a losing action. As in World War I, American resources of raw materials and weapons had reached Great Britain after changes were made in US neutrality laws in November 1939, and from 1941 the Soviet Union also received ever-larger shipments.

Beginning in 1941, the German Army increased the number of its motorized infantry divisions and doubled the number of panzer divisions, but in the latter case by halving the number of tanks per division, which reduced their combat value. Divisions were no longer deployed in regiments and battalions but in the form of battle groups of regiment or battalion size, equipped with half-track vehicles, self-propelled artillery and assault tanks. As its strength declined, the Luftwaffe could intervene less in land battles and the self-propelled artillery became all the more important. But all this depended on adequate supplies of spare parts and fuel, two items which were in short supply on the Eastern Front.

Two important new weapons for defense against tanks were also introduced into the German infantry's armory from 1943 onward. The *Panzerfaust* was a recoilless antitank projectile fired from a light, easily manufactured metal tube. The *Panzerschreck* was virtually a direct copy of the American bazooka rocket launcher (first used in North Africa) and was operated by two men. These three weapons and their British counterpart, the PIAT, could be used only at close range – usually 100 yards or less – which required considerable nerve in those using them.

In postwar literature the German Army is often described only in terms of tanks and motorized units. This is entirely invalid. Horse and cart and sheer hard foot-slogging were often the rule. Motorization was far from standardized. True, there were a number of standardized army vehicles, but the bulk were requisitioned in Germany and the occupied countries. The only thing they had in common was their camouflage. Standardization to the extent carried out by the Western Allies and the Russians did not exist.

The US and British armies were fully motorized and mechanized. When the draft was introduced in the United States the army was faced with an apparently insoluble problem. Its regular officer corps was well trained but small, too small to train an army of millions. The solution was to use the regular officers to prepare detailed training programs which were distributed to all recruitment camps. There, people who had previously occupied managerial positions in industry were commissioned and given the task, with the aid of these manuals, of training the conscript army. Every officer had his 'Master-Lesson' according to which recruits were to be trained. The short-term disadvantage of this system was that the officers who actually took these fresh forces into combat had had little or no previous contact with them, which initially led to inferior performance. But as the lessons were learned the hard way on the battlefield, this drawback was soon eliminated. Neither American nor British forces during World War II fully adopted the German concept of *Auftragstaktik*; only after the war was it adopted in the US Army. However, the British and Americans had an efficiently functioning integrated command structure that was totally lacking between Germany and her allies.

When the German Army launched Operation Barbarossa on 22 June 1941 the army leadership's picture of the enemy forces and his military and economic capacity was vague, or even nonexistent. What did exist was a vast underestimation of the Soviet potential. The German attack, contrary to current opinion, did not come as a surprise to the Soviet Union. The Red Army had almost completed the forward assembly of its forces, the first wave of which consisted of some 130 divisions, the second wave of 80 divisions and the third wave of 33 divisions and five brigades. Added to this were the forces that could be transferred west after the conclusion of the Russo-Japanese Pact in April 1941 – mainly elite Siberian units. By the middle of October the number of divisions in the Red Army had increased to 240. To some extent the Russian divisions were still in the

process of re-equipment. However, the entire southern wing was already equipped, to the shock and surprise of the German Army, with the new and formidable T-34 tank. In the central and northern areas this process was still under way. The Russians could recruit 1.2 million men per year, the Germans only 430,000. In other words, if Germany failed to achieve victory in 1941 it would find itself faced by ever-increasing Russian man-power, while the German reserves would dwindle. The Russians had over 20,000 tanks in service, but these included many of outdated types. In 1941 alone the British and Americans supplied the Russians with more tanks than the whole German Army possessed.

The German attack forced the Russians onto the defensive at first. The Soviet artillery was not as experienced as it would be 12 months later. Instead of supporting its infantry by concentrated fire, it tended to fire over the entire width of a battlefield. Nor had the Red Army organized its defense in depth; its antitank screens were rarely deeper than 3 miles compared to 15 miles in 1943. However, the Russian tank guns were vastly superior to anything the Germans had. The 3.7cm gun was still used in most German tanks, whereas the Russians already had 76.2mm weapons.

The attacking German forces found an enemy who fought with a tenacity and bravery never before encountered by the Germans, but in the initial phase the German leadership proved more flexible and superior in communications. Even the powerful T-34 did not normally carry a radio set. The German aim was to defeat Russia in a single *Blitzkrieg* campaign. The OKH centered its hopes on the capture of Moscow. But the OKW and Hitler failed to clarify the actual objectives. The army was still dominated by the concept of the battle of annihilation, in its mistaken interpretation of Clausewitz. Hitler gradually came around to the view that economically it was more important for Germany to capture the Baltic countries and the Ukraine, with their immense agricultural and industrial resources. He believed that only the possession of these reserves would make it possible for Germany to sustain a war of attrition. Only at a slightly later stage was Hitler prepared to make the decisive thrust toward Moscow. As allies, Germany had the Finns, the Rumanians and two Italian divisions, as well as Slovak and Hungarian contingents.

At the propaganda level, the campaign was proclaimed to be a 'Crusade against Bolshevism' which had to be carried out with all the ruthlessness attendant on a war of religion, including the

Above: US Marines on Bougainville in the Solomon Islands chain. 'Island hopping' was the favored US strategy from 1943, when the Americans began to push back the Japanese from the South Pacific islands. Above right: Claire Chennault, commander of the American air squadrons operating against the Japanese in China. Right: One of hundreds of Japanese aircraft wrecked in the South Pacific island battles. Below right: One of the most useful aircraft of World War II, the Catalina flying boat. Built in the USA for both the American and British air forces, this machine's long range made it ideal for naval reconnaissance, and it also had its uses as a submarine hunter.

Above: On a visit to the Eastern
Front in 1941, Mussolini
accompanied by Hitler inspects
Italian troops in the Ukraine.
Below left: Speer, Hitler's minister
responsible for arms production,

immediate execution of all captured Russian Commissars. The attacking German armies advanced over the entire front without producing a desirable *Schwerpunkt*. Their ranks included volunteers from Spain, France, Belgium, Flanders, the Netherlands, Denmark and Croatia. Until 1943 the Luftwaffe retained supremacy in the air, a supremacy which it lost in the summer of that year, but which was still in effect over specific areas such as the Baltic and the Black Sea. The Russian Navy, on the whole, remained in a passive role in both these areas.

The German Army Group South was assigned to penetrate in the direction of Kiev and to destroy the enemy in the western Ukraine. For the first time in World War II, the German Army with its armor failed to break through and obtain the necessary operational freedom. But then Army Group South had encountered the best-equipped segments of the Red Army. They had come across the T-34 for the first time.

Army Group Center operating in Belorussia was to reach Smolensk as quickly as possible, destroying the Russian forces north and south of Minsk on the way. Then it was to detach some of its armored formations and transfer them to Army Group North to support it in its operation to capture the Baltic countries and Leningrad. Army Group Center achieved its goal, but several weeks behind schedule due to the fierce resistance of the Russians plus some supply problems. The pocket battles of Bialystok and Minsk were its major engagements, but in spite of capturing huge numbers of prisoners and quantities of equipment, at no time were the German pincers strong enough to prevent sizeable Russian contingents from escaping their encirclement and forming new defenses.

Army Group North was to destroy the Red Army in the Baltic countries, capture the various ports and ultimately take

inspects a captured Soviet T34 tank. It was thanks to Speer's energy that German industry was belatedly mobilized for a long and expensive war. He lived long enough to enjoy some years of freedom after release from post-war imprisonment as a war criminal, and his penitent memoirs are a rich source of information.
Below: Soviet partisans in action.

Leningrad. It made headway without, however, being able to destroy any significant number of Russian forces.

The Russian leadership replied to the German invasion with a policy of scorched earth and the formation of partisan units to operate in the rear of the German Army. Early in July the Germans launched their attack in the south upon Uman, and the following month the battle for Smolensk was fought and won. In the north, the original Russo-Finnish border had been recaptured. But then the northern operations came to a halt. The terrain, largely swamps, was unsuitable for armored warfare and Hitler decided to lay siege to Leningrad instead of capturing it in a bitter house-to-house battle. Army Group North had also failed to interrupt the important rail link to Murmansk. In the northern sector, therefore, both armies dug in, and remained in much the same positions until 1944.

At this point Hitler decided to rest the armored formations for urgent repairs and then to move southward into the Ukraine and capture the oilfields of the Caucasus. But the dream of defeating the bulk of the Russian forces was over. After seven Russian armies had been defeated at Kiev in September, Hitler changed his mind again and ordered the attack upon Moscow. Early in October Army Group South attacked both the Donets Basin and the Crimea, while Army Group Center, en route to Moscow, achieved a brilliant victory at Vyazma and Bryansk. Although Stalin remained in Moscow, the government offices were transferred to Kubishev. General Zhukov was appointed to lead the defense of Moscow.

Just as the preparations for the attack on Moscow were completed, the weather changed for the worse. Incessant rainfall made the land virtually impassable for the German vehicles. Then, late in November 1941, freezing temperatures set in, ranging between minus 20 and minus 40 degrees Centigrade. The German troops were not equipped with winter uniforms, though these were stocked in the areas to the rear. Weapons failed, and the oil in the tanks and other vehicles froze. Only 25 percent of the necessary daily supply trains could be run. Still, after overcoming many difficulties, 'Operation Typhoon,' the attack on Moscow, was launched, the vanguards penetrating as far as Moscow's suburbs. There, on 6 December 1941, they came face to face with the Russian counteroffensive launched by Zhukov.

The German front seemed on the point of collapse when Hitler intervened and dismissed Brauchitsh, the Commander in Chief of the Army, and a number of other generals. Hitler himself assumed direct control of the conduct of operations in the East. Hitler's order to hold fast prevented a retreat from becoming a rout. The front stabilized itself again. At Demyansk and Kholm, two sizeable contingents of the German Army were encircled by the Russians and cut off. They were supplied by the Luftwaffe and managed to hold out until relieved by German counterattacks in the spring of 1942, an experience which undoubtedly influenced Hitler's decision later in 1942 to hold Stalingrad.

The Battle for Moscow was decisive, because from that moment on the German Army in the East could no longer take the offensive over the whole length of the front. Its overall offensive capacity had been broken and the turning point of the war had come. The German defeat at Stalingrad served only to confirm this. For Germany, the war on two fronts had become reality. From 22 June 1941 until 31 December 1941 the German Army in the east had lost 1,073,066 men, 276,540 of them killed. This exceeded by far the available reserves. The Russians now began to apply *Blitzkrieg* tactics. The Soviet artillery increased in firepower, armor operated independently in depth and infantry attacked in narrow sectors.

Below: An Allied convoy at sea. An escort carrier can be discerned in the background. In the foreground is an anti-aircraft gun platform of a US warship. Unlike World War 1, the convoy system was adopted right from the beginning of hostilities by all belligerents, with the partial exception of the Japanese. Bottom left: A U-boat at sea. For much of the war U-boats made their attacks on convoys while on the surface, several submarines forming a 'wolf pack' and relying for surprise on their low profile and poor visibility or darkness. However, improved radar enabled convoys to cope with these tactics in the later years of the war. Bottom right: Von Manstein and his staff. General (later Field Marshal) von Manstein was possibly the most competent of Hitler's generals.

The German policies in all the occupied territories were such as to drive the population into the arms of the emerging partisan movements. This was especially the case in the Soviet Union. However, in areas entirely under military administration, the Germans could depend upon a considerable amount of collaboration, to the extent that some Russians even joined the German Army. By the end of 1941, unknown to Hitler, over 1 million Russians were serving as auxiliaries within the German forces, but much of the existing good will was destroyed when, in 1942, a policy of compulsory labor in Germany was introduced and males and females in eastern and western Europe were deported to Germany. So far as its labor force was concerned, Germany still lived in a virtual peacetime economy. Total war had come, but those directly affected by it should preferably be foreign workers and not German women, whose British and Russian counterparts worked around the clock in their war industries.

By 1942 German strength was no longer sufficient to maintain offensive actions over a 2000-mile front. But Army Group South captured the Crimea and Sevastopol. Then began the attack which was to carry the German Army to the summit of Mount Elbrus in the Caucasus, to Maykop and to Stalingrad. The oil-fields found at Maykop had been destroyed, and they could not be used by the Germans.

The German lines of communication had not only become overextended but extremely undermanned as well. The advance upon Stalingrad exposed the entire German flank in the south. Neither rail nor trucks could solve the supply problems of the Sixth German Army under Paulus at Stalingrad. The city was to be taken by a pincer movement, but the Germans, once in the city, had to engage in fierce house-to-house fighting. What Hitler had feared in the case of Leningrad became reality in Stalingrad. In the course of August Hitler also became aware of the vulnerable points at which the Sixth Army could be cut off by the Russians. Orders were issued to the Chief of the General Staff, Halder, to build up a 'corset' consisting of antitank guns deployed in depth behind the Rumanian and Italian units holding the exposed sectors. The transfer of a panzer division from France to this sector of the front was also ordered. Halder did nothing and precisely at the point which Hitler had predicted, on 19 November 1942, Russian armored corps broke through the lines and closed the circle around the Sixth Army. Hitler, who meanwhile had parted company with Halder and appointed General Zeitzler Chief of the General Staff, was in two minds about what to do. To hold or to break out? Göring's promise that the Luftwaffe would supply Stalingrad resulted in the decision to hold on to the city at any price. However, the Luftwaffe was quite incapable of meeting the supply demands of over 300,000 men. Of the defenders of Stalingrad, 100,000 were killed in action. Ninety thousand became prisoners of war, of whom 6000 survived the ordeal – including the commanding generals, Field Marshal Paulus and General von Seydlitz-Kurtzbach. In December 1942 Manstein had led a relief operation and came as close as 30 miles from the city. He waited for the garrison to break out, but Hitler forbade them to do so. On 2 February the rest of the Stalingrad garrison capitulated.

Hitler took the responsibility for the disaster upon himself, and in recent years his decision has been vindicated by none other than General Chuikov, the Soviet commander of the Stalingrad defense, who argued that the siege of Stalingrad tied up so many Russian forces as to make it impossible to bring about the total collapse of the German Army Group South. As it happened, Manstein managed to build up a new defensive line and the Russian advance farther west was prevented for the better part of another year.

Before the fall of Stalingrad, the Casablanca Conference between Roosevelt and Churchill had resulted in three major conclusions. The first was to demand 'Unconditional Surrender' from Germany and her allies, and the second was to put an end to the threat of the German submarines. Thirdly, they placed priority on strategic bombing in order to undermine Germany's morale and industrial production. What had been achieved by the blockade in World War I was to be achieved by bombing from the air in World War II.

In fact, the principle of area bombing of German cities had already been approved by Churchill upon assuming the premiership in May 1940. He had advocated it in 1917. We have it on the authority of the then Principal Assistant Secretary in the Air Ministry, J M Spaight: 'We began to bomb objectives on the German mainland before the Germans began to bomb objectives on the British mainland. That is an historical fact which has been publicly admitted. Yet because we were doubtful about the psychological effect of propagandistic distortion of the truth that it was we who started the strategic offensive, we have shrunk

from giving our great decision of May 1940 the publicity which it deserved. That surely was a mistake. It was a splendid decision. It was as heroic, as self-sacrificing, as Russia's decision to adopt her policy of "scorched earth." '

The strategic air offensive against Germany started in May 1940, though with bomber forces of an insignificant size compared with the armadas of the air that appeared over Germany beginning late in 1942. But even in 1940 public opinion samples collected by members of SS Security Service, the SD, express time and again the concern of the people in the Ruhr about being bombed and machine gunned.

The Allied air offensive could not break the resistance of the German civilian population any more than the German bombing had affected British morale in 1940. Industries were dispersed, but Germany was still far from conducting a total war. Goebbels was its propagandist, but could not make much headway in practice, even after he had been appointed Plenipotentiary for Total War after 20 July 1944. However, largely because of the efforts of Albert Speer, Armaments Minister from February 1942, German output of arms and weapons in 1944 was many times that achieved in 1940.

The last large-scale offensive mounted by Germany in the east was the Battle of Kursk which began on 5 July 1943.

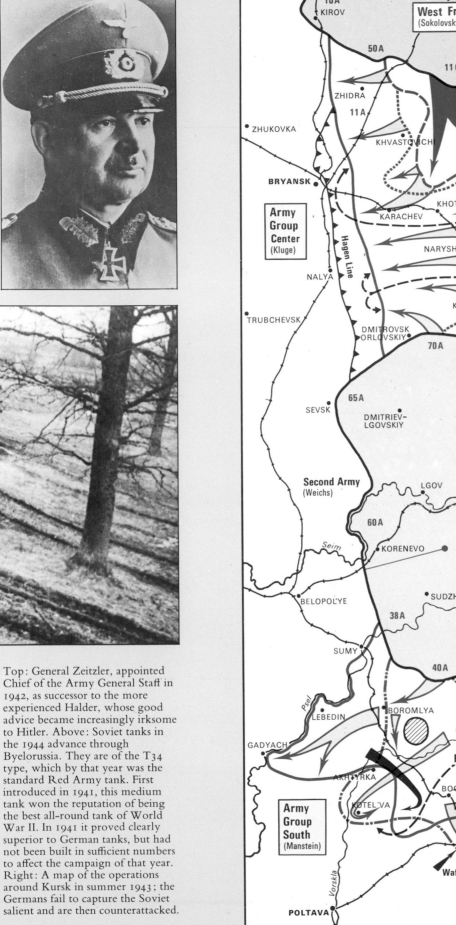

Top: General Zeitzler, appointed Chief of the Army General Staff in 1942, as successor to the more experienced Halder, whose good advice became increasingly irksome to Hitler. Above: Soviet tanks in the 1944 advance through Byelorussia. They are of the T34 type, which by that year was the standard Red Army tank. First introduced in 1941, this medium tank won the reputation of being the best all-round tank of World War II. In 1941 it proved clearly superior to German tanks, but had not been built in sufficient numbers to affect the campaign of that year. Right: A map of the operations around Kursk in summer 1943; the Germans fail to capture the Soviet salient and are then counterattacked.

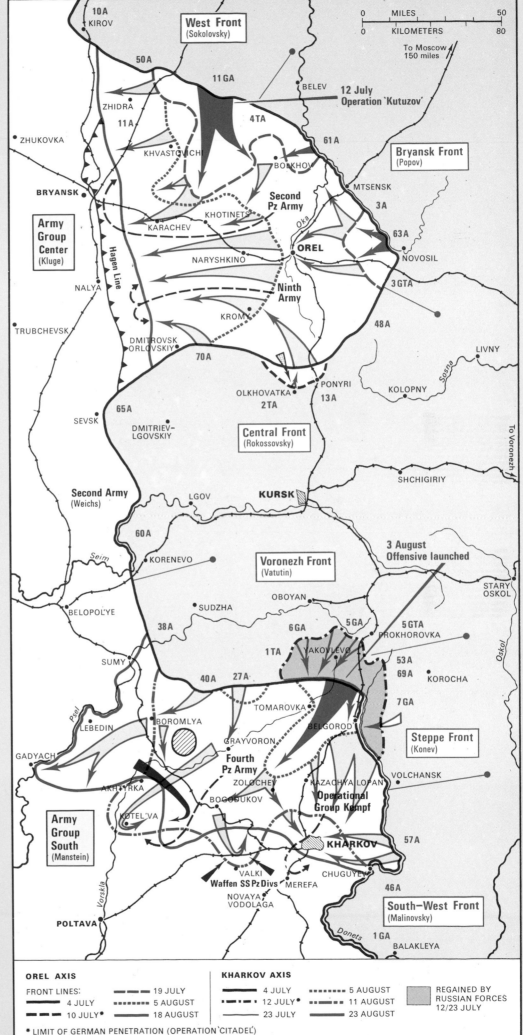

West Front (Sokolovsky)

Bryansk Front (Popov)

12 July Operation 'Kutuzov'

Army Group Center (Kluge)

Second Pz Army

Ninth Army

Central Front (Rokossovsky)

Second Army (Weichs)

KURSK

3 August Offensive launched

Voronezh Front (Vatutin)

Steppe Front (Konev)

Fourth Pz Army

Operational Group Kempf

Army Group South (Manstein)

KHARKOV

South–West Front (Malinovsky)

Waffen SS Pz Divs

POLTAVA

10A KIROV · 50A · 11GA · BELEV · 61A · MTSENSK · 3A · 63A · NOVOSIL · 3GTA · 48A · ZHIDRA · 11A · ZHUKOVKA · KHVASTOVICHI · BOLKHOV · KHOTINETS · Oka · OREL · BRYANSK · KARACHEV · NARYSHKINO · Hagen Line · NALYA · KROMY · LIVNY · TRUBCHEVSK · DMITROVSK ORLOVSKIY · 70A · PONYRI · KOLOPNY · Sosna · SEVSK · OLKHOVATKA · 2TA · 13A · 65A · DMITRIEV-LGOVSKIY · SHCHIGIRIY · LGOV · 60A · SEIM · KORENEVO · STARY OSKOL · BELOPOL'YE · SUDZHA · OBOYAN · 6GA · 5GA · 5GTA · PROKHOROVKA · 38A · 1TA · YAKOVLEVO · 53A · 69A · KOROCHA · SUMY · 40A · 27A · TOMAROVKA · 7GA · Psel · LEBEDIN · BOROMLYA · GRAYVORON · BELGOROD · GADYACH · AKHTYRKA · ZOLOCHEV · KAZACHYA LOPAN · VOLCHANSK · KOTEL'VA · BOGODUKOV · VALKI · MEREFA · CHUGUYEV · 57A · NOVAYA VODOLAGA · 46A · Vorskla · Donets · 1GA · BALAKLEYA

OREL AXIS

FRONT LINES:
— 4 JULY
— — 10 JULY *
— · — 19 JULY
···· 5 AUGUST
— 18 AUGUST

KHARKOV AXIS
— · — 4 JULY
— · · — 12 JULY *
— 23 JULY
···· 5 AUGUST
— — 11 AUGUST
— 23 AUGUST

REGAINED BY RUSSIAN FORCES 12/23 JULY

* LIMIT OF GERMAN PENETRATION (OPERATION 'CITADEL')

Below: British aircrews join their Stirling bombers at an airfield in England. The Stirling was the RAF's first four-engined bomber and for a time was the workhorse of the bomber offensive against Germany. But it was soon superseded by the Lancaster and Halifax; it was not an easy aircraft to pilot, and its bomb bays could not accommodate the very large bombs which soon became standard weapons. Left: General Eisenhower and his colleagues. Right: The US Air Force in Britain. The pilot is sitting in a P-51 fighter. This, the Mustang, was the best US fighter of World War II, although originally designed for the RAF by North American Aviation. Far right: The observer at his post in a US bomber; bomb-aiming was his major function.

However, the Russians had detailed advance knowledge via an espionage group, the so-called Red Orchestra, and made their preparations accordingly. The offensive bogged down in the deep network of Russian defenses and had to be broken off. The initiative had come to rest firmly in Soviet hands. The time had come to make peace, but who could make peace with Hitler? In an ideological war as total as was World War II, this was no longer possible. The agony was to go on for another two years, until the German armies had been thrown back to Berlin.

Shortly after the Kursk Offensive had begun, Mussolini was toppled from power on 19 July 1943 and the Italian government taken over by Marshal Badoglio. The Allies had already landed in Sicily, and the campaign in Italy which followed was marked by hard defensive battles of which Monte Cassino serves as but one example. A decisive Allied breakthrough was not achieved until April 1944, and the Allies' entry into Rome occurred only two days before the D-Day invasion of the coast of northern France. Right up to the capitulation in May 1945, the Germans, though being steadily pushed back, maintained their foothold on the Italian peninsula. Mussolini had been rescued by a German commando raid, but he no longer played a role of any political significance.

Operation Overlord began in the early hours of 6 June 1944. Now it was no longer the Luftwaffe which dominated the skies but the Allied air forces, and under their protection the Normandy beachhead was consolidated, though it was nearly two months before General Patton could break out into the open country. Coinciding as all this did with the Russian offensive of June 1944, those German officers who formed a resistance to Hitler believed that the last possible moment had come in which to act. A bomb planted by a Colonel Stauffenberg exploded in Hitler's conference room, but Hitler survived with a few minor injuries. From that moment on, he was utterly convinced that Providence had selected him to lead Germany to final victory. There was not a chance. The Russians crossed the East Prussian frontier, and although they were thrown back for a time, Russia proper was liberated and the Russian armies stood at the gates of Warsaw. After Patton's breakout in the west the German Army disintegrated until it came to a standstill again at the frontiers of the Reich.

Hitler's last hope was the Ardennes Offensive launched on 16 December 1944. But Antwerp, his objective, was out of reach of the German armies. Once the weather changed and clear skies allowed the Allied air forces to intervene, the German forces were quickly thrown back to their points of departure. In March 1945 the British and Americans crossed the Rhine, and in spite of using the last German reserves, children and old men, there was no escape from defeat. After Hitler's suicide on 30 April 1945, shortly before Berlin fell to the Russians, Grand Admiral Dönitz became his successor. Under his guidance, the German forces in north-western Germany surrendered to Montgomery and on 7 May General Jodl, on Dönitz's behalf, signed the instrument of unconditional surrender of the German Army in the presence of General Eisenhower at Reims, a procedure repeated by Field Marshal Keitel before Soviet representatives in Berlin the following day.

During the last few years of the war, the techniques used had changed considerably. Although capable of conducting the war Blitzkrieg-style, on the whole the Soviet forces preferred a battle of attrition, to which they resorted time and again. In contrast to the German plan at Verdun, they also aimed at the conquest of considerable slices of territory. When forming up for battle, the Russians deployed what they called a 'long-range battle group' consisting primarily of armored units as their leading formation. Accompanied by motorized rifle formations, they had to take and hold important geographical points. Objectives and directions were described in minute detail by the Soviet High Command and were to be adhered to to the letter. This deprived the army of the flexibility which they might have had otherwise and provided the Germans at a local level with repeated opportunities to launch effective counter-attacks. The bulk of the Russian infantry, with its supporting armor, was to keep as close as possible to the long-range battle group, which in effect slowed down the armor and reduced the speed of the attack. Moreover, although the Soviets had held air supremacy since the summer of 1943, battles were marked less by cooperation between armor and air force (as had been the case in Poland and the west in 1939 and 1940) than by the cooperation between armor and artillery. This led to a Russian concentration of artillery which had never been seen before. During his offensive of 1918, Ludendorff had concentrated 100 pieces of artillery per $\frac{3}{4}$ mile of frontage, but the Russian offensive operations, on the average, concentrated over 500 guns on the same size sector. Their firepower was immensely increased by their rocket artillery, the 'Stalin Organs.' The Germans, too,

question. Instead, defense with mobile forces was conducted in depth in the form of battle zones, a development which pointed to the future of defensive warfare.

The defenders had the task of stopping an enemy attack in the depth of the battle zone and gaining time for further evacuation. Behind the immediate front line was a system of small strongholds consisting mainly of two-man bunkers which was to wear down the attack. Concentrated enemy artillery fire thus often hit areas of no importance. Broad belts of minefields were to play a key role in slowing down the advance of enemy armor and/or pointing it in the direction desired by the defender. It was of primary importance to recognize the beginning of an enemy attack. Once this was done, the bulk of the forces moved to the rear of the battle zone, the artillery moved into their prepared positions and the armored reserves waited for the moment to intervene. Much depended also on expert camouflage, a lesson which the Germans learned from the Russians, who are past masters of this art to the present day. What had above all to be hidden from the enemy's eyes was the point of concentration of the defensive armor. This new type of defense proved its value.

Mainly *Volksgrenadier* divisions were used for the defense of

Above far left: Otto Skorzeny, leader of the SS airborne detachment that snatched Mussolini from his Italian captors after the fall of his Fascist regime. Above left: General Rommel, shortly before his enforced suicide, inspects German troops manning defenses on the northern French coast. The self-propelled gun has French-built chassis. Left: Generals Patton, Bradley and Montgomery in France, summer 1944. Right: Allied troop-carrying gliders, their life-cycle accomplished, await disposal in Normandy.

had rocket artillery, the *Nebelwerfer*, but not in the necessary numbers, and only a very few were self-propelled, as they were mounted on half tracks. The same was true of American rocket launchers, of which only relatively few had been mounted on the turrets of Sherman tanks. But the principle of using the rocket or rocket-powered weapons was firmly established during World War II, ranging from the bazooka to the rocket-propelled Me 163 fighter and the rockets of the V1 and V2 types.

During the last few years of the war air forces were dominant. In the course of the breakthrough operation from the Normandy beachhead at Avranches, the Allies used 1500 four-engine bombers, 500 twin-engine bombers and 500 fighter bombers which concentrated their attacks on a German defensive area measuring 4.8 miles by 1.5 miles. This amounted to an increase in firepower which surpassed anything known during World War I.

Although 1944 witnessed the highest output of German arms, including armor and vehicles, there were neither adequate fuel reserves nor a transport system sufficiently intact to carry them to the forces in the field. This necessitated a new type of defense – but not from fixed and firmly held positions as during World War I. For that type of defense, the German manpower reserves no longer sufficed. Defense on a wide front was out of the

these battle zones, each of which was about one-third experienced infantry men, the rest being hastily trained recruits. These divisions had no effective offensive power, but their equipment was superior to that which the German Army had had in 1939. They were more than adequately supplied with light machine guns and the newly introduced fully automatic assault rifles and *Panzerfausts*. What they lacked were antitank guns, but forces thus equipped could be quickly assembled to form a concentrated defense against attacking armor.

At the operational level, the German Army conducted its battles on the defensive most expertly, especially under Field Marshal von Manstein and General Model, as long as resources were available and Hitler did not intervene with one of his 'hold at any price' directives. Defense was carried out in 'wandering pockets' cut off by the Russians until they had succeeded in breaking through the Russian lines from the rear and rejoining the main front. When this was no longer possible, linear defense was reintroduced by Hitler, but the lines were so thinly manned that it was a relatively easy matter to break through them. Mobile defense, however, had shown its value and once again pointed to a new confirmation of the primacy of defense.

The most important German infantry weapon issued during the final phase of World War II was the *Sturmgewehr 43*, the

fully automatic assault rifle already mentioned. Although its range was shorter than that of a light machine gun, its firepower was considerably greater. The rocket-propelled antitank missiles already mentioned gave the infantry added protection against enemy armor. Among German battle tanks the tendency was toward heavier and heavier vehicles. Possibly the best was the Mark V Panther, which mounted a 75mm long-barreled gun and weighed just over 40 tons. The Tiger, mounting an 88mm gun, initially weighed 58 tons (in its final radically-different Tiger II version, 70 tons) while still powered by the same engines as the Panther. Its fire was accurate and deadly. With the exception of the Soviet Joseph Stalin Mark III, there was no Allied tank which could match it in this respect, but firepower was not matched by great mobility; this was its chief disadvantage. While the Mark IIs and IIIs in 1940 had no difficulty in using the roads through the Ardennes, during the Ardennes Offensive of 1944 the very weight of the new German armor transformed the road system into a quagmire, which made it impossible for the supply columns to follow.

The Luftwaffe, from early 1944 on, was equipped with the first operational jet fighter, the Me 262. Much has been made of the delay in the deployment of this plane being caused by Hitler's demand to transform it into a fast bomber. That decision was not as nonsensical as it seems at first glance. Air combat at speeds approaching Mach 1 requires different training and different

Above left: A US battleship
bombards land targets with its
16-inch guns. In the Pacific war
gun engagements between battleships were rare but the effectiveness
of naval artillery against coastal
objectives provided an important
role for both old and new US
battleships. Left: 'Big Three'
meetings between Roosevelt,
Churchill and Stalin (here shown
with their foreign ministers
standing behind them) took place
at Teheran and Yalta, and also at
Potsdam with different American
and British participants. Right: For
defense against low-flying aircraft,
external machine guns were fitted
to several tank designs. Above,
inset: Rocket launching arrays, of
which the Soviet *Katyusha* was the
first to see widespread service, were
also developed for the US Army,
as shown here.'

tactics but low-level bombing runs, compared with combat in the air, are relatively simple. Special training proved to be time-consuming. Nor were the existing jet engines completely free from defects. More German jet fighter pilots died because of engine failure or generally inadequate handling of the aircraft than by being shot down by the Allies. Added to the Me 262 was the Me 163 aircraft which was rocket-propelled. This type was used mainly for the defense of the Leuna synthetic fuel installations at Magdeburg. Its unprecedented rate of climb and speed allowed it to penetrate far above the bomber formations, then glide down upon them and open fire with rockets and cannon from a distance out of range of the aircraft gunners.

Other German jet aircraft which came into operation in 1944–45 were the Arado 234 *Blitz* bomber and the *Volksjager* He 162. However, the ultimate weapon of World War II, fortunately for Germany, came too late to be used over Europe: the atomic bomb, first used at Hiroshima and Nagasaki.

To sum up, the image of war, the *Kriegsbild*, had profoundly changed by 1944 from what it had been in 1940. During the first few years of the war, armor supported by tactical aircraft could make a breakthrough and achieve operational freedom. Later in the war defensive positions were built in increasing depth and in stages, providing the manpower to keep them functional was still available. What in World War I had been

Top left: A German *Volkssturmer* does his gallant best with a *Panzerfaust* one-man missile launcher, in May 1945, the month of Germany's surrender. Above left: General Bor-Komorowski surrenders to the SS general in Warsaw, after the final defeat of the insurgents, in November 1944. The captured Poles, members of the Home Army, were treated as regular prisoners of war by the Germans; Bor-Komorowski was imprisoned at Colditz, but finally settled in Britain. Above: The main street of Bastogne, in the Ardennes, in January 1945. Taken at the height of the Ardennes campaign, this picture illustrates the high degree of motorization in the US Army. Above right: An obvious publicity photograph of a US three-man combat team.

the role of the barbed wire entanglements was, in World War II, largely taken over by extensive mine fields.

In 1944 infantry in an attacking role had weapons with a much greater rate of fire than had been the case in 1940. Nonetheless, support from armor, especially self-propelled assault guns, provided the backbone for any infantry counterattack as well as for its defense. The task of the attacker was first to destroy the enemy antitank positions, as well as the armor held in reserve in the rear, before attacking armored wedges could begin to smash their way through the defensive system. The intensity of firepower had a higher priority than mobility, a reversal of the position held in 1940. The air force supplemented the fire of the artillery while the mechanized infantry followed close on the heels of the armored formations. Tactical fighter bombers held down the enemy's artillery and, wherever possible, attacked its reserve armor. Other air force formations attacked roads, bridges and intersections to prevent supplies from reaching the enemy. The United States Army Air Force, and to a lesser degree the RAF, attacked vital centers of communications in the enemy's hinterland where American precision bombing succeeded in almost destroying Germany's synthetic fuel production.

The Red Army was still highly dependent on railroads and horse-drawn carts for its supplies, which meant that the Russians were forced to pause after every offensive, giving the Germans the chance to reorganize their disrupted defense. The American and British Armies, however, were supplied largely by trucks to the extent that their advancing forces could move as far as 360 miles from their base. Transport aircraft and fuel pipelines made them partially independent of the railroads, and this model has determined the pattern of warfare ever since.

Psychological warfare played a major role in the war. At first the initiative seemed to be in the hands of the dictatorships. The Soviet Union, as well as National Socialist Germany, were one-party states. A *Politruk*, a political commissar, was attached to every unit in the Red Army right down to the company level. The Germans sought to emulate this from 1943 on by the introduction of the *Nationalsozialistischer Fuerhrungsoffizier*, the National Socialist Leadership Officer. At first Allied propaganda about German atrocities was relatively ineffective because much the same propaganda had been used during World War I and afterward had been shown to be blatant lies. Therefore, the perpetration of genuine atrocities had not been completely believed even in high official quarters. The real stories, such as the 'Final Solution of the Jewish Problem,' were revealed in their full gruesome details only after the war. They were products of an ideological warfare, and only wars of religion, which essentially belong to the realm of ideological warfare, have ever been conducted with anything approaching equal ferocity and bestiality.

The real victors of World War II were the United States of America and the Soviet Union. The Great Powers of Western and Central Europe have disappeared, insofar as their greatness depends on their ability to impose their will upon any of their neighbors. But the military consequences of World War II are still shaping and influencing not only Europe, but the entire globe.

Left: A US aircraft carrier with escorting destroyer in the Pacific theater of operations. The naval war in the Pacific was essentially a war between the seaborne aircraft of the US and Japan, whose outcome was decided by the superior productive strength of the US, which guaranteed a numerical preponderance both of aircraft carriers and of aircraft. Below left: The first Soviet tanks enter Berlin. Above: 'Enola Gay', the bomber entrusted with the dropping of the first atomic bomb, during training in New Mexico. The aircraft flew the mission from a Pacific island base, to which the bomb had been delivered earlier by a US cruiser.
Below: A bomb-damaged Japanese drydock at the time of surrender, crammed with midget submarines.

9. The Nuclear Age

In this final chapter, it will be our task to examine the emergence of the *primacy of the defense* from an historical perspective and then to look at the role it plays at present and consider the lessons NATO and the Warsaw Pact countries have learned from the past.

The primary problem in the conduct of conventional warfare in Central and Western Europe in the past resulted, other factors apart, from the nature and the character of defense in a given geographic area. Throughout the latter part of the 19th century and the first half of the 20th century, the geography of these areas has become more and more complicated and is at this very moment going through changes in its urban structure. It is still in a process of transformation such that a future battlefield in Western and Central Europe will bear little resemblance to that which existed at the end of World War II.

Apart from this, the definition of the concept of conventional warfare provides some difficulties, because it is not only a question now of whether or not it includes tactical nuclear weapons, but also of whether conventional warfare includes guerrilla warfare. This problem can be left open for a time while we turn to warfare in the past and look first of all at the basic change in the role of defense. From the historical perspective of the last 160 years, one major change is clear – a much smaller number of troops is needed to defend a given line and hold it successfully. Wellington's army at Waterloo had approximately 20,000 men per mile of defense line. In the American Civil War this ratio decreased to 12,000 men per mile, and during the last two years of the Civil War the forces of the Confederacy repelled attacks successfully with 5000 men per mile, even though these attacks were doubled in strength. The army of General Lee defended, for over nine months, a long line between Richmond and Petersburg, yielding only when its strength had declined to 1500 men per mile.

The Franco-Prussian War seemed to contradict this development, but superior strategy and greater tactical maneuverability resulted in the defeat of the French forces before they were able to organize an effective defense within a large framework. Nevertheless, the bloody and successful defense against the German attack at Gravelotte shows the potential power of the defense in isolated local actions.

If we turn to the Boer War we find a further decline in the defensive strength necessary to hold a given line. The Boers, with forces ranging between 600 and 800 men per mile, successfully repelled attacks carried out by the flower of the British professional army. Near Magersfontein the Boers held a front of around six miles with only 5000 men, and at Colenso a front of over seven miles with 4500 men. During the Russo-Japanese War, in the Battle of Mukden the Russians defended with 7450 men per mile a front that stretched over 40 miles, until the Japanese succeeded, by threatening the Russian flank, in driving them from their positions.

After the Battle of the Marne in World War I there was a defensive line of roughly 450 miles from the Channel coast to the Swiss border. In 1915, when the German armies on this front were on the defensive, they held it with roughly 90 divisions – there was one division approximately every five miles, or 3480 men per mile. This, however, requires qualification because the Vosges Mountains were at the southern end of the front, approximately 100 miles long and considered by both sides as unsuitable for major attacks. There the strength of the defense was lower than elsewhere on the Western Front. This circumstance enlarges the defense figure on the main sectors to almost 6000 men per mile. Since, however, these figures include strategic reserves, logistical personnel and so forth, this means that the effective defensive strength amounted to one division

per $5\frac{1}{2}$–6 miles, which brings us back to the actual ratio which ranged between 4475 men and 3000 men per mile of front including local reserves. This line of defense stopped the major autumn offensive of the Allies, an offensive which in individual sectors was carried out with a superiority of five to one.

In the face of the growing superiority of the Allies, particularly in medium and heavy artillery, the German Army leadership changed its defensive tactics; it grouped its divisions in depth rather than in width. In practice this meant that now only one-third of the combat strength of a division held the first line while the rest stood in reserve. The Allied artillery bombardment, which usually preceded every attack, in effect hit a defense line which was either not manned at all or manned very thinly. Attacks could be absorbed immediately and repelled by counterattacks from depth, preferably at the weakest points of the Allied attack.

Previous page: An underwater detonation, one of the series of atomic weapon tests staged by the US government at Bikini Atoll in 1946. The ships, anchored at varying ranges from the device, include several well-known survivors from both the US and hostile navies of World War II. Below: An air view of a Bikini test. The circular line is the rapidly advancing shock wave, and this is followed by a dust storm.

The problem for both sides was how to get out of a war which had become stuck in the mud of the trenches – in other words, to return to mobility. The British found their answer in the development of tanks, but it would be wrong to name the tank as the weapon which, in a military context, was the decisive instrument in World War I. As already mentioned, its operational radius was relatively small, roughly 20 miles, and its technical defects were many. Large numbers of tanks were put out of action before they could become really effective. The German Army had its own answer for bringing about greater mobility in warfare, the shock troops. They realized that mass infantry attacks would lead only to mass butchery, and therefore they changed their offensive tactics by dividing them into two stages. The first stage was to consist of a wave of shock troops deployed against key points of the Allied defense. A shock troop could range in strength from platoon to company size – from about 30 men to 120 – comprised of expert marksmen, hand grenade throwers, machine-gun units, trench mortars, flame throwers and engineers who were to penetrate the first line of defense and largely clear out the first trenches before the second wave, the bulk of the division, would follow. Ludendorff supported this development enthusiastically and gave the shock troops a key role in the March Offensive of 1918.

It was precisely this offensive, in which the British confronted a German superiority of three to one, which demonstrated the

real value of the defense, because the bulk of the German attacking units could move forward only relatively slowly. The German attack finally failed to exploit the initial breakthrough. In other words, the German forces could not maintain in depth the original impetus of their attack; the farther they went, the weaker this impetus became until the attack was halted. The attackers, once again, were compelled onto the defensive.

In the late summer and autumn of 1918, when the Allied Forces obtained a superiority of three to one over the German Forces, it allowed them to develop multiple leverages, thanks to which the German defensive line could gradually be pushed back. However, Field Marshal Haig, as well as Winston Churchill, estimated the remaining German fighting capacity as high enough to be able to continue the war for another year.

Neither tanks nor shock troops were the real solution to the problems of trench warfare. They represented partial solutions, but together, as mobile armored units and mechanized infantry, they became the answer. This development changed the strategy and tactics of land warfare and could be applied in the attack as well as in defense.

Again, one could take the German successes of World War II in Poland and in France as examples contradicting the idea of the primacy of the defense. However, the defeat of Poland, other factors apart, was caused in large part by the deployment of the Polish forces in forward positions which lacked the depth necessary for defense. The Poles became quick victims of an enemy who used the new concept of the *Blitzkrieg*, which combined the mechanized speed of the armored units and the tactical support of aircraft.

As we have seen, this concept was first developed by Major General Fuller and Captain Liddell Hart. But the prophet is never recognized in his own country. Also, in Germany, General Beck, the Chief of the General Staff of the Army until 1938 and the Commander in Chief of the Army, General von Fritsch, were rather reluctant to support these ideas as expounded in their country by Guderian. But in the end, Guderian was successful. On 10 May 1940 the strength of the German and Allied units was evenly balanced, with roughly 140 divisions on each side, while the Allies had more – and in many respects, more powerful – tanks. One element in which the German armor was superior to that of the Allies was speed. But much more important was the fact that the Allied tank forces played a role subordinate to the infantry and did not represent an integrated, independently operating unit that could penetrate in depth or be deployed as a kind of fire brigade at critical points on the front.

The Allies, especially the French, were not only the victims of the *Blitzkrieg* concept, they were also the victims of their ignorance of how to deploy the available materials and the mechanized forces so as to adapt them to the requirements of a new kind of warfare. They had six armored divisions available, with two more in reserve, as well as a considerable number of motorized divisions, compared with 10 German armored divisions and 7 motorized divisions, all deployed near the Ardennes sector. The German breakthrough was carried out by only a small number of the German divisions before the mass of their forces entered the fray. The ordinary infantry divisions were still marching on foot and using horses and carts for transport.

The French had mobility; they possessed the means for a flexible defense without realizing it. Among the reasons which Fuller enumerates for the German success, and which also illustrates the essence of the *Blitzkrieg* concept, is the strategy of annihilation, because under favorable conditions the advantages of this strategy outweigh those of attrition. As deployed by the Germans, this strategy was unwittingly favored by the French because of their belief in solid fronts – the so-called Maginot complex – but also because the French did not realize that this idea had been overtaken by rapid armor operations supported by a tactical air force. This deprived the French forces of any initiative and handed it over to the enemy.

There were also the tactics of speed which the strategy of annihilation requires for consistent maintenance of the impetus of the attack. The German forces were not only organized so that they could maintain this impetus, but they also included engineers and building troops. In fact, the entire logistical apparatus was structured in such a way that it could be present at any point where it was required, whether this meant refitting tanks, overcoming fortifications, securing the road network, rebuilding bridges, regulating the traffic or the supply of fuel and ammunition at all times. The German Stuka dive bombers paralyzed the French rail network, but where possible they avoided the destruction of roads and bridges upon which the German advance was to be carried out.

This new kind of warfare required the integration and co-operation of all service branches in order to maximize the effective power, the power at the point of contact, which, during the western campaign, was between 100 and 200 miles away from the point of departure of the attack. The German Air Force had been built up almost exclusively for a tactical role. The speed of the attack required the concentration at the point of contact and in this context the German dive bomber was, in the last analysis, nothing other than a flying field howitzer. In this function, integrated with the panzer units, it doubled the impact of the latter.

There are other factors which played a role, such as the demoralization of the French staffs by the superior German strategy and tactics and that psychologically imponderable will to victory which many British and German observers of the time found lacking in the French Army.

Therefore, we come to the conclusion that France fell because she did not recognize the antidote to the concept of the *Blitzkrieg*, and this antidote brings us back to the rise of the defensive over the offensive, a remedy which the Soviet forces used, at first reluctantly and then increasingly, toward the end of 1941 and 1942, until they had successfully regained a position in which they could return to an offensive strategy.

The campaign in North Africa provides further examples of successful defensive actions, including those in April and May 1941 when the 9th Australian Division held Tobruk against Rommel's German and Italian forces. The Australians defended a badly built position roughly 30 miles in circumference with a strength of 800 men per mile against two German armored divisions and three Italian divisions. About a year later, at Alam Halfa and El Alamein, the defensive showed its great potential

Right: Berliners celebrate the arrival of the first truckload of oranges after the lifting of the Berlin Blockade. Below: Douglas Skymasters, 4-engined transport aircraft which were a mainstay of the Berlin airlift, await their next flight. The German failure to air-supply Stalingrad in 1942 probably encouraged Stalin to undertake the Berlin Blockade, which failed because of the number and size of transport aircraft available to the US and Britain. Below right: A time-exposure photograph tracing the navigation and signal lights of supply aircraft circling a Berlin airfield.

once again. In both cases there were no open flanks, and at Alam Halfa in September 1942 Montgomery repelled Rommel's attack with a plan that had actually been drawn up largely by his predecessor, Auchinleck, and carried out with roughly the same force as that available to the defender. At El Alamein in October the Afrika Korps tried to hold a defensive line of 40 miles with a strength of roughly one division per eight miles of front. Montgomery opened his attack at El Alamein with a superiority in combat troops of three to one (or eight to one if the Italian forces are excluded) as well as a six-to-one superiority in the number of tanks over the Germans. In spite of this overwhelming power of attack, the intention of which was to wage a battle of annihilation, the British achieved their breakthrough only after 13 days of hard fighting. British tank losses were three times greater than those of the defenders. However, one must

not forget that in this battle the German tank units were already very weak and in the course of this engagement were almost annihilated. The British operational aim, to destroy the Afrika Korps, was not achieved. The Germans made their retreat and in the course of the following seven months were in a position to inflict serious losses upon the British Eighth Army and the British and American forces in Algeria and Tunisia.

In Normandy in 1944 there was a similar situation. Although the Allies enjoyed almost total superiority in the air, it took virtually two months for them to succeed in breaking out from the Normandy beachhead. At that time the Allies had a superiority of five to one over the German defense. As an example, on 30th July 1944 an unsuccessful attempt was made by the British Second Army to achieve a breakthrough at Caumont, coordinated with the American attempt to break through at Avranches to the west of the bridgehead. This 'Operation Bluecoat' faced a German front about 10 miles wide. The German forces were low-grade divisions, but nevertheless they held. Local breakthroughs were achieved only in the western part of the sector, and these were eliminated by German reserves three days later. The British Official History comments upon this episode with the words, 'It is a measure of the German soldier's fighting quality that notwithstanding these disadvantages he continued to offer effective opposition and to make skilful use of country that is in itself an obstacle to rapid movement.'

The German strength in Normandy amounted to roughly one German division per eight miles of front on a front which totalled almost 80 miles. It must also be borne in mind that most of these divisions were understrength and in France for refitting. When Patton succeeded in breaking through at Avranches eight weeks after the Normandy landing, the German reserves were so reduced that they could no longer threaten the Allied flanks and Patton broke out into territory ideally suited for large-scale armored operations in depth. The German reserves were so thin, and the area in which to outflank them so large, that the Allied armies could press forward for a time almost unhindered. This was all the easier since the bulk of the German infantry divisions were still not motorized, in contrast to those of the Americans and the British. Nevertheless, near the frontier of Germany, they held once again with forces of highly various quality, and a counteroffensive was waged which, although it failed, yet provided examples of holding frontal sectors with fewer men than had been thought feasible a few years earlier.

On the Eastern Front, as we have seen, the German attack had first splintered the Soviet armies and the German armored units penetrated into the depths of Russia. Russia's most important allies, the geography and climate of the country, gave the Red Army an amount of time much beyond that which France had in 1940 – the time necessary to reform as well as rethink, to adapt to the *Blitzkrieg* concept strategically and tactically. In the history of World War II Stalingrad is described, almost without exception, as a turning point in the east. But the turning point had already been reached in the winter of 1941 during the attack on Moscow. After the unsuccessful attempt to conquer Moscow, the German forces were no longer in a position to mount an offensive over the entire front in the East. Signs of exhaustion in the German offensive power increased month by month, and Stalingrad was nothing more than the dramatic confirmation of this development. After Moscow, and even more so after Stalingrad, the Russians, with new and growing reserves, could turn to the offensive. However, they faced an enemy who immediately adopted the concept of the flexible defense – a defense which might have been even more flexible had Hitler allowed it. In some instances the Germans defended successfully against a superiority of seven to one.

Left: The war in Korea; US medium artillery in action. The USA and her allies had a preponderance both of artillery and of ammunition supplies, but this advantage could be decisive only in rarely occurring tactical circumstances, set-piece battles in which the enemy did not have overwhelming manpower. Below: MacArthur and Truman meet during the Korean War. The General advocated all-out war against China and the President disagreed. This classic conflict between civil and military authority ended with the dismissal of MacArthur. Below center: MacArthur surveys his master-stroke, the landing at Inchon. This combined operation threatened to cut off the advancing North Koreans and forced them into a retreat which continued almost up to the Chinese frontier, at which point China intervened to turn the tide and, indirectly, bring MacArthur's military career to an end. Below, center right: US infantry in Korea clean their rifles and check ammunition belts. Bottom left: A wounded US soldier evacuated by helicopter. Bottom center: US tanks await orders in Korea. Bottom, right: United Nations infantry moves along a highway in Korea. The two files and extended order of march suggest that this is an area subject to enemy ambush.

Three conclusions emerge from all of this. First, in an age of mass armies combined with a development of arms and weapons and weapon systems which can almost be described as revolutionary, the effectiveness of the individual soldier has increased to an extent that one is almost tempted to speak of the primacy of the defensive over the offensive. Second, the *Blitzkrieg* strategy proved its value in World War II, at a time when the necessary technological and organizational preconditions for its application did exist. Third, although the *Blitzkrieg* concept achieved success, its preconditions could also be applied in the defensive, which had thereby gained a new dimension – that of flexibility. And so we come to the question: To what extent have the tactics and techniques of World War II been adopted and adapted by the forces of the Warsaw Pact countries and by those of NATO, even in a modified form?

In trying to answer this question, one thing becomes immediately apparent – the position of the Soviet Union today is not dissimilar to that of the Third Reich of 1939, in whose military thinking it was important to remember that the economic position of Germany and its poverty of essential raw materials for armaments did not allow a long war. The concept of the *Blitzkrieg* was not only a product of the military technological development, it was also a product of economic conditions. By comparison with the economic structure of the NATO powers – although they too have their weak points, for instance, in oil resources – the Warsaw Pact powers are still underdeveloped. In the long run, they are not yet in a position to mobilize those economic resources which NATO can mobilize in the short term.

The economically weaker side cannot attack the stronger side and expect to be victorious, except, of course, when maximizing and concentrating all its resources of men and material with the aim of defeating the enemy in one mighty blow before the enemy can unfold its full economic resources. Warsaw Pact military maneuvers over a number of years have shown that the Soviet leadership has adopted the maxim that the decisive battle must be fought within the first 48 hours. In short, the Soviet military leadership has adopted the *Blitzkrieg* concept, and only this concept explains why the Russian and East German Army units are deployed as they are. It explains why in recent years

there has been extensive new road and rail construction in certain areas, and why an air base has been built near Parchim within 35 miles of the West German border capable of dealing with large transport aircraft. The maneuvers which preceded the building of the Parchim Air Base had demonstrated that Soviet and East German armored units could not reach their operational bases in the necessary record time. Prior to the construction of the Parchim Air Base the second strategic wave from Russia had to disembark in Berlin and Dresden.

Two factors, therefore, determine Soviet planning: first, the fuller development of a superior military system based on the German panzer division of World War II, and second, the development of a system of mobilization which allows overwhelming the enemy before he is in a position to gather his forces. It is the aim of Soviet strategy to prevent full expansion of the military potential of NATO by quick offensive action with an irresistible force. While a mass attack by tanks spearheaded any offensive movement until a few years ago, present Warsaw Pact maneuvers demonstrate that the Warsaw Pact powers have not ignored recent advances in antitank defense technology. Now the tank formations are widely spread out, with self-propelled artillery and antiaircraft units interspersed among them, so that the artillery within the tank units can

effectively clear the line of attack by concentrated fire and thus pave the way for the armored units. This scheme could also include the use of tactical atomic weapons. Consequently, the *Blitzkrieg* strategy can be applied to our atomic age without any real difficulty.

All in all, one can say that the Soviets have succeeded since 1946 in keeping the superior strategic power of the US in check while simultaneously extending and consolidating their control over their satellite states and building up an atomic arsenal equal to that of the US. At the same time the Soviet Union has modernized its conventional forces and those of its satellites and turned to the third dimension of warfare: the fleet. Today, in spite of its lack of large aircraft carriers, the Russian Navy represents a considerable threat to NATO's rather weak northern and southern flanks. Particularly in the organization of its land forces, the Soviet Union has achieved the maximum of effective combat strength in its divisions, especially through a logistical reorganization which increased the combat strength of the division. The logistical personnel of a Soviet division comprise roughly 25 percent of its strength, as compared to 50 percent per division of the NATO unit.

In spite of the smaller number of soldiers per Soviet division, its combat power can be estimated as equal to or even greater than that of a NATO division. This increased effectiveness has been achieved by centralizing the logistical apparatus and by integrating many of the training units into the organizational structure. The net result is that units at all levels, as compared to those of NATO, are smaller but at no sacrifice of effective combat strength; moreover, cadre divisions have been retained on an active basis. If one divided the total strength of the forces by the

number of divisions, it would be seen that within the American Army there are 60,000 men per division, in the Russian 11,000, or, if one considers the American forces stationed in the German Federal Republic, it means 41,000 as compared to 21,500 in units of the Warsaw Pact.

The Soviet variation on the *Blitzkrieg* concept envisions a massive, but narrow, breakthrough of a defensive front which is lacking in depth. This means that they look for a decision on the battlefield before large-scale replacements of men and material become necessary. Compared with this, NATO, with its highly complicated logistical apparatus, is at a serious disadvantage. Quite apart from the costs involved, the oversized logistical units of NATO really obstruct the mobility of the combat units. *Blitzkrieg* divisions require relatively little logistic support and also need relatively little indirect fire support except during the breakthrough. After that has been achieved, it is expected that logistical and artillery support will be needed to a small extent in a theater of war in which the enemy forces have presumably been split asunder. To supply each division in an operation of this kind with its own logistical apparatus is therefore unnecessary.

An armed force built up with the aim of overwhelming the enemy quickly and effectively does not require a complicated infrastructure. The centralization of the logistical apparatus of an army on the offensive under the command of higher staffs has the advantage that the support necessary can be directed to any division where it is required, according to the prevailing situation. And since losses among the logistical personnel are naturally fewer than among combat troops, there is also a reserve of combat troops among the logistical troops.

The land *Blitzkrieg* is supported in the air, a dimension in which the NATO forces have so far seemed to enjoy a high degree of superiority. However, in central Europe, particularly over the North German Plain, the prevailing weather conditions are such that they can neutralize the use of the air force. The technology involved in building all-weather aircraft is very complex, but it is being developed and the trinational Tornado may prove to be a satisfactory answer.

The concept of a successful *Blitzkrieg* also presupposes an efficient command structure, which is naturally much easier to create in a national army than in a complicated alliance-and-pact system. Even among the best of allies, as in the case of the British and the Americans in World War II, personality problems and other factors can reach a pitch that obstructs operations rather than assisting them. From this perspective, of course, the Warsaw Pact powers carry a much heavier burden, and the Russians experienced the consequences of this when they occupied Czechoslovakia in August 1968. The result was a thorough reform in the command structure of the Warsaw Pact.

Until 1969 the chain of command ran from the Headquarters of the Warsaw Pact powers to the respective national ministries of defense which, as the example of Rumania or Czechoslovakia between January and August 1968 demonstrated, were not always willing to comply with Soviet wishes. Having learned from this experience, the Soviets realigned the entire command structure. Since 1969 the most important forces have been directly subject to Warsaw Pact Headquarters, that is, to Russian command. The Russians also supply the liaison staff between headquarters and the respective national contingents of the Warsaw Pact forces. The role of the national ministries of defense has been virtually reduced to training and supervising logistical functions. This process of restructuring is the military consequence of the Brezhnev doctrine, according to which any internal threat in a socialist brother country is a matter to be dealt with by all nations in the Warsaw Pact. In practice this means that should another situation arise similar to that of the spring and summer of 1968, the Kremlin is no longer in a position that forces it to ask its allies for support. In 1968 the Rumanians refused, while the Hungarians reacted only after considerable delays. The Kremlin now has the freedom to act when it sees fit. Among other things, the Kremlin also retains for itself the right to intervene in Germany's western half, a right derived

Post-war Soviet weapons. Far left: SA4 ground-to air missiles on their launchers. Left: T55 medium tank. This successor to the wartime T34 appeared in the 1960s and is used by the Warsaw Pact forces. Above: BTR-50P armored personnel carrier accompanied by scout cars. Below left: Mi-24 assault helicopter. Below: The nuclear-powered guided missile cruiser *Kirov*, the most formidable ship in the growing Soviet fleet.

from the Potsdam agreements of 1945. This means that the restructuring is not limited only to the internal affairs of the Warsaw Pact countries – Germany, Austria and Yugoslavia could be potential victims.

General Steinhoff, a retired former NATO commander, listed the most important criteria for a successful defense of Europe, namely a common military concept, standardized weapon systems, joint arms development, joint technological development, common logistical apparatus and common training methods. If one measures the Warsaw Pact powers and those of NATO by these criteria, obviously the Warsaw Pact powers are much more advanced.

At the risk of overgeneralizing, one can say that while the Soviet Union has adopted the *Blitzkrieg* concept of World War II, NATO adopted the concept of flexible defense after the doctrine of massive retaliation (1950s and early 1960s) had proved to be politically as well as militarily unusable. But there appear to be different opinions as to what flexible defense means exactly, and some influential experts, including General Fourquet, actually reject the value of conventional defense in principle. General Fourquet's objections were based on the

excessive expenses necessitated by conventional armaments. From his point of view, conventional forces should only be strong enough to recognize and test the intentions of the enemy. Once these are recognized as predicting a major attack, the nuclear threshold has been crossed and the use of atomic weapons becomes necessary. Fourquet understood that the conventional forces' sizes, which had first been laid down in the Lisbon Conference in 1952 and obliged NATO to keep 50 divisions in arms, were an attempt to match the Soviet and Warsaw Pact forces numerically. This, in fact, does not seem to be necessary, because today it would amount to almost doubling the size of existing NATO forces. The problems are: how can the available and potential strength be converted into actual combat strength, what kind of combat strength is required, which tactical doctrine and organizational form results from it and to what extent technological developments compensate for fewer troops. In other words, can NATO, with its present strength, organization and weapon systems, repel an attack from the east?

One objection to a stronger conventional defense points out that by increasing conventional forces, the atomic deterrent is weakened as an operative factor, since it is a sign that the West is not prepared to use its atomic weapons as quickly as possible. According to this assessment, the atomic threshold has to be kept as low as possible in order to prevent an attack – this is a return to the doctrine of massive retaliation. This argument is popular with French military leaders who, before they left NATO, had objected to any reduction in the US military presence in Europe, while at the same time they objected to any enlargement of the general conventional forces because of the costs involved.

Another argument against conventional warfare in Europe points to the extent of the destruction that would ensue. This argument directly contradicts the prevailing conviction in NATO staffs that a war in Central Europe will necessarily be a short one. This conviction has been confirmed so far by all maneuvers of the Warsaw Pact countries. The picture of an extensive long-term strategic air offensive belongs to the past. Wastage of bombers and fighters at rates comparable to those occurring in World War II is simply no longer possible. The technical development of the aircraft into highly complicated integrated arms attack and defense systems has reached a point which not even the economic capacity of NATO as well as that of the Eastern Bloc countries could cope with in terms of the losses and replacement figures of World War II.

General Gallois' main objection to the strengthening of the conventional forces of the NATO armies is based on the assumption that strong conventional forces and atomic warfare are mutually exclusive. Nuclear weapons are bound to triumph over conventional ones. In his view, with the system of conventional defense based upon a concentration of men and material, firepower stands in a direct relationship to troop concentration. That, in turn, requires a complicated logistical system to deal with the masses of men and material. Therefore, in a conventional war, a long time is needed to mobilize all military and economic reserves fully. This argument, again, is really based on World War II thinking and ignores the fact that the defensive tactics of mechanized units and the application of tactical nuclear weapons do not mutually exclude one another.

There is also the objection to strong conventional forces based upon the assumption that the Soviet Union in a European conflict will fight from the outset on a nuclear basis; thus strong conventional armaments amount to a waste of money and effort. There is Marshal Sokolovsky's maxim that every war in Central Europe will inevitably escalate into a nuclear war, since the conventional NATO forces are too weak to check the forces of the Eastern Bloc countries so that NATO will be forced to use its atomic arsenal. Yet this argument underlines the importance of strong conventional forces in order to heighten the atomic threshold once again.

Apart from that, all these arguments against strong conventional forces are based on a false understanding of their function. Conventional forces were once the means by which the sovereign state defended itself. This is only the case in very limited instances today, and it does not apply to Europe at all. NATO's present conventional forces are a means of crisis management, designed to meet a smaller danger effectively before it can transform itself into the danger of atomic warfare. An atomic power without strong conventional forces occupies an immensely weaker position than the power which possesses them. Lacking the strength which could reduce the risk of a conventional war escalating into an atomic one, weaker conventional forces actually help increase the instability that can give rise to a situation in which one is forced to use atomic weapons.

We have mentioned before that NATO has adopted the concept of flexible defense within the framework of what is called the flexible response, consisting of the triad of conventional forces, tactical atomic forces and strategic nuclear weapons. The only question is whether this triad does exist – whether or not the definition of conventional warfare does already imply tactical atomic weapons. Among the Warsaw Pact forces there are many indicators that the use of tactical atomic weapons are automatically included in the *Blitzkrieg* concept and this is also believed to be the case within NATO plans for land warfare. For economic reasons, but also for strategic and tactical reasons, the concept of flexible defense has been given some credibility by giving NATO units greater mobility, as, for instance, recent structural reforms of the Federal German Army demonstrate. Since these reforms are still in their infancy, we will have to see what effects they have. However, there is cause for concern, because the reforms imply reduced forces in actual readiness. If one confronts an enemy who operates on the basis of the *Blitzkrieg* concept, who is determined to enforce a decision within the first 48 hours, then the amount of time it takes cadre units to achieve their full strength is irrelevant; it does not matter with what speed the main power of the western alliance, the USA, can bring its reinforcements, as in the Reforger exercises, from their home bases in North America to the bases in Western Germany. What counts in this situation is the number of effective combat units available at the critical moment and the locations at which they are available.

Much has been written about these problems in the last few years, among them the book by General Close, *Europe Without Defense*, and General Hackett's *The Third World War*. Hackett's book is really based on a presumption that cannot be taken for granted, namely, that at D-Day or Day X or whatever we may call it, NATO will be fully equipped with all its forces available, that American forces can be brought from the USA to Europe without any serious interruption and so on. By comparison, General Close is rather more skeptical, basing his arguments on the situation as it is now and not as it might be. Taking into account the time necessary to transport Belgian and Dutch forces into the theater of operations, and for the Federal German Army, the British Army of the Rhine and the Fifth and Seventh United States Armies in Western Germany to mobilize, it is clear that the result on Day X would be a series of highly complicated movements in all directions before units could reach their operational areas. The main weight of the defense within the first 36–48 hours would lie on the shoulders of the NATO air forces, who must prevent a breakthrough from the east.

At the present moment, and probably for some years to come, effective use of the NATO air forces will be dependent on weather conditions. However, if we look at the Soviet Air Force, we see that until the end of the 1960s its main emphasis lay on the development of a tactical air force to defend Soviet airspace. But with the recent introduction of the MiG-25 and the SU-24, there is a change of emphasis toward neutralizing Western airpower as well as increasing offensive capacity, a capacity which not only complements the offensive capability of the land forces, but in fact increases them. NATO dominance of the airspace of Central Europe is now far from assured.

Even assuming its practicality the when and where of flexible defense is also open to question. In answer to the question *where*, one ordinarily sees the short formula – forward defense – a formula which does not answer this question but actually circumvents it. One must understand the demarcation line between east and west in Central Europe. That this is often misunderstood is demonstrated by the fact that the kill zones of the tactical atomic weapons of the Seventh American Army all lie within West German territory. This is supported by the observations of the former Deputy Supreme Commander of the American Forces in Europe, General Collins. According to his argument, tactical atomic warfare will occur first in Western Germany; only later will it extend into Eastern Germany and other Soviet satellites. From that one can conclude only that NATO's conventional defense is no longer in a position to absorb an attack carried out on the *Blitzkrieg* concept.

Defense in depth to the Pentagon means defending the whole of Western Germany and part of western Holland. In spite of the signs of erosion appearing in the units of several NATO allies, this does not mean – at least not yet – that NATO does not have the conventional strength to absorb such an attack; what it does mean is that its forces are located in the wrong places and cannot be at hand immediately to deal with such an attack successfully. The reason for this unfortunate situation is a legacy of the former zones of occupation of Germany and of the early phase of West German rearmament, when NATO still planned to stop any attack west not east of the Rhine. This would have meant that the West German forces would have to withdraw to their own western border in order to reconquer their own national territory at a later time.

Forward defense, therefore, still belongs to those formulae with which one tries to cover up the existing discrepancy between that which is necessary and that which, for whatever reasons, one is prepared to do for defense. The instruments of defense do exist, but in the wrong places. Add to these contradictions the complication referred to by the American defense expert, Paul Bracken of the Hudson Institute, which is likely to modify both the *Blitzkrieg* concept and that of flexible defense as well. All existing scenarios of a war in Central Europe take as their point of departure the conduct of a battle in the North German Plain where, according to the old *Blitzkrieg* concept, the aggressor would circumvent densely populated areas. This precondition is in the process of fundamental change by virtue of changes in the urban structure of this area. Urban development has extended to the point where the suburbs of various towns virtually merge with one another, connected by a road network on which the enemy could move forward under the protection of tall buildings.

A typical NATO brigade is deployed to cover an area 15 miles square containing approximately 85 villages. Villages and woods make up 60 percent of West Germany. This makes it more difficult for the aggressor to circumvent towns and villages. But he can turn their existence to his own advantage by what Bracken calls 'urban hugging' tactics, thereby making

Above right: A captured US
bomber pilot is presented to the
world through a press conference
staged in Hanoi. B-52 bombers were
occasionally brought down over
North Vietnam, although for the
most part their bombing missions
in the Vietnam war were carried
out with impunity. However, even
with modern target finding
techniques, heavy bombers were
not suited to this kind of war;
advanced technique and sheer
weight of munitions expended did
not prove to be war-winners.
Above far right: A US infantryman
in Vietnam. High temperatures and
vigilance is well conveyed in this
picture, which does not, however,
fully explain why this war was so
unpalatable for the ordinary US
soldier. Added to climatic and other
physical discomforts, and
knowledge that a determined
enemy might be lurking anywhere,
was the feeling that local friends by
day might be enemies at night, that
unnecessary cruelties were being
inflicted on innocents, and that the
war lacked strong moral incentives.
Center right: Firefighting crews at
work on the deck of a US Navy
aircraft carrier after an accident during
operations off the coast of Vietnam.
Below: A US type M48 tank bogged
down while accompanying supply-
carrying personnel carriers, in
Vietnam.

Left: An American B-52 bomber emptying its bomb bays over Vietnam. Below left: US helicopters over Vietnam. The picture well illustrates the kind of terrain over which the war was fought, and which was well suited to guerilla warfare: paddyfields, copses, and densely-wooded hills. Right: A CH-54 helicopter delivers a field gun to US forces in Vietnam. Even more than the Korean War, the Vietnam campaign emphasized the role of helicopters. Below right: Assault rifle held high, a US infantryman fords a watercourse in Vietnam. Bottom right: A file of US infantrymen ford one of Vietnam's seemingly innumerable watercourses.

248

Top left : An Israeli A-4 Skyhawk fighter bomber, one of the many aircraft supplied to the IDF by the United States. Far left: Ariel 'Arik' Sharon led his forces over the Suez Canal to cut off Ismailia during the 1973 Yom Kippur War. He subsequently became Minister of Defense in Menachim Begin's government, but was forced to resign after the refugee camp massacres which took place in Beirut after the Israeli invasion of Lebanon in 1983. Near left: Moshe Dayan was the architect of Israel's victory in the 1967 Six-Day War. He also became Minister of Defense after leaving the IDF. Above: An American built F-16 fighter of the IDF. Above right: Two Kfir C2 fighters. These aircraft are built in Israel and are a home-built

derivative of the French Mirage V
using General Electric J79 engines.
Below left: An Israeli-modified
Centurion tank moves through the
Sinai Peninsula during the Yom
Kippur War of 1973. In spite of the
early Egyptian successes Israel
managed to recover from a surprise
attack and force the Arabs back.
Below center: A Reshef-class fast
patrol boat of the IDF. Below right:

US Marines enter Beirut as a peace-
keeping force in 1958. In 1983 they
were again called upon to fulfill
this role in the aftermath of the
Lebanese Civil War and the Syrian
and Israeli invasions.

Below: Crew and Royal Marines relax on the flight deck of HMS *Hermes* on their journey south to the Falkland Islands in Spring 1982. Below center: A Wessex helicopter lands Marines on East Falkland. It is armed with Milan anti-tank rockets.

Bottom: The Atlantic Conveyor with Sea Harriers and Chinook helicopters on deck. This vessel was later destroyed by Argentinian Exocet missiles fired from Super Entendards.

Above center: Sea Harriers in the below-deck hangar of the carrier HMS *Invincible* on her way to the Falkland Islands. Superior British training and equipment enabled the Task Force to defeat the Argentinian troops occupying the Islands despite heroic efforts by the Argentinian Air Force. Above right: British paratroopers leap ashore at dawn on East Falkland. The landings were accomplished with remarkably light casualties, considering the inherent risk involved in amphibious operations. Center right: A Sea Harrier on the deck of a Royal Navy assault ship. These V/STOL aircraft proved their worth during the Falklands campaign, shooting down more than 30 Argentinian planes. Below: HMS *Hermes* makes a triumphant return to Britain after the Argentinian surrender.

Left: A modern ground attack and interceptor aircraft, the SAAB *Viggen*. Designed and built in Sweden from the 1960s, this carries air-to-surface or air-to-air missiles and can operate from 500-metre runways. Below: Belgian F.16 fighters, whose long, slim radar noses illustrate the electronic nature of modern warfare, in which instant information about the enemy is so crucial. Left, inset: A military communications satellite undergoing final checks. Bottom, inset: A US ballistic missile submarine, showing its launching tubes open; much of the strategic significance of such vessels lies in the ability to launch missiles underwater.

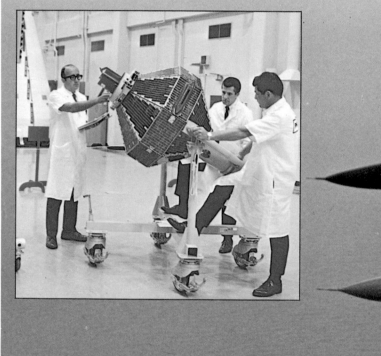

himself less vulnerable to the use of nuclear weapons. At the beginning of the 1980s the urban Rhine/Ruhr complex has almost merged with the Dutch area, a stretch of about 190 miles reaching from Bonn in the south to the Hook of Holland. From a strategic point of view, this development would make it impossible to repeat the pincer movements of the past, due to the concentration of buildings which does not allow the assembly and unfolding of mass forces. More important, however, is the fact that this development is also noticeable in an east-west direction, parallel to that of a Soviet attack, which could facilitate the urban hugging tactics already mentioned. We must also take into account the reforestation in this area which amounts to 0.8 percent annually, and the extension of the road network by 1 percent per year. This trend increases the tendency for armies to stick to well-built roads – a fact confirmed in recent Eastern Bloc maneuvers which featured very strong armored cars as a prominent factor.

However, in a 1975 report by the American Secretary of Defense to Congress on the nuclear forces in Europe, no reference was made to the significance of this growing urbanization.

Perhaps this is understandable, because who will take seriously a doctrine of deterrence that requires the firing of several thousand nuclear weapons upon one of the densest urbanized areas in the world? It also seems that the time for panzer battles conducted over ranges of several thousand yards is a thing of the past. In fact, even the new generation of guided missiles is almost useless in street fighting in urban areas, compared with such older antitank weapons as the bazooka or the German *Panzerfaust*. There is no NATO antiarmor weapon that can actually be fired in a closed room without injuring the soldier who fires it. This includes the otherwise excellent Milan missile. Rockets guided by wires, such as the American TOW rocket, are not stable in flight when fired at the close range demanded by any conflict within an urban area. On the other hand, this development seems to favor a kind of super Maginot Line for defensive purposes. Whether it is worthwhile to develop this possibility further is another question, but in any case, the training of the soldiers would have to place much greater emphasis on urban fighting. Appropriate new weapons are needed, and consideration of the Maginot concept requires the beginning of planning to evacuate the civilian population. No such plans exist at this juncture.

Under whatever aspect one looks at the problem of a defense of Western Europe, one confronts the apocalypse. Even such alternatives as those proposed by Carl Friedrich von Weizäcker and Horst Alhfeldt are not real alternatives but only a new variation of the Bonin concept. General von Bonin, in the early 1960s, suggested the elimination of any offensive features in the Federal German forces by doing away with strong battle tanks and replacing them with much cheaper self-propelled antitank guns, placed and disposed in depth according to the model of Soviet defense in the Battle of Kursk. Adherents of this strategy suggest a new variation which they call Techno-commandos. Armed with antiarmor weapons, the commandos are supposed to be deployed in depth with the object of halting the Eastern armored nations. They lack any offensive capacity but have the alleged advantage of lower cost. However, even assuming that an attack could be halted by this means, the possibility arises that the enemy will attempt the breakthrough with all available weapons. The most important question is, can the Soviet Union afford to fail in even a limited attack on Central Europe? To take such a risk, the Soviet leaders would have to be fairly convinced that it would succeed, with all the consequences which that would imply for us all, because a failure would completely alter the relationship between the Soviets and their satellites and might well bring fundamental political changes in the Soviet Union itself. This risk would appear to add to the security of the West, but we must remember that this would not be the first time that a state tried to solve its internal problems by external warfare. The temptation to this can be especially strong if the potential aggressor has reason to believe that the enemy is badly prepared to resist and has a weak or divided leadership.

Although the political situation was much more relaxed in the 1970s, the military argument that this should not be confused with a permanent change should be borne in mind. Politics, especially in systems where power is concentrated in the hands of a few, can move suddenly and unexpectedly in new directions, and the primary question for the soldier is how he can adapt the instruments of defense at hand to the changing conditions so as to guarantee security at any time. Whether the primacy of politics in Clausewitz's sense will be maintained, not only in Europe but in the numerous trouble spots throughout the world, is a question not even the superpowers can answer with confidence. Their means of control are limited; the possibilities for irrational action are limitless.

INDEX

Acknowledgments

American Red Cross 33 (above left) 90 (left below)
Bayer Haupstaatsarchiv 38 (top), 184 (below)
Bison Books 27 (below), 35 (top), 49, 52 (top), 54-5 (below), 87, 92 (center), 130-1, 134 (center), 142 (both insets), 142-3, 154-5, 156, 164 (top and bottom), 164-5, 166 (below), 171 (below), 172 (below), 173 (center), 178 (both insets), 180-1, 191 (inset), 192-3, 194, 194-5, 195, 198 (all 3), 202-3, 206, 207 (both), 212 (below) 218-9, 218 (both insets)
Anne SK Brown Military Collection 6-7
Brown University, Rhode Island 8, 60 (above and below), 63 (above), 80-81 (all), 84-5, 85 (inset), 88-9, 92, 96-7 (all), 100-101, 108-9, 120, 121 (above and below right) 124-5, 128-9
Bundersarchiv 27 (top left and right), 29 (below), 44 (above and below), 45 (above and below), 47 (below left), 70-1, 122 (below), 130 (below), 131 (left), 132, 133, 134 (top right, left below), 135, 137, 196, 196-7 (below), 202-3 (insets), 204-5, 224 (above right), 228 (above)
ECPA 115 (top right), 123, 184 (above)
General Electric 35 (below right)
General dynamics 252-3
Robert Hunt Picture Library 28 (both), 29 (top), 42-3, 46 (bottom), 160 (below), 161 (above), 164 (center), 166 (above), 167 (left), 168-9, 170-1, 172 (top), 177 (below), 183 (top), 188 (above, below), 200-201, 204, 216 (top), 220, 221-2, 226 (below), 241 (above right and left)
Imperial War Museum 34 (center right), 36-7, 38 (below left), 42 (below), 131 (right), 132-3, 183 (below), 186 (inset), 187 (inset), 203, 208, 212 (above), 216-7, 225 (below)
Lauros Giraudou 10-11
Library of Congress 25 (below), 30-31, 33 (below), 40 (above), 45 (top), 47 (above), 64 (above left), 138-9, 140 (above), 141 (all 3), 143 (inset), 144 9 (top), 145 (both), 146-7 (all 4), 148 (all)
MARS 34 (top), 59, 61 (above and below), 78 (bottom), 79 (both), 84 (inset), 86 (both), 90-91 (both), 93 (top), 94 (both), 116 (below), 126 (above and below), 127 (below), 154 (both inset)
Musée de l'Armée, 64 (above right), 65 (above), 117 (both), 121 (left),
Musée de la Guerre, 196 (below)
National Archives, 36, 37, 43 (above), 46 (below right), 53 (left), 54-5 (top), 150, 151, 192, 186-7 (above), 187 (above), 199, 222 (inset)
National Army Museum 12 (below), 13 (below), 16, 111 (top), 153 (top)
National Maritime Museum 24 (top left), 186-7
Richard Natkiel (maps), 52 (bottom), 62, 83, 144 (below), 157 (above), 171 (above), 177 (below), 193, 209, 221
Peter Newark's Historical Pictures 18 (top), 26, 33 (above right), 34 (center left), 34 (bottom left), 53 (right), 63 (below), 65 (below), 67 (all), 68 (above right and below), 69, 74-5, 77 (below), 90 (top), 93 (below), 19, 98, 102-3 (all 5), 104, 105, 106-7 (all five), 116 (below), 118-9 (all 4), 129 (above right), 142 (below), 152, 153 (below), 157 (below), 158, 159, 162 (inset left), 178-9, 182-3, 190-1, 190 (inset)
Novosti 160 (above), 161 (below), 162-3, 162 (inset left), 163 (inset), 167 (right), 173 (top bottom), 189, 230 (below).
SAAB 252 (top)
SADO 224 (above left)
Ullstein Billerdienst 24 (below), 25 (top, 40, 41, 46 (center), 68 (above left), 110-1, 111 (below right and left), 112-3 (all 3), 114, 115 (above right and below), 122 (above), 127 (above) 128, 129 (below), 136 (above and below), 236-7 (all 3), 240 (both)
Victoria and Albert Museum 12 (top), 13 (top), 17, 21, 24 (top right), 58, 76
USAF 215 (top below), 222, 232-3, 234-5, 245 (top left) 246
US Army, 210 (inset right), 211 (inset), 224 (below), 226, 228-9, 238-9 (all 7), 245 (bottom), 246-7, 247 (top center)
USIS 188-9
US Marines 38 (below right), 43 (below), 47 (below right), 52 (right), 214-5, 245 (top right), 247 (bottom)
US Military Academy 50-1 (center and below), 51
US Naval Academy 50 (top)
US Navy 35 (below left), 149, 210 (inset left), 210-1, 226-7, 230 (above), 242, 242-3, 245 (center) 252.